# LA CHINA

duilorusi

apvilocho

bolcaneto

illadiladri

abarien

illadicorali

zamall

hibulon

zeilon

furnuno

cali

matoles

lozon

anzitos

cangarj

mellana

matnai

lotov

caul

calange

tocol

zubur

chipili

buauan

bitaubota

joj

barbat

laranBanj

tabima

cachingan

lipan

monaripa

naju

illapicola

caGaiani

tidori

illaguad

muliv

tapj uas

tiudaja

# Pacific

An ocean of wonders

For Joshua and Brendan

Published in the United States of America by
University of Washington Press
uwapress.uw.edu

ISBN 978 0 295 74679 1

Designed by Goldust Design
Picture Research by Sally Nichols
Printed and bound in Italy
by Printer Trento

FSC
www.fsc.org

MIX
Paper from
responsible sources
FSC® C015829

# Pacific

## An ocean of wonders

### Philip J. Hatfield

University of Washington Press
Seattle

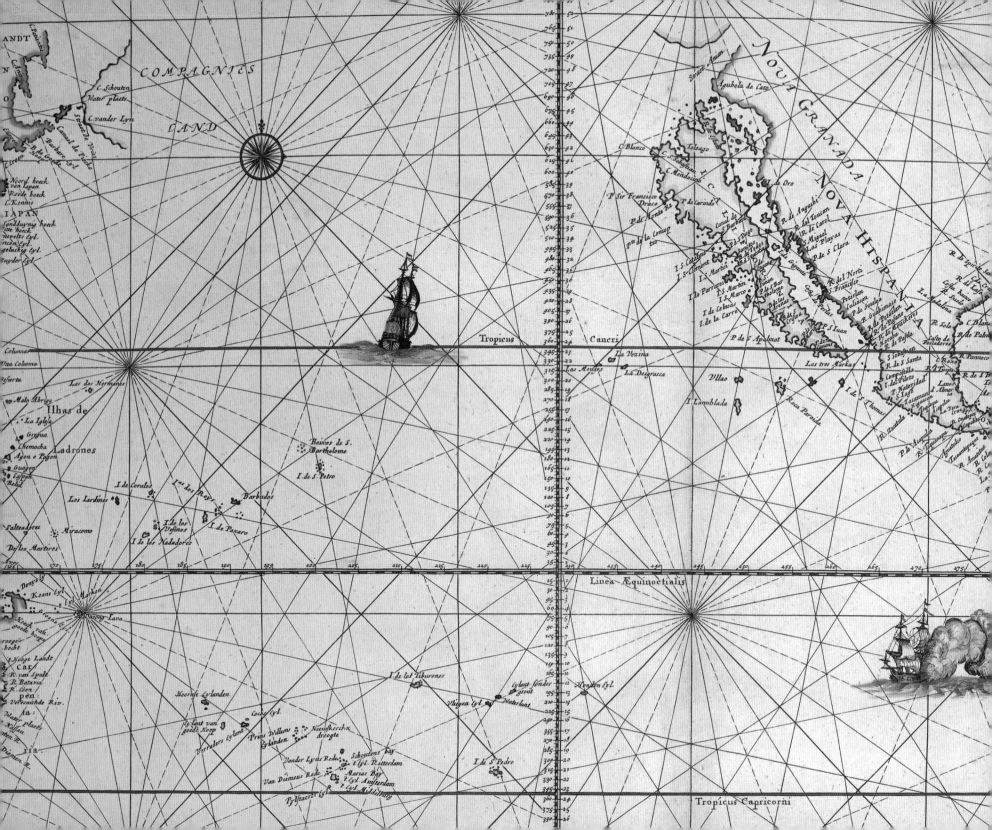

# Contents

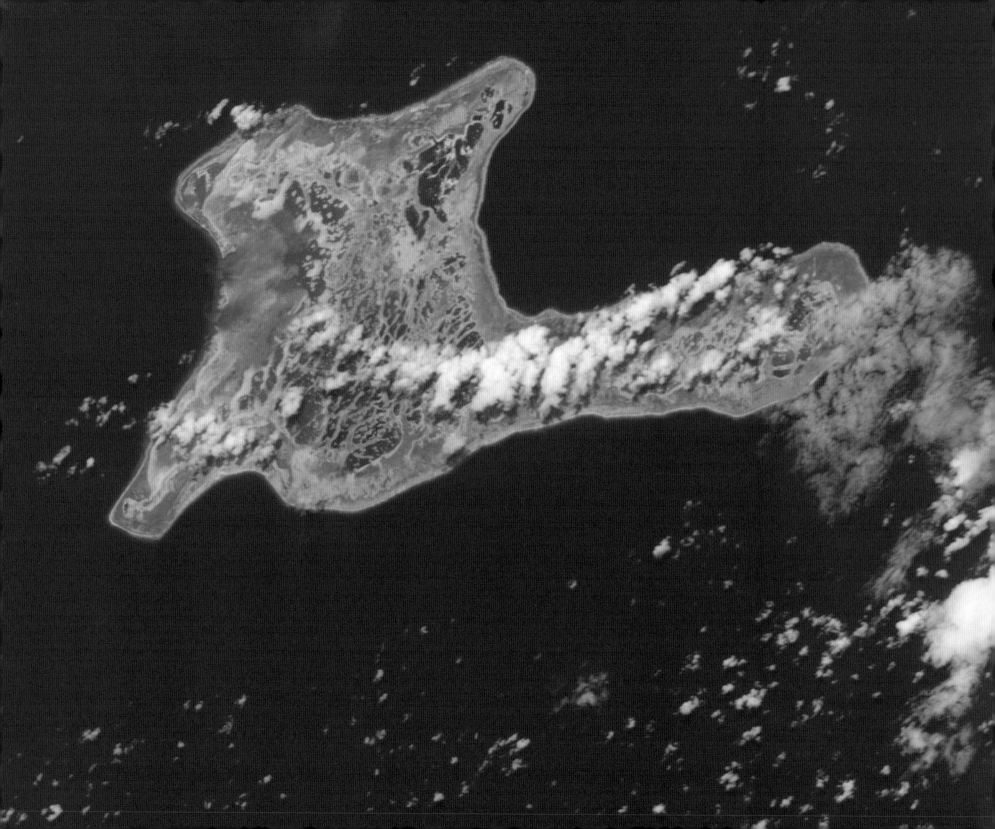

# Introduction

If you centre a globe on Kiritimati (Christmas Island) all you see around it is a vast expanse of ocean. Islands of various sizes float in view while glimpses of continents encroach on the fringes, but this is a view dominated by water. This is the vast expanse of the Pacific Ocean.

The Pacific Ocean is inhabited by a diverse array of peoples and cultures, each with its own history. These include Japanese, Polynesian, Aboriginal Australian, Malay, coastal American First Nations and Aleut communities, as well as many other groups who live in the lands in and around the Pacific Ocean. These peoples are bound by a common thread: their relationship with the sea. In recent centuries, into this world came European explorers, traders, whalers, missionaries: men and women with a whole host of other motives for travelling around the world. Early European interest was broadly driven by trade and the desire for trade goods, the exploration of the Pacific being the end goal of other endeavours of exploration from the fifteenth century onwards, be that the rounding of the African

An aerial view of Kiritimati (Christmas Island).

Cape or the search for Arctic trade routes via the Northwest and Northeast Passages. Trade in the Pacific meant money, and money meant political advantages in the cut-throat world of European politics, and so the Pacific began inexorably to shape and change European society, as it had already shaped those societies around it.

This ocean had a powerful hold on European minds before explorers even knew it existed. In the rush for dominance in a world of increasingly globalised trade, Spanish and Portuguese explorers sought access to the goods and markets of the kingdoms of China, Japan and elsewhere in Southeast Asia: kingdoms to which the Pacific is a key route of access. Spanish and Portuguese sailors were later joined by those from the Netherlands, England, France, Russia and, later, the United States as the Pacific became a hub of global political relations. Over centuries the Pacific has inspired European imaginations with desert islands, beachcombers, piracy, surfing, castaways, mutineers, nuclear weapons tests and kaiju. Even more profoundly, the Pacific has stimulated new ages in scientific enquiry as the specimens and ideas brought back by expeditions such as Captain Cook's

*Endeavour* provoked interest in cities such as London and Paris.

This legacy of dynamic seascapes, imaginative landscapes and influential historical events has developed through one Pacific landscape in particular: its islands. From vast territories like Vancouver Island, to the tiny atolls and reefs of the South Pacific, these hotspots of the Pacific Ocean have had an indelible impact on global history. More significantly, global history has had a huge impact on these islands. While travellers from outside the Pacific have traded, bartered, explored, waged war and much else, they have influenced the recent history of peoples who live in and around the Pacific. These people, their islands and the ecosystems they support have also borne the tremendous consequences of the actions of those who come from outside the boundaries of this ocean.

Indigenous peoples from South Pacific atolls, Vancouver Island and many other locations have been displaced from their land. Disease has ravaged populations. People have been dispossessed by nuclear testing. Today, the consumption practices and lifestyles of other countries threaten to submerge some islands beneath the waves and markedly change the environment of others. Such has been the consequence of a rapidly globalising world for many peoples, but the Pacific experience is marked by a particular intensity in terms of how people were affected by, and affected, other cultures. It is also marked by how dynamically many Pacific peoples engaged with this new world of contact, be that through trade, bringing Europeans into local conflicts or travelling the world with European sailors. Indeed, from the earliest Spanish voyages to the travels of Captain Cook and onwards, people from Pacific islands were frequent sights on European and American ships as sailors, hunters, factotums and notable travellers.

Those who have travelled this ocean, be they people indigenous to the Pacific or those sailing in from oceans on the other side of the world, have shaped its history and its environment. They have indelibly written themselves onto the landscape. Today, the Pacific is seen as a focal point for witnessing the effects of climate change and human-induced environmental degradation, but it is important to note that the effects of human habitation on Pacific islands have long been in evidence. Humans are not truly native to any of these isolated spaces and wherever they have arrived, as seen in the histories of the early settlement of Japan or the much later Polynesian settlement of Aotearoa/New Zealand, they have dramatically reconfigured the environments they have come into contact with. This impact has accelerated over the

centuries, perhaps most powerfully illustrated by the testing of atomic weapons on Pacific atolls. When once it took humans centuries to eradicate the ecology of an island, by the mid-twentieth century it took only seconds.

This ocean of islands, then, particularly after contact with Europeans in the late fifteenth century, provides an opportunity to see how human societies impact, shape and destroy the environments that surround them. In

particular, it illustrates how the resulting age of empires and the post-colonial aftermath of this extended period of history generated flows of goods, capital and people that have long-term and potentially catastrophic effects on the environments around us. In short, capitalism, empire, the development of global superpowers and conspicuous consumption all combine to become a driving force behind what some scholars see as a new geological age, the Anthropocene. While the need

of the Pacific and early human impact on its islands, but it focuses particularly on the sixteenth century and onwards. This is the period when Europeans first encountered the Pacific and began a new link in the chain of global engagements with the Pacific that endure up to the present day.

The book is divided into three sections which focus respectively on the early history of human engagement with the Pacific, the period of empires begun by the work of Captain Cook and others, and the modern period, stretching from the late nineteenth century to the present day. Each of these sections will focus not just on how Europeans saw the Pacific but also on how Pacific islanders engaged with the world around them too. They will also show how, through the work of figures like Tupaia, Charles Darwin and Sir Joseph Banks, the Pacific has had a profound effect on how we understand the world around us, and it should continue to inform our understandings today. This ocean and its islands are not done teaching us. The book will, in short, highlight the importance of an ocean that covers very nearly a third of the surface of the globe and has dramatically shaped the world and people around it.

for change looms large in this book, even a brief history of the interconnected spaces of the Pacific offers insights into how human societies can also act to conserve and protect the world around them.

*Pacific* is an illustrated history of such impacts and the intense relationship between the islands of the Pacific and the rest of the world. Through maps, photographs, books and other objects it shows how the peoples of

the Pacific have created this interconnected ocean which has seeped into the imagination of the wider world. It also reflects on how the rest of the world was understood by the peoples and cultures of the Pacific. Crucially, the book considers how the Pacific has seen waves of settlement, suffered experiments in colonialism by outsiders and provided a beachhead for the development of indigenous politics and anti-colonialism. The book covers a long history, contextualising the settlement

# Part I
## An Ocean of Peoples

It is impossible to look at the islands of the Pacific without seeing the dramatic impacts of human habitation. Island ecosystems are delicate things, often evolving without the presence of significant carnivores or providing refuge to zoological and botanical systems which have been out-competed on landscapes closer to continental landmasses. Such was the zoological and ornithological situation encountered when Polynesian navigators first began to settle Aotearoa/New Zealand. When early Maori began to settle the two main islands they were the domain of giant, flightless and herbivorous birds as well as the terrifying raptors which hunted them. Within a few centuries of human contact with these islands, and the ecologies they contained, many species originally present had disappeared. This was not solely because of the hunting and farming practices of Maori settlers, but also because of the wide range of biological actors they brought with them. New plants and invasive species have travelled in train with all human migrations, reshaping the ecosystems they encounter, and those of the various peoples who settled Pacific islands were no exception.

When we combine these factors with the diverse actions of human societies themselves we begin to understand why the Pacific islands discussed in this book are undeniably human-moulded landscapes. This brief history of the Pacific attempts to shift our gaze away from European-centric histories of the ocean and to look more broadly at how a wide range of interconnected peoples have engaged with the Pacific, its ecologies and the other human cultures which exist within it. In so doing it owes a great deal to Epeli Hau'ofa's idea of a 'Sea of Islands', where the key to understanding the human history of the Pacific is to perceive the interconnectedness of its islands and the cultures that exist across this vast expanse. This theory runs counter to the demographic distinctions applied to the Pacific by European theorists, which obscure our understanding of the Pacific as a space of linkages, where voyagers and navigators from across the centuries have explored, settled, traded, warred and coexisted by using the ocean, its currents and winds as means of connection. In taking on Hau'ofa's idea and looking at the historical record of Pacific encounters, we not only perceive this interconnection but clearly begin to

understand the impact of various human societies on the Pacific and its islands.

This first section of *Pacific* surveys how that history of human engagement with the Pacific began, and the rich cultures that existed there before the arrival of European explorers and adventurers, as well as the changes that the arrival of Europeans began to bring to this gigantic portion of the globe. 'An Ocean of Peoples' will highlight that the arrival of Europeans in the Pacific is a dramatic and often traumatic event for the region but that it does not instigate as many changes to life on the ocean as we may assume. Contact accentuates the interconnection of the Pacific and its islands with the rest of the world and, by accident or design, extensively reshapes many societies around the ocean; but the arrival of Spanish, Portuguese, Dutch and other sailors creates little that is truly new.

Instead, Europeans force themselves into a world of diverse societies, valuable trade goods, complex interconnections and various interdependencies that was well established prior to their arrival.

# An ocean of vessels

This book is a history of islands and human interaction with them, but those islands exist in a vast ocean that human societies also engage with. It is difficult, almost impossible, for island societies to exist in isolation; they require connection to other cultures, food sources and trade goods, to name a few necessities. Without outward connections cultures can stagnate, social stratification can lead to civil unrest or even war and, as we will see within this history, population pressure can overwhelm an island's ecosystem. To counteract this, peoples who live in island societies need to be able to use the waters around them as a way of connecting to the wider world, as an extra source of food and for trade in other materials for day-to-day life. This means that, for island societies, sea- and ocean-going vessels are key tools enabling them to survive and thrive.

The montage shown here is a small representation of the diversity of craft used by Pacific peoples in order to undertake a variety of activities on the ocean. Some craft, like the Aleutian *bidarka*, were designed for transit and to allow people to hunt by land, sea and ice. Japanese and Chinese vessels played important roles in day-to-day life

and the running of empires, allowing not just for fishing and communication but also trade, moving goods and resources around the Pacific Ocean. Vessels on the Pacific also had ceremonial, social and belligerent aspects to their use, with vessels from islands such as Tahiti and Aotearoa/New Zealand being outfitted for use in ceremony and war, to name a few functions. Crucially, these vessels also moved societies around the ocean, as exemplified by Polynesian *wa'a kaulua* and wayfinding techniques.

The scenes illustrated here are all from later in the history of the Pacific, taken from the records and accounts of European explorers and those who accompanied them. Nonetheless these works suggest to us the variety of craft which operated in the Pacific and the range of functions Pacific peoples required their vessels to undertake. The amount of time given to illustrating the vessels of the Pacific also highlights the fascination these vessels held for European explorers, which is perhaps an indication of how common a part of European experience of the Pacific these indigenous ocean-going craft were. The centrality of boats and the water to Pacific life is also highlighted by

another illustration from the period of explorers, but one that is produced from an indigenous perspective. Tupaia, a Ra'iātean religious figure, who left Tahiti with Cook on the *Endeavour* expedition, produced 'A Scene in Tahiti': one of a number of his illustrations which became part of the collection of Sir Joseph Banks.

Tupaia produced illustrations of places and peoples during his time with Cook, many with an emphasis on the social structures and religions of various cultures. Within that context what we can see in Tupaia's illustration is the significance of water and the craft which sailed on them within indigenous perspectives of the Pacific too. These were not just European pre-occupations. Instead, the various vessels which sailed the Pacific before, during and after the arrival of Europeans are the driving force of this ocean of islands; they facilitated the use of the water, reading of the skies and developing sea routes which crafted a tapestry of human exchanges across the Pacific.

A selection of vessels used in and around the Pacific Ocean.

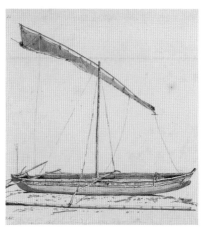

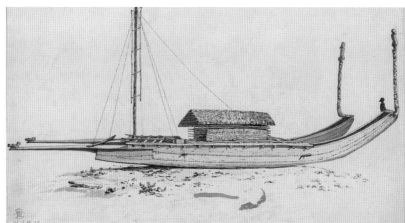

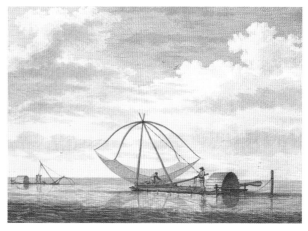

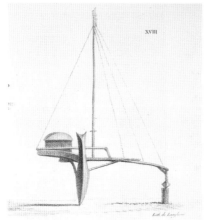

# Human connections

Human settlement of the Pacific was an ancient and complex process driven by the broader patterns of human dispersal across the globe. The settlement of many islands in the western and southern Pacific was driven by the expansion of human populations across Asia, while the settlement of more northerly and easterly islands was driven by the movement of human populations towards and into the Americas. However, even far east in the ocean, in places like Rapa Nui (Easter Island), there were populations which owed elements of their heritage to the complex migrations from the ocean's west, by peoples archaeologists characterise as Austronesian and, later, Lapita.

Archaeological evidence suggests that around 3000 BCE a wave of peoples known as Austronesians spread into Taiwan and then to the south, southeast and southwest of the island. These were not always the first human inhabitants of the islands they settled, as they seem to have encountered existing populations in places like New Guinea, but Austronesians had a formative impact on the islands they came into contact with. They brought with them plants and animals that would change the ecology of islands, they developed commodities precious to various cultural groups and, as a result, they began to undertake voyages of trade, connecting islands and further intermixing their populations.

The Austronesian settlers and the other cultures they came into contact with gave rise to a cultural network that would encompass much of the modern Solomons, Kanaky (New Caledonia), New Guinea, Vanuatu, Fiji, Samoa and Tonga. This was the Lapita cultural complex. The name, derived from the site in Kanaky (New Caledonia) where the pottery was first encountered, is given to a group of cultures which produced and exchanged this distinct style of earthenware pottery. The pottery is distinguished by its repeating geometric patterns and by the infrequent use of anthropomorphic faces and figures. For many Pacific peoples, especially those later grouped by Europeans as part of the Melanesian, Micronesian and Polynesian cultural groups, the pottery is a direct ancestor of the artistic and cultural practices still used today.

The geographical spread of Lapita pottery is also an illustration of how interconnected the islands of the Pacific Ocean were, even early in the history of human settlement. Its geographical spread, across today's Melanesia, Micronesia and Polynesia, suggests at least the exchange of knowledge and skills across large distances but is more likely to evidence the existence of significant and regular trade routes over these distances. In short, from the time of earliest settlement Pacific islanders from this part of the ocean maintained dynamic, socially driven connections between the islands. Populations from other Pacific islands have long done the same, with evidence from modern Indonesia, Japan, the Aleutian Islands and others suggesting complex relationships with other islands and the proximate mainlands these cultures were adjacent to. The pottery also reminds us of the impact these cultures will have had on the islands and seas that supported them, as all industry requires people, resources and a means to circulate. These resources must all be extracted from the natural environment and so even the earliest settlers of Pacific islands will have had significant impacts on the islands they called home.

Newly reconstructed Lapita pot at the Vanuatu National Museum.

# Navigators and early empires

These networks on the Pacific Ocean were liable to grow and change over time, sometimes prodigiously. The settlement of Aotearoa/New Zealand by Polynesian navigators was one such exceptional expansion which redrew the map of human habitation in the Pacific. Underpinning this navigation of the ocean and the settlement that resulted from it was the technique of wayfinding. The principles of wayfinding are complex, using the wind, ocean currents, the position of the sun, moon and stars, and the presence or absence of certain fauna, particularly birds. As a whole they form a complex web of practices used to navigate around the ocean.

Maori histories of the settlement of Aotearoa are driven by the historical figure of Kupe. Kupe hailed from Hawaiki, possibly part of modern Tahiti, and arrived at Aotearoa after the prodigiously long pursuit of an octopus that was troubling his community. Many Maori place names owe their root to Kupe's history, as does the name Aotearoa (translated as 'Land of the Long White Cloud') which was bestowed upon the North Island by Kupe's wife, Kuramārōtini. The *punga* (anchor stone) 'Maungaroa' illustrated here is believed to have been left at Porirua harbour after Kupe exchanged it for a different stone he could return to Hawaiki, and it served for centuries after as an anchor to indigenous narratives of the voyage of Kupe.

Kupe's voyage and the resulting settlement of Aotearoa shows the ways in which Pacific networks could grow. Elsewhere in the western Pacific we see how island networks in the ocean developed into complex networks of increasing scale. In Vanuatu around the beginning of the twelfth century CE, the chief and political figurehead Roi Mata used complex political and cultural processes, reinforced by the use of ceremonial rituals, to bring peace to various warring groups and to ensure harbours and routes of safe passage so that the connections and networks of this region could continue to thrive. Prior to Roi Mata's rise, the Tuʻi Tonga Empire had begun to develop a cultural complex and political hegemony that would shape this region of the Pacific for over five hundred years and still does today. The Tuʻi Tonga was an island network underpinned by trade and tribute while being held together by tightly woven family groups. These family groups and the chiefly figures who arose from them were also the leaders of trade between the islands, with culturally valuable commodities such as woven mats both circulating on the network and providing prestige to those who held them.

Kupe's wayfinding culture, the networks of exchange that strengthened the Tuʻi Tonga Empire and the ceremonial practices that formed the basis of Roi Mata's power all developed from the cultural intermixing that had arisen from the distribution of the Lapita peoples. This group, the settlements they developed and the relationships they established with other cultural communities in proximity to them led to the development of the cultures often grouped together today as Melanesian, Micronesian and Polynesian peoples. The continued development of this culture, through instances such as those discussed here, would eventually give rise to an idea of a shared, interconnected community across much of the southern and western Pacific. This idea still exists in many circles today and will be seen throughout *Pacific*.

Carving depicting Kupe with a paddle. Part
of Waipapa Marae, University of Auckland.

# Living off the ocean

All island peoples need a connection to the sea. Even the ecology of larger islands can struggle to support significant human populations living on them permanently, and so seas and oceans become an important source of food and resources, not to mention particular minerals which can be difficult or impossible to obtain on land. As a result, island communities across the Pacific have always maintained extensive and often distinct ways of exploiting the bounties of the ocean.

For island-based indigenous peoples in North America, such as the Nuu-Chah-Nulth and other groups from today's Vancouver Island, the bounty of the ocean is found in greatest abundance during the annual salmon run. The magnitude of the salmon run, even today, is such that it provides sustenance through the winter for whole communities and a wide range of animals in the food web of North American ecosystems. Communities harvest the fish using boats, lines, nets and various other local methods but the final result is the same, a store of calories and minerals which can be dried and used to nourish people through the leaner parts of the year. Elsewhere in the Pacific, whale-hunting has historically provided an important source of

calories and developed the cultural heritage of various groups. Aleutian Islanders and Japanese whalers are just two of a number of groups who have at points in history relied on hunting various species of whale to support their food intake and commodity cultures.

As technologies for whaling and fishing in the Pacific have improved over the centuries,

human pursuit of these activities has become problematic, pushing species to the brink of extinction and wreaking havoc on the ecosystem of parts of the ocean. The result is that we restrict the continuation of some activities, such as whaling, while fishing is increasingly regulated and controlled by the nation states who lay claim to Pacific waters. Nonetheless it is important to understand the fundamental significance of hunting and fishing on the ocean to many Pacific peoples. Even whaling has been a significant connecting thread for the ocean and its peoples, bringing them into contact with each other and the wider world. It has shaped this watery world and our understanding of it.

The extraction of and trade in resources from the ocean has also created histories that remind us of the long history of human interconnectedness across this seascape. Although there is a popular misconception that European exploration of Australia resulted in the first external contact with Australian Aboriginal peoples, for centuries the bounty of the ocean meant this was not so. The north coast of Australia had long seen the arrival of traders from the islands of today's Indonesia who were looking to acquire trepang (sea cucumbers) to cater to expensive tastes in China. As a result, Torres Strait Islanders, such as the Muralag, and north coast Aborigines, such as the Yadhaigana, were part of the complex trade and exchange networks of the Pacific before the arrival of Europeans on the continent. Here too we see the importance of the resources of the ocean in maintaining human societies around the Pacific and as a means of connecting these communities together in a vast web of interdependence and exchange.

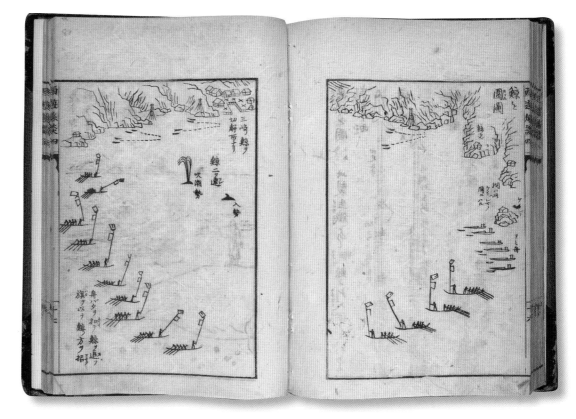

(*Left*) 'Whaling off the Coast of the Goto Islands', by Hokusai.

(*Top*) Aleutian Islanders hunting whales.

(*Bottom and overleaf*) A Japanese whale hunt, by Ezu Saiyudan, 1803.

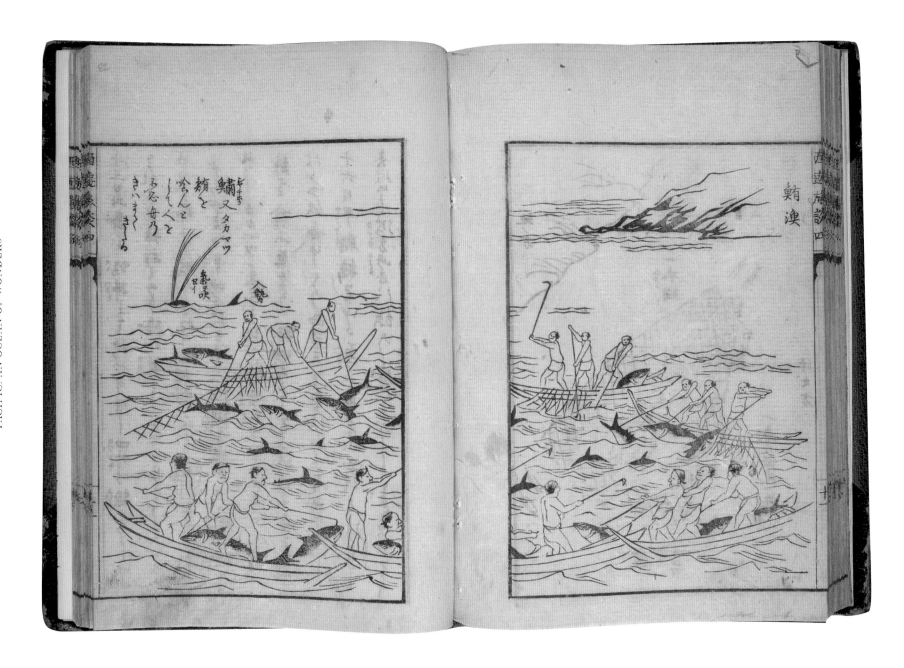

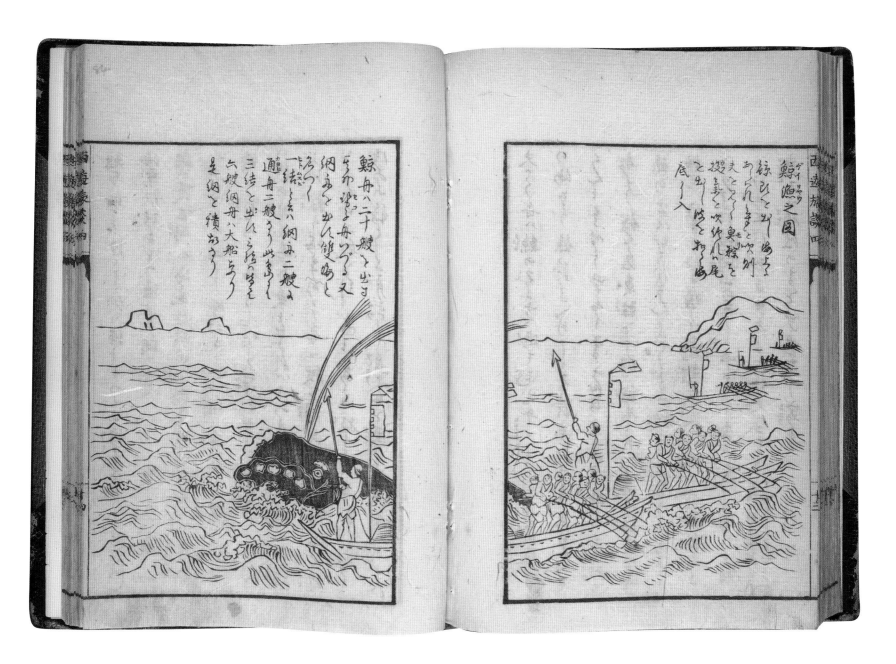

# North America's islands

In the early history of an interconnected Pacific, the islands of North America sit apart from those in the western and southern Pacific. As a result of their geographic situation these islands, composed of bodies such as the Aleutian Islands in the northern Pacific and Vancouver Island on the western rain coast of North America, maintain different connections from those discussed previously. The Aleutian Islands are most likely the remnants of the land bridge that allowed human settlement to move from Eurasia to North America, and thus hold an important place in the history of human expansion around the globe. Similarly, islands like Vancouver Island formed cultural hubs in the network of diverse indigenous cultures that would develop in North America.

The communities that formed on islands like Vancouver Island, developing into various members of the Nuu-Chah-Nulth and Coast Salish cultural groups, depended on the ocean in different ways from the Pacific communities discussed previously. The ocean and its seas were still important conduits for communication, trade and social mixing. The vessels of coastal indigenous peoples, even the simple plank canoe (*tiat*) depicted

Native Americans fishing at an unspecified location in California.

(*Right*) Salmon weirs of the Kenaitze.

AN OCEAN OF PEOPLES

in Harris's *Navigatum* and used by various groups such as the southern Californian Chumash, were employed in networks of exchange that plied coastal areas, offshore islands and inland waterways.

However, in North America the bounties of the ocean had a different relationship with the land. This is perhaps best illustrated by the importance of the annual salmon run that would head to rivers on Vancouver Island and elsewhere on the Pacific coast of North America. After years feeding in the ocean, salmon would return to the rivers they were born in to breed, undertaking prodigious journeys upstream so they could spawn in gravel beds that would harbour their young through their early days. The effect of the salmon run is to disperse the Pacific Ocean

into the lands of North America. Nutrients ingested from the ocean by the salmon are transported across vast distances before becoming part of the food web of humans and animals inland.

For communities around Vancouver Island this has meant the development of distinct relationships with the ocean and cultural practices. The ocean not only provides an annual bonanza of food but also contributes to elements of the ecosystem that groups such as the Nuu-Chah-Nulth may rely on later in the year for food. The salmon run also meant the development of societies that were relatively self-sufficient, fixed to key locations and lived in large groups. These were the communities first encountered by Europeans as the traders and missionaries

discussed later in this section began to work their way up the Pacific coast of North America.

Unfortunately, the relative isolation of Pacific islanders based around North America meant their immunity to introduced diseases was possibly lower than those living in other areas of the Pacific. Introduced disease was a looming danger for all islanders in the Pacific, especially as Europeans began to expand their interests around the ocean, but those in proximity to exchange networks linked in some way to the Eurasian continent had a greater chance of not being completely vulnerable to continental disease. Islanders from around North America were not so fortunate and the arrival of Europeans often proved catastrophic.

# Connected by imbibing

Drinks and drinking cultures are another thread which has long provided connecting tissue for the Pacific world and its constituent islands. *Malok*, *yaqona*, *sakau*, *'awa*, *'ava* and *kava* are some of the many names applied to a drink derived from the root of the kava plant. In societies across Polynesia, Micronesia and Melanesia the drink is used as a means of conducting ceremonies, reaffirming bonds and beginning new relationships. As well as this, the plant itself is illustrative of the sea of interconnectedness of the Pacific and the peoples who lived on it, as it must have travelled, as many plants and animals did during the colonisation of the Pacific, from island to island with new groups of settlers. As a result, it is one of the many invasive introductions made to island ecosystems that humans have facilitated across the centuries.

The drink and ceremonies that surround it were and are integral to many societies in the region, providing a means of social, cultural and political bonding that could be conducted at various scales. For many today, kava and the kava bowl are still means through which friendship groups and family meet, discuss and bond. Kava can provide a formal, connective element in even informal situations. The illustration by John Webber reproduced here shows how the drinking of kava also operates across the social spectrum, being a social and political tool used by kings in formal ceremonies as well as a part of day-to-day family life. As a result, the kava bowl was often an early means of social bonding for Europeans who visited islands where people used the libation and its vessels as a cultural tool.

Ceremonies underpinned by drinking are common across the world and are present in many Pacific societies, a further example being the role of sake in Japanese society. It is important to note how such drinks and their associated cultures show how Pacific peoples have connected to the wider world around them. In this regard the circulation of *tuba*, an alcoholic drink distilled from the fermented sap of the palm tree, is illustrative. Commonly drunk in the Philippines before the arrival of Spanish explorers and traders, the drink became bound up in the ocean-spanning circulations these same explorers instigated. As a result, this drink of the Philippines quickly found its way to mainland South America, where it is still drunk to this day.

Such cultural export and assimilation has been an important part of the exchange between Pacific islands and their continental hinterlands for centuries, with products and practices mediating encounters and exchanges with new groups. In short, sharing drinks, knowledge and experience has long been part of the experience of the peoples of the Pacific and those who come into contact with them.

'Poulaho, King of the Friendly Islands, Drinking Kava', by John Webber.

# China, engine of the Pacific

The economy, culture and commodity trades of China's empires have long been a driving force behind flows of people and products around the Pacific Ocean – as we saw earlier with the trade in trepang. Across the various imperial dynasties, China's effect on the ocean to its south and east has been complex but ever present in some form. Prior to the arrival of Europeans in the Pacific, a number of islands in the ocean were drawn into China's network of commodity exchange for goods like trepang and spices, and their polities were also part of tributary networks that ebbed and flowed with the power of particular dynasties.

Among the most significant expressions of early Chinese dominance in the region were the voyages of Admiral Zheng He (鄭和), the Ming Dynasty mariner, explorer and diplomat. Between 1405 and 1433 Zheng He was tasked with carrying out multiple expeditions across the western Pacific and the Indian Ocean, even travelling far enough to receive tribute from an African kingdom in the form of a giraffe. The admiral's work in the western Pacific was intended to underline Ming power in the region, enforcing networks of tribute on the various smaller empires, city states and islands he encountered as part

of his voyage. The result was a rich tributary network that acquired rare spices, minerals and trade goods for the empire. A voyage with such aims required scale and spectacle in order to succeed, and Zheng He's fleet had this in excess. The fleet consisted of hundreds of ships fulfilling different functions, and individual ships were marvels of the technical achievements of the age. Archaeological evidence suggests that the main vessels of the expedition were hundreds of metres long, with as many as four decks and seven masts to keep the ship moving. In shape and form, these ships were the *Irish Rover* without the lyrical exaggeration. A wide range of mariners and other workers enlisted for the voyages – including cooks and tax collectors, for example.

China's extraordinary maritime engagement with the Pacific under Zheng He would not continue beyond the admiral's career. Subsequent emperors were less keen on enforcing control on the maritime sphere, but the relevance to the Chinese empire of Pacific networks of trade, tribute and interaction nonetheless endured in various forms across the centuries. It is also worth dwelling on what Zheng He's expeditions can tell us about the cultures of the Pacific then and in the centuries since his expeditions set sail. The Admiral himself was a Muslim and was tasked with extracting tribute from the many Muslim states that were developing in the region of today's Philippines, Indonesian islands and the Malay peninsula. He also travelled with thousands of personnel in his service, his fleets veritable floating cities on the high ocean. It is impossible to believe that these bodies of mariners and other workers were a homogeneous group or that they all entered service in China and remained in this labour until the end of the expedition.

Instead, some of those serving the expedition would have departed on various islands, while others were enlisted in cities and ports visited by the admiral. As a result the expeditions of Zheng He must have been significant factors in the cultural mixing of the western Pacific Ocean, not only bringing peoples of diverse backgrounds into contact, as the admiral himself illustrates, but also distributing and mixing these individuals over a vast seascape as part of the tributary networks of the Chinese Empire.

(*Left*) Zheng He on a boat, from *Records of the Western Ocean*, c. 1600.

(*Right*) Zheng He's ship and route, from *Wubei Zhi*, c. 1644.

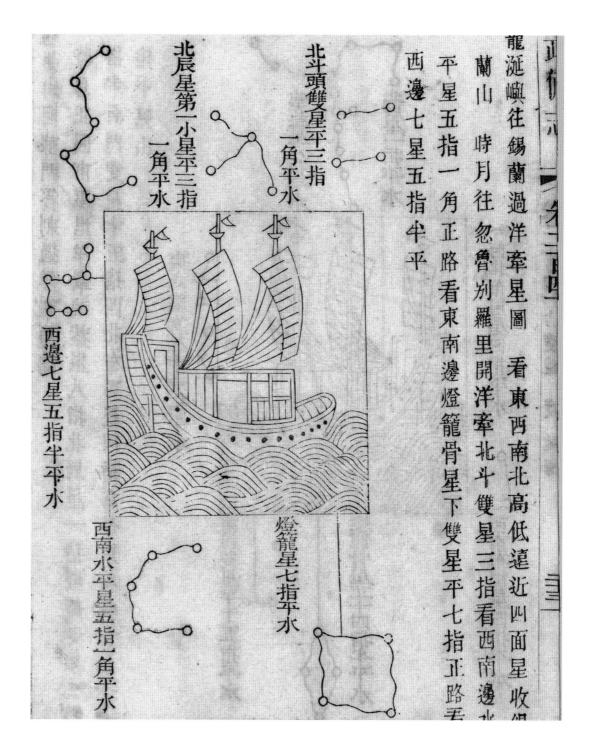

# Marco Polo's 'Locach'

European interest in the Pacific in the early modern period had many motivating factors, not least, as we will see, the desire to connect by sea to the spice trade and the market for other precious trade goods coming from Chinese markets. Until at least the eighteenth century another search also motivated the explorers of Europe to head to the Pacific: the pursuit of *Terra Australis*, the Great Southern Land. The idea of *Terra Australis* has many intellectual threads, such as the idea among cartographers and speculative geographers that the continents of the northern hemisphere needed a counter-balancing landmass to the south, but early motivations to search for the continent were financial in origin.

The seeds for this driving influence were sown by the voyages of Marco Polo (1254–1324) and subsequent interpretations of his travels. In his account of his time in the court of the founder of China's Yuan Dynasty, Kublai Khan, as illustrated in *Li Livres du Grant Caam*, Marco Polo makes mention of lands to the south of China, those of 'Locach' and 'Beach', which were the source of fantastic riches, troves of gold and the seat of great kingdoms. Many influential readers of Polo's account interpreted this to mean kingdoms

and empires akin to China in size, scale and wealth and so these must, surely, require a whole other continent to support them. As a result, the idea of the continent of 'Locach' or *Terra Australis* began to take hold of the European imagination.

The map illustrated here is a 1571 version of Paolo Forlani's map of the world, itself derived from Giacomo Gastaldi's 1546 map of the globe. It shows the vast expanse of land *Terra Australis* was thought to represent and

also reproduces Marco Polo's nomenclature for the part of the continent south of Asia, here labelled 'Terra De Lvcach [Locach]'. Forlani's map also suggests the riches to be found in the land, not by marking possible kingdoms but by showing a landscape populated by camels, rhinoceroses and even unicorns. As a result, it articulates and perpetuates the fascination of Europeans of this period with the imaginary continent. Such ideas would encourage various expeditions, including those led by the English navigator Captain James Cook, to be sent in search of this land. The hope was to find, if not kingdoms to trade with, vast lands opulently furnished with valuable natural resources.

How the story of the search for *Terra Australis* unfolds will be detailed throughout this book, but for now the important detail to focus on is scale. Modern scholarship suggests that the vast and affluent kingdoms Marco Polo was referring to were those of the Khmer Empire, with the 'golden towers' and other notable details possibly referring to historic sites such as Angkor Wat. These were, no doubt, significant monarchies with vast resources at their disposal, and we can imagine stories of them filtering through to

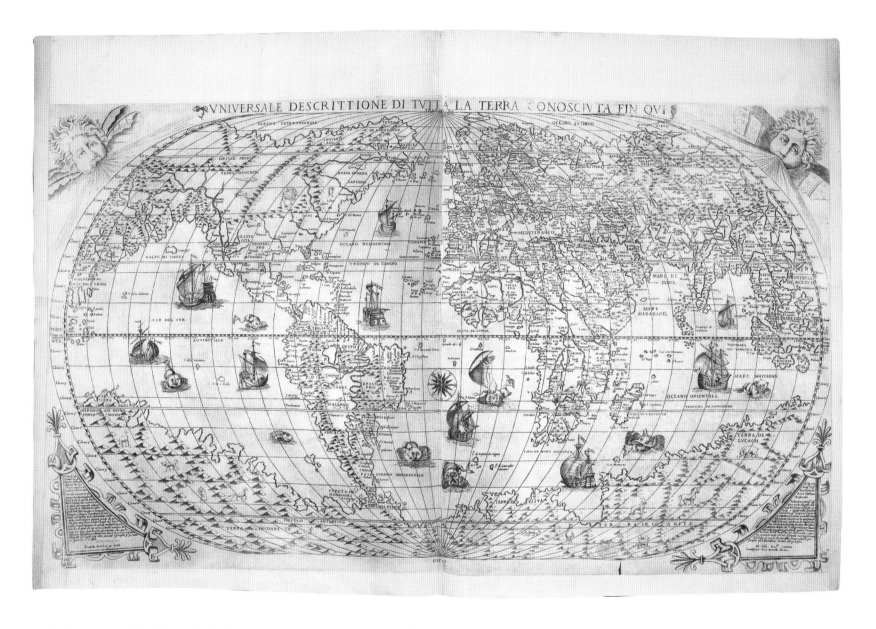

UNIVERSALE DESCRITTIONE DI TVTTA LA TERRA CONOSCIVTA FIN QVI

and being reported by Marco Polo. However, the kingdoms and the lands they occupied are markedly different in scale from those sought by European explorers. Indeed, as the feasibility of such kingdoms existing,

uncontacted, by European navigators waned, the desire to find a vast land of rich resources continued. The search for these lands would shape European understandings of the Pacific and its islands.

(*Left*) Miniature of the Great Khan from *Li Livres du Grant Caam, or Travels of Marco Polo*.

(*Above*) Paolo Forlani's map of the world, 1571.

31

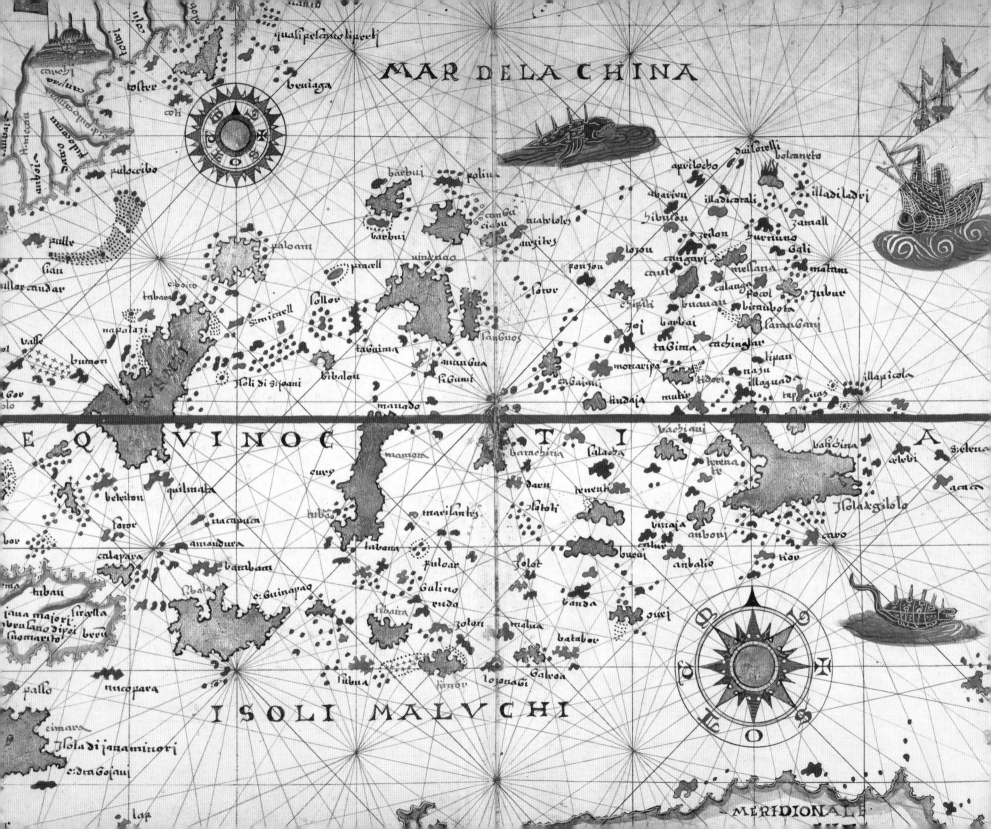

# Europeans, the Pacific and trade with China

Trade with the east had formed a significant part of the European economy for centuries before Portuguese and Spanish navigators attempted to find a new way to Asia. Before the fifteenth century this trade was based on overland routes that entered Europe via Asia, making city states like Venice incomparably wealthy owing to their status as a gateway to the products of the Orient. For Europeans, the east was the source of fine ingredients for cooking, spices such as pepper and nutmeg, as well as desirable hand-made commodities, such as silk garments.

While the economy of this trade was complex – consisting of various local centres and competing products, and distributed over a large geographical area – for Europeans two names loomed large in their imagination of the Asian trade: 'Cathay' (China) and Japan. Historic accounts of travels in Asia, such as those by Marco Polo, gave Europeans a sense of the riches and trade opportunities to be found, especially in China. However, to the European mind both these kingdoms were

still shrouded in mystery, part of a vast east of the world which, along with the kingdom of Locach on *Terra Australis*, required not just exploration but the establishment of direct trade links that would benefit western European kingdoms. For the monarchs of these nations there were too many barriers – and too many enemies – between them and the eastern trade.

Fifteenth- and sixteenth-century maps of the world show the preoccupation Europeans had begun to develop with the east. *Mappae mundi*, and their Middle East-focused world, had become increasingly marginalised, replaced by portolan charts – nautical navigation aids first used in the Mediterranean region – and even the seminal maps of Gerard Mercator, which provided lines of constant course. This reflected a shift in how the world was seen. Europeans now focused on oceanic trade routes and the commodity-rich kingdoms of the east, rather than a world framed around continents and religious geographies. Such imaginations still existed but they moved to the margins of an increasingly mercantile world. The charts shown here, copies from the atlas of Joan Martines, are illustrative of this shift.

Martines was cosmographer to King Philip II of Spain, and produced an atlas of the world as it was understood by the end of the sixteenth century. What he conveys is the result of the endeavours of previous centuries, works by explorers who set out to encounter and open up trade with Asia. As a result, the atlas focuses strongly on the geography of the western border of the Pacific, with maps showing Japan, China and the islands of the Philippines and Indonesia. Despite the relatively late date of the map, the geography of this region is still depicted with significant errors, such as the alignment of the islands of Japan. This hazy geography, even of parts of the world in contact with Europe, suggests why the idea of a mystical continent in the south could exist for centuries.

The maps do, however, show us that this region of the world was of significant importance to European explorers and the kingdoms they represented; these adventurers would keep trying to find a way to Asia and so they would, inevitably, reach across the Pacific Ocean.

Chart of Indonesia by Joan Martines, 1578.

# Controlling the Spice Islands

For all the riches offered by trade with China, it was perhaps the 'Spice Islands', today's Maluku Islands which form part of Indonesia, and the ports that controlled them that held the greatest allure for European explorers. Spices were big business in Europe, with vast profits to be made selling to European markets in spite of the vastly inflated cost of acquiring the goods after they had travelled across continental trade routes and arrived in markets like those in Venice. The idea of forcing down acquisition costs by sailing to the East Indies, acquiring the spices directly and then sailing back was of immense interest to the seamen of kingdoms like Portugal and Spain. As a result the Portuguese began attempting to sail to Asia in the late fifteenth century, rounding the Cape of Good Hope in 1488 and reaching India in 1497 during an expedition led by Vasco da Gama.

The ability to trade with Asia directly was now open to the kingdom of Portugal, but there was the looming issue of Europeans having little of value to trade with Asian markets in order to acquire the spices which they so desired. Violence and extortion became an inevitable recourse, and it was an effective tactic, with important ports like Malacca beginning to fall to Portuguese control in the early sixteenth century. From this point there was no turning back for the Malay peninsula and, as time went on, the western Pacific as a whole. Europeans were here to stay and would continue to explore, probe, intimidate and extort what they could from the ports, islands and kingdoms they encountered. The Portuguese explored key parts of the Malay peninsula while, as we will see later, the Spanish attempted to reach the spice islands by sailing across the Pacific. Later, the Dutch, English and other nations would seek to muscle in on the trade, with varying degrees of success.

Dutch interest in the Spice Islands is well illustrated by the account *Oud en Nieuw Oost-Indien Vervattende* (1724), which recounts the actions of the Dutch East India Company in various locations but especially focuses on the Malay peninsula. The account illustrates the various spices desirable to Europeans – pepper, cloves, nutmeg and so on – as well as the principal locations and fortifications of the region. By the eighteenth century, when this work was published, the balance of power in the region had shifted away from the Portuguese, but European dominance of the islands was established. As a result the Malay peninsula was now a highly militarised space characterised by indentured and even enslaved labour, plantation economies and the destruction of entire ecosystems in the name of trade.

While plantation economies often ravage the environments they are based in, the spice trade was destructive on another level. In trying to regulate the production and sale of spices, companies controlling the trade decimated entire regions so that spices could be acquired only from plantations, rather than in the wild. The establishment of the trade not only meant the entrenching of European explorers and financial interests in the Pacific, but it also heralded dramatic, human-driven changes to the ecosystems of islands across the Pacific Ocean.

Map of Banda Islands, from *Oud en Nieuw Oost-Indien Vervattende*, 1724.

(*Overleaf*) Petrus Plancius, 'Insulae Moluccae' (Spice Islands), 1617

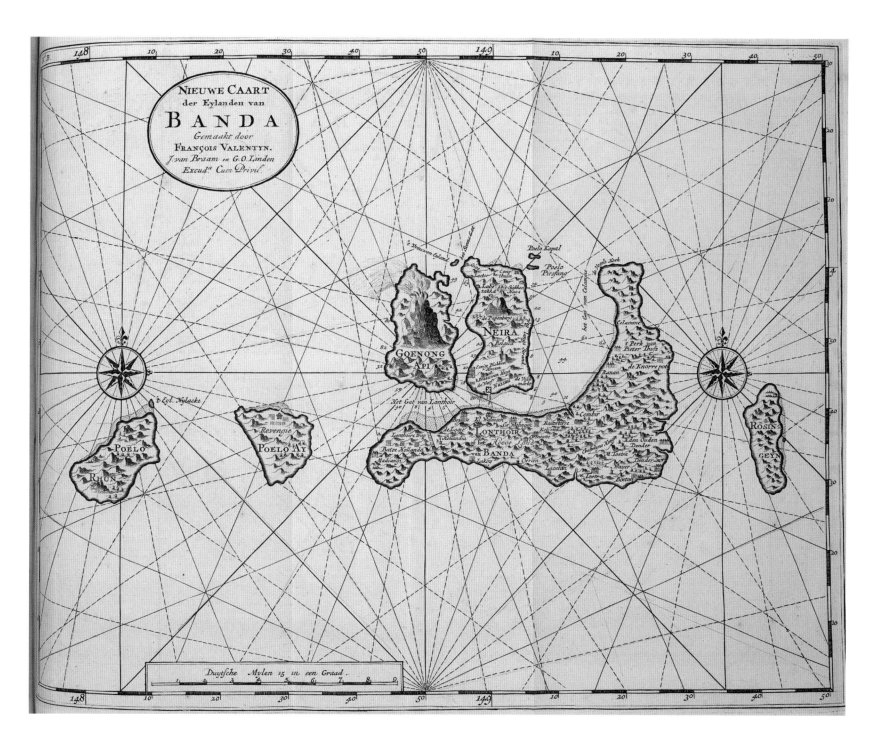

NIEUWE CAART
der Eylanden van
B A N D A
Gemaakt door
FRANÇOIS VALENTYN.
J. van Braam en G. O. Linden
Excud.<sup>t</sup> Cum Privil.

GOENONG
API

NEIRA

Poelo Kapal
Poelo Piesfang

POELO
RHUN

Revengie
POELO AY

Het Gat van Lonthoir

LONTHOIR
of het
Hooge Land
van BANDA

ROSIN
GEYN

Duytsche Mylen 15 in een Graad.

ARI

I: de los Salteadores

Miracomo Vãs

De los Martires

I: de Aves

Barbudos

I: de Paxaros    I: de Dõ Alogo

De los dos Vesinos

I: de los Nadadores

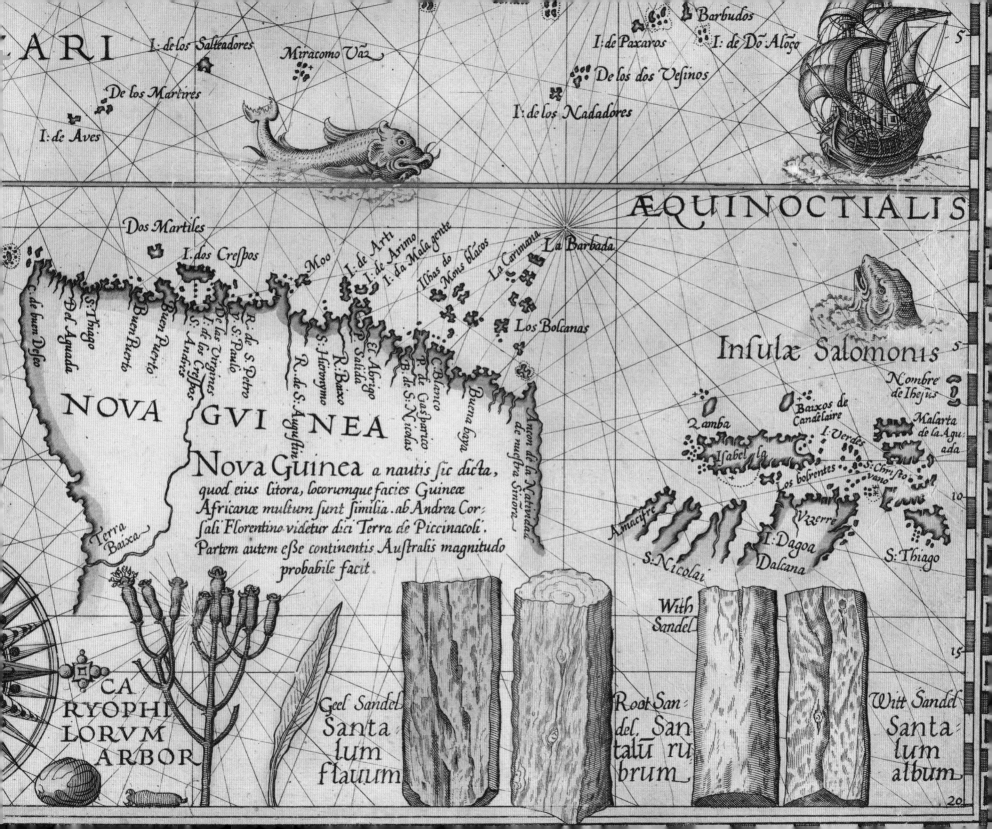

AEQUINOCTIALIS

Dos Martiles

I: dos Crespos

Moo    I: de Arti

I: de Arimo

I: da Mala gente

Ilhas do

Mons blacos

La Carimana    La Barbada

Los Bolcanas

Insulæ Salomonis

Nombre
de Ihesus

C: de buen Deseo

S: Thiago

Del Aguada

Buen Puerto

Buen Puerto

Buen Puerto

I: de los Crespos

S: Andres

De las Virgines

R: de S: Petro

P: S: Paulo

S: Hieronymo

R: de S: Augustin

R: Baixo

S: Salida

El Abrigo

El Abrigo

C: Blanco

P: de Gasparico

B: de S: Nicolas

Buena baya

Ancon de la Natiuidad

de nuestra Señora

Baixos de
Candelaire

Malarta
de la Agu-
ada

Zamba

Isabel la

I: Verdes

los bol-rentes

S: Christo
vano

NOVA    GUINEA

Nova Guinea a nautis sic dicta,
quod eius litora, locorumque facies Guineæ
Africanæ multum sunt similia. ab Andrea Cor-
sali Florentino videtur dici Terra de Piccinacoli.
Partem autem esse continentis Australis magnitudo
probabile facit.

Amacifre

S: Nicolai

Vzerre

I: Dagoa

Dalcana

S: Thiago

Terra
Baixa

With
Sandel

CA
RYOPHI
LORVM
ARBOR

Geel Sandel
Santa
lum
flauum

Root San
del. San
talũ ru
brum

Witt Sandel
Santa
lum
album

# Islam and the Pacific

The religious networks of the Pacific are complex and existed for centuries before the arrival of Christianity. As well as the various religions which were unique to islands within the Pacific, a number of global religions had, by the fifteenth century, become part of Pacific cultures, including Hindu, Buddhist and Islamic traditions. The Islamic world in particular has a long-established relationship with the western Pacific, with Arabic records attesting to contact with the Spice Islands and beyond by at least the tenth century. By the fifteenth century many significant islands and ports in the western Pacific, such as those in the Malay peninsula which formed the principal points of trade for exotic spices, were governed by rulers who were members of the Islamic faith.

The early history of Islam in the Pacific is one of preachers establishing themselves in the ports and towns of the spice trade, but by the fifteenth century the dynamics were significantly changed. Powerful individuals who were followers of Islam set themselves up in opposition to the great kingdoms of Southeast Asia, such as Siam, and established their own settlements or operated as pirates,

raiding the trade vessels and settlements of the region. An illustrative example is that of Parameswara (1344–1413), who set himself up in opposition to the Majapahit Empire and other parts of the sphere of Siamese influence and eventually founded the settlement and trading port of Malacca in

1402. Malacca quickly became an influential trading port in the region, managing trade in and out of one of the most significant, but narrow, entrances to the sphere of the Pacific Ocean. It was also representative of a number of significant trading ports and islands in the region which would be controlled by sultans,

and were therefore nominally Islamic in their faith and culture, by the time Europeans began sailing to the Malay peninsula and the Pacific Ocean.

This would lead to conflict between European Christians and Muslims of the Pacific, with Europeans using coercion and force to insinuate themselves into the profitable spice trade and wider trade with the likes of China and Japan. Despite this, and the zealous work of the Christian missionaries who followed

in the wake of the adventurers, Islam remains a significant faith in the region. This is illustrated by later accounts which recount or depict the people, architecture and practices of Islam in the Pacific region.

Islam has its own history of aggressive expansion and conflict in the Pacific, as do many religions which have expanded across the region, but it was also established and, in many areas, politically dominant at the time Europeans began to arrive. As a result, the

faith and the sultans who upheld it have often been regarded as defenders of the region against colonial aggression from Europeans. This creates divisive, complex relationships in the contemporary Pacific but tells us a great deal about the religious, cultural and political networks into which Europeans ventured from the late fifteenth century onwards.

Illustration of mosque at Ternate, produced during the voyage of Jules Dumont d'Urville, 1837–40.

(*Left*) Chart showing Ache and mosque on the island of Sumatra.

# The first circumnavigator

The hunt for sea-based trade routes, largely driven by the Portuguese and the Spanish, resulted in the Treaty of Tordesillas (1494), which divided the world between these two rapidly growing European powers. Broadly speaking, routes to the east via Africa were to be the domain of the Portuguese Crown and trading interests, while lands and routes to the west (excluding part of modern-day Brazil) were to be the domain of the Spanish Crown. While this gave Spain access to the riches of the Americas, it gave Portugal control of the ocean-going trade with the east. Portuguese traders made the most of this and had a significant impact on the political structures, trade networks and cultures of the Spice Islands, with Malacca falling to Portugal in 1511. One man who was present at this important moment for Portuguese trade was Fernão de Magalhães (Ferdinand Magellan, 1480–1521).

Later, Magellan transferred his loyalties (and career prospects) to the Spanish cause and sought to lead an expedition to the west of the Americas. In 1513 Vasco Núñez de Balboa (c. 1475–1519) had waded into the Pacific Ocean and claimed the waters for Spain. There was also the significant issue of where the border for the Treaty of Tordesillas lay on the other side of the world: where did the western and eastern hemispheres of the Treaty meet? This border would be somewhere west of the Americas, and may be so far west that some of the most easterly Portuguese territories, including the Spice Islands, could in fact fall within the sphere of Spanish control. This needed investigating and Magellan, believing a passage to the Pacific existed towards the south of the Americas, insisted he was the commander for the job.

Departing Spain with four ships in September 1519, Magellan spent the next year probing the eastern coast of South America before rounding Cabo Virgenes in October 1520 and encountering a strait below the continent. The journey was long and arduous, bedevilled by fog, reefs and icebergs, but eventually Magellan and his crews entered a large body of water on the other side. Joyful at his success and the tranquillity of the waters encountered, Magellan referred to them as 'the Peaceful Sea' (*Mar Pacifico*). From this point Magellan's journey was fraught with difficulties. While the Pacific is an ocean of many islands the course set by Magellan brought him into contact with nothing until he reached the Philippines, an epic journey marked by hardship, starvation, disease and death. After encountering the islands in the west of the Pacific, Magellan then became embroiled in local conflicts while attempting to Christianise the indigenous inhabitants. This resulted in his death on the island of Mactan in April 1521, and the remainder of his crew completed the famous circumnavigation.

One member of this crew was 'Enrique de Malacca', who had been in Magellan's service since his time in the East Indies. Enrique was, in fact, from the Malay archipelago, most likely Cebu in the Philippines, and so when Magellan's expedition arrived on the islands in March 1521 it was possibly Enrique who became the first person to circumnavigate the globe. Despite missing almost all of the islands in the Pacific Ocean, the expedition and Enrique earned a unique place in world history.

Battista Agnese's map of the world showing the route of Magellan's fleet, 1540.

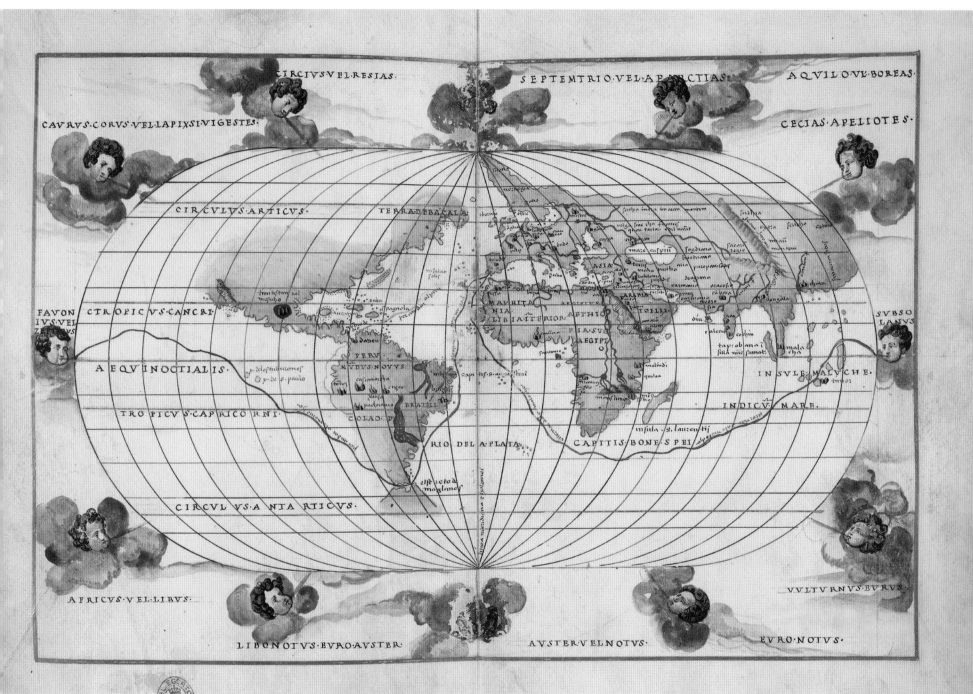

CIRCIVS·VEL·RESIAS.    SEPTEMTRIO·VEL·APARCTIAS    AQVILO·VEL·BOREAS.

CAVRVS·CORVS·VEL·IAPIXSI·VIGESTES.    CECIAS·APELIOTES.

CIRCVLVS·ARTICVS·    TERRA·DE·BACALA    iberna    serha india in aurum montem    scythia

CTROPICVS·CANCRI    ASIA    ARABIA    TOELI

FAVONIVS·VEL·ZEPHIRVS    AEQVINOCTIALIS·    MVNDVS·NOVVS    MAVRITA NIA    AEGIPTVS    SVBSOLANVS

LIBIA·ITERIOR    AETHIOPIA·SVB·AEGIPTO    INSVLE·MALVCHE·

PERV    casimarcha    cusco    BRAZILL    INDICVM·MARE·

TROPICVS·CAPRICORNI    COLAO·P    insula·s·laurenty

RIO·DELA·PLATA·    CAPITIS·BONE·SPEI

CIRCVLVS·ANTARTICVS·    elstreto·d maglanes    linea meridiana ptolomei

AFRICVS·VEL·LIBVS·    VVLTVRNVS·EVRVS·

LIBONOTVS·EVRO·AVSTER    AVSTER·VEL·NOTVS·    EVRO·NOTVS·

# The kingdom of Japan

The Sea of Japan and the wider Pacific Ocean in which the islands of Japan sit have defined the country's relationship with mainland Asia for centuries. These islands and the various kingdoms and governments they have accommodated since humans first settled them are undeniably part of Asia, connected to its politics, culture and wider economy, but they also sit apart from it. This separation is physically created by the bodies of water that form the greater Pacific, and it has facilitated the development of cultures and political structures that are significantly detached from their neighbours.

The relationship between the islands of Japan and their respective populations is complex and dynamic, but of broader global significance is how Japan has historically related to the mainland kingdoms near to it, China and Korea especially. For much of Japan's history the relationship with China was that of a tributary kingdom on the outskirts of the Chinese Empire. Envoys, like those shown in Taishokkan's illustration, would periodically visit the islands, reminding Japanese rulers of the responsibilities and duties owed to the emperor. This dynamic had started to change by the time Europeans arrived on the islands; Japan became increasingly combative and sought to develop its own sphere of influence at the expense of other islands and mainland kingdoms, most notably Korea.

For Europeans the islands of Japan were another site of potential wealth in the east, but wrapped in more mystery than China and the Spice Islands off the Malay peninsula. By the time the Portuguese arrived in Tanegashima in 1542, Europeans had been in

Chinese envoys approaching Japan, by Taishokkan.

(*Left*) Sketch of the Dutch envoy and retinue from Kaempfer's *History of Japan*.

contact with other parts of the greater Pacific Ocean for almost half a century. The Japan they encountered was a feudal society that was initially eager to trade with Europeans for weapons and goods acquired as part of the broader trade in the Pacific. Despite the close tributary ties Japan had maintained with China across the centuries, when Europeans arrived on the islands Japan was actually cut off from trade with mainland China and so luxuries like silk and porcelain were hard to acquire in the country.

This provided Portuguese traders and those who came later, like the Dutch, with a unique opportunity, ferrying goods to Japan and installing themselves as intermediaries in the commercial cycle of the Pacific Ocean. Japan's experience of European interest would be markedly different from that of many other parts of Asia and the Pacific but it was nonetheless influenced by the actions of these *gaijin*, or outsiders. While the history of the Pacific islands had always been one of circulation, trade and oceanic politics, the arrival of Europeans was slowly changing the rhythm of the previous centuries – even for a relatively isolated group of islands like Japan.

# Gateways to the Pacific

In the wake of Magellan's circumnavigation it was clear there was more than one way to reach the East Indies and the western Pacific, but the known routes were still under the control of two European powers. The Portuguese controlled the routes via Cape Horn, using a passage via Malacca to reach the Malay peninsula, while the Spanish were establishing control of the Philippines and beginning to explore the possibility of developing the galleon trade across the Pacific.

The European right to enforce control over these passages was to be underpinned by the edicts of the Treaty of Tordesillas for many years to come, which meant that other Christian kingdoms from Europe were denied the use of these routes. Nonetheless, waterways like those that flowed between the archipelagos off the Malay peninsula were used by many non-European cultures and would remain the major conduit into these waters for some time. They represented a rich cultural melting pot, with ships, traders,

missionaries and fishermen from many cultures plying their trade using the waters and the settlements that surrounded them.

This world was increasingly influenced and controlled by Europeans, however, and not just through the means of a politico-religious contract like the Treaty of Tordesillas. These powers were underscored by armed ships and fortified harbours, the key to Portuguese and Spanish control of their respective gateways to the Pacific. Faced with such military and political barriers, not to mention the significant economic and political gains which controlling these routes gave Portugal and Spain back in Europe, other European powers needed to find their own gateways to the Pacific.

For the English and the Dutch, early interest focused on the possibility of passages via the Arctic and the North Pole, most famously the Northwest and Northeast Passages. Adventurers like Martin Frobisher and Henry Hudson became bound up in a centuries-long quest to find a route via the frozen waters of the Arctic into the East Indies, while also hopefully discovering resources and other trading opportunities

The East Indies route, by Joan Martines, 1540.

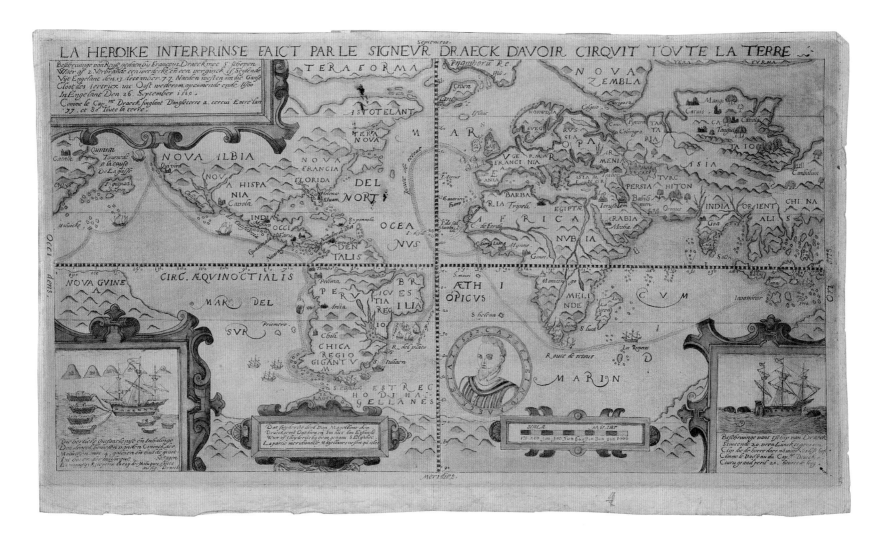

along the way. This became of increasing importance as political and religious pressures in Europe brought nations into direct conflict with the powerful kingdom of Spain. Whether it was through the religious turmoil of the Reformation or, in the case of the Dutch, the desire for independence from Spanish control, the sixteenth century would give rise to numerous reasons why other European kingdoms needed to compete against and to subvert the trading monopolies of the Spanish and Portuguese Crowns.

Practically, Arctic routes were not a solution. Numerous expeditions made little progress to the Pacific, although they did open up handsome opportunities for trapping and whaling. For now, privateering and overt aggression would be the key, especially using other Pacific gateways such as Drake's Passage, which passed south of the Strait of Magellan via Cape Horn.

Map of the world showing Drake's journey and Drake's Passage, probably published in Antwerp, 1581.

# Missionary politics

Following and accompanying the explorers, adventurers and traders now arriving in the Pacific from Europe were Christian missionaries and others tasked with establishing the faith in the lands they encountered. This should come as no surprise, as Christianity, specifically Roman Catholicism, was central to the Treaty of Tordesillas which Portugal and Spain used to divide the world between themselves. Under the Treaty, the kingdom of no Catholic monarch was to be colonised or conquered by the European powers but all other lands were available for subjugation and claim. It was implicit that the Portuguese and Spanish adventurers would facilitate the spread of Catholic teachings to the lands and peoples they encountered.

This meant that the conversion of local populations to the Catholic faith became an important mechanism for enforcing not just moral control in a region but also political control. As discussed earlier, the western Pacific entered by Europeans was a complex patchwork of religious beliefs, and those beliefs often underpinned local political control, be that in the form of sultans controlling significant trading locales or

the role of indigenous island religions in supporting the authority of chiefs and ruling families.

When European missionaries and religious figures arrived in the Pacific, then, they brought with them not just a faith but a means of political destabilisation. The conversion of people indigenous to the islands was a way of creating conflicting loyalties between a person's faith and the political body that ruled them. It was also a means of exacerbating tensions between European and local political interests. Throughout the history of European engagement in the Pacific, the defence of members of Christian faiths has repeatedly been used as a reason for belligerently engaging with established political bodies, especially in the case of the Islamic rulers of the western Pacific. The creation of significant Catholic communities in island groups like the Philippines, therefore, was a means of developing and ensuring European control in a locality and the region as a whole.

Illustrations such as this bird's-eye view of Manila articulate the role of religion in ensuring control of an island. The various

church spires that dot the landscape are the agents of Christianisation, moral redoubts that support the castles, walls and ships which defend the island as a whole from physical attack. The significance of the spread

DE STADT MANILHA.

of religion and the work of missionaries in changing the workings and political balance of the Pacific Ocean are perhaps best illustrated through Japan, where local rulers worked to make sure Christian missionaries did not establish lasting footholds on the islands. As we will see, this was key to maintaining Japan's independence in the coming centuries.

Bird's-eye view of Manila with various church steeples in the landscape, by Johannes Vingboons, c. 1665.

(*Left*) Michael Rogerius and P. Matthaeus Riccius arriving in China, engraving after A. van Diepenbeeck, 1682.

47

# The return journey

The successful circumnavigation of the world instigated by Magellan's expedition, and the discovery of the Strait of Magellan, was not as significant for Spain as you might expect. Yes, a route into the Pacific from the Atlantic had been found, and Magellan and his crew had made their way to the Philippines and the archipelagos of Southeast Asia. However, the distance to those islands had been much further than the Spanish had hoped, not only making the journey dangerous but challenging the original idea that the Spice Islands could fall within the Spanish sphere of influence defined by the Treaty of Tordesillas. On top of this Magellan had encountered no other landmass on his journey across the Pacific, and therein lay another critical problem: there was no immediately apparent and expedient way back across the Pacific.

Since Magellan's expedition, other Spanish navigators had set out to reach the lands encountered in 1521. They reasoned that easterly winds which would lead back to the Americas must exist. This was based on their knowledge of the gyre winds in the North Atlantic, circular currents of air that ran clockwise around the northern part of the ocean (and later drove the Triangular Trade) and which Portuguese navigators had already begun to understand. Surely similar flows of air must exist in the Pacific; but for over forty years, attempts to find them failed. The 1564 voyage of Don Miguel López de Legazpi, which was accompanied by the navigator André de Urdaneta, made progress that would change how Europeans related to the Pacific and begin the creation of the 'Spanish Lake'.

After Legazpi's expedition reached the Philippines, Urdaneta was involved in proselytising and establishing some of the first Christian sites of worship on the islands before being dispatched home by Legazpi. Urdaneta was a famed navigator before the departure of the expedition, and Legazpi entrusted him with finding a route across the Pacific and back to the Americas. Dividing his ships, Urdaneta reasoned that the prevailing North Pacific winds worked

A view of CAPE ESPIRITU SANTO, on SAMAL, one of the Philippine Islands in the latitude of 12.40 N° Bearing WSW distant 6 leagues. In the position here represented his Majestys Ship the CENTURION engag'd and took the Spanish Galeon call'd NOSTRA SEIGNIORA DE CABADONGA, from ACAPULCO bound to MANILA.

The *Centurion* attacking the Spanish galleon *Notra Signiora de Covadonga*.

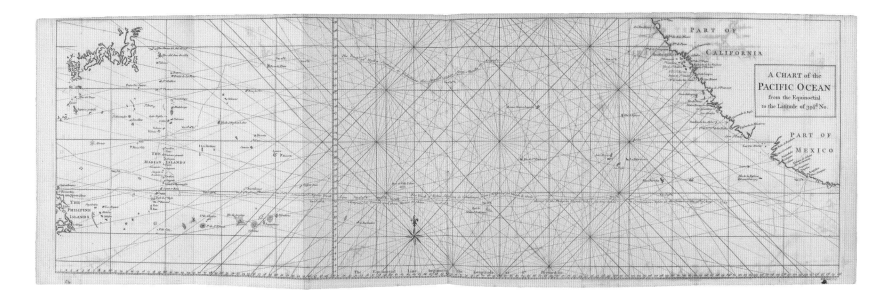

in the same clockwise direction as those in the North Atlantic. Thus, the most likely successful route was to head north towards the latitude of Japan before hopefully picking up gyre winds that would take him to the Americas.

The reasoning was sound although the journey that awaited Urdaneta and his crew was long, dangerous and stalked by starvation and death. Nonetheless Urdaneta and the remainder of his crew reached Acapulco in October 1565, having travelled 20,000 kilometres in 130 days. The achievement made trade across the Pacific possible, and therefore allowed the shipment of silver from Spain's mines in the Americas to China. Suddenly Spain was able to transport to Asia a resource the Chinese Empire actually wanted, and so began the Spanish galleon trade, shipping silver from the Americas and returning via the gyre winds laden with valuable manufactures. Spain now controlled the most profitable trade route in the world, and if it could keep it well defended it would be able to dominate European and global politics. Of course, as the map here suggests, this would not be easy. Inevitably the ships on the route would be tempting targets to Spain's competitors, as this ship, taken by George Anson during the War of Jenkins' Ear (1739–48), and many others, would find out.

Map of the route of a captured galleon.

# The galleon trade and the 'Spanish Lake'

As the Spanish discovered how to use the currents of the Pacific to their advantage, the resulting galleon trade became big business. Between 1565 and 1815 ships plied a route that ran from Acapulco to Manila and back again, taking silver from the Americas and using it for trade in Asia. This route particularly focused on trade in China and the same vessels returned laden with silks, porcelain, spices, ivory and other

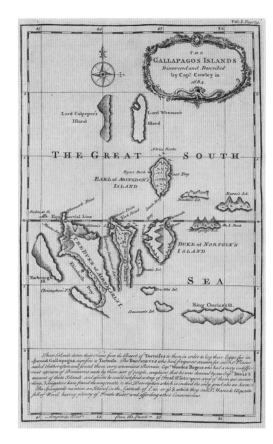

(*Above*) Map of the Galápagos, from Harris's *Navigantium*.

(*Left*) Drake's capture of the galleon *Nuesta Señora de la Concepción* (the *Cacafuego*), March 1579.

valuable commodities. The ships were of such significant value that soon after the inception of the trade, many travelled with battle-ready armadas supporting them. In theory Spanish monopolisation of the galleon trade routes, along with the military presence that accompanied the galleons, would make the main body of the Pacific a 'Spanish Lake', a domain under the sole control of the kingdom of Spain.

Such an endeavour had dramatic consequences for the economies, cultures and populations of the Pacific. The galleon trade became a major source of cultural mixing and exchange as huge numbers of peoples travelled on the ships along with the commodities they transported. It is the galleon trade that disseminated the drinking of *tuba* (discussed earlier) to South America and that is responsible for so many words originating in the Americas finding their way into use in the Philippines and Southeast Asia more widely. Furthermore, the galleons brought not just Europeans but the indigenous peoples of the Americas and Southeast Asia into increasing contact with each other, with populations moving across the ocean and settling in centres of the trade. This is perhaps best illustrated by the role of Filipino shipwrights in the construction of the galleons. During the 250-year period of the trade, construction focused on Manila, but ports in mainland South America also constructed galleons, often using labour and overseers who were originally from the Philippines.

A trade of such vast wealth and social impact could not hope to operate unseen for long, and soon the sailors of other nations were beginning to view the galleon trade with interest. Nations like England, at war with Spain for many of the years the galleon trade operated, saw in the galleons an opportunity to give the Spanish Empire a bloody nose. It was the rich Pacific coast of South America and the galleon trade that drew Sir Francis Drake to the Pacific, resulting in his charting of Drake's Passage and, after a failed attempt to find the Northwest Passage, his circumnavigation of the world.

The illustration here, depicting the capture of the *Cacafuego*, shows the galleons the English hoped to prey on as well as their success in doing so. The desire to prey on the trade also brought the English into increasing contact

with the Pacific, although their engagement with the ocean was significantly different from that of the Spanish. While the Spanish relied on the winds of the ocean and often ignored islands in the vast body of the Pacific, to the English these islands were hubs where their privateers could hide and resupply in order to continue their quest to capture Spanish riches. The map John Harris published in *Navigatum*, while from a later period of English privateering, shows the

concerns of English sailors, such as deep harbours and fresh water, and how the islands of the Pacific could be used to undermine the 'Spanish Lake'.

Galleon in a bay in the Philippines, from Theodor de Bry.

Arcipelago di S. Lazaro.

Baixos de S. Bartholome
I. de S. Petro.

OCCI-

La de Seyrouechada

Corral de Pracelas
I. de Pracelas

Barbudos
I. de Don Alonco

De las dos Ve̅
sinos

I. de Paxaros

DENTALIS.

Miracomo Vas

I. de los Nadadores

La Ballena
De la buena paz
Elabrigo

I. de hóbres
blancos
I. de la
Madalena
Triango

La Carimana

La Bardula

Islas de Salamon.

De la
malagète
Elabrigo
Elbolcan

De la Madre de
Dios

La Redon

R. de S. Pietro et paulo
De las Virgines
R. de S. Ieronimo
R. Baxo
S. Augustin
R. Salido
C. de Galfario
B. d. S. Niculas
Blanco
Buena Baja
Anco̅ de la nattiui
dad de n. fimora

Baixos de Candelaire

Nombre de Ibesus

Nova Guinea.

Vista de
Lexos

Zamba

I. Verdes

Malarta

De la Aquada

S. Xpoual

Sic a nautis dicta, quòd
littora illa, conditioq̃ terra,
Guineæ in Africa multùm
similia fint. Continensnè
ad terrã Auftralẽ, an In-
fula fit, incognitũ eft.

Amacfre

Los bolcètes
Ysabella

S. Nicolai

Vizerre
I. Dagoa

Dalcana

S. Thiago

I. de la Tubarones

# Europeans come to Oceania

While trade across the 'Spanish Lake' was instigating profound changes for islanders at its edge, the beginning of heightened European interest in the Pacific was passing many populations of islanders in the Pacific by. In particular, many of the descendants of the Lapita peoples – the diverse cultural groups Europeans later named Melanesian, Micronesian and Polynesian – were ignored by Spanish traders chasing circular routes and the privateers who followed them. Towards the end of the sixteenth century, however, this situation began to change as enthusiasm to explore and, crucially, the desire to locate *Terra Australis* reared its head again.

The search for the Great Southern Land that Europeans believed Marco Polo hinted at never truly died away after the Portuguese and Spanish entered the Pacific, but interest in locating the continent certainly diminished. Reasons for this were purely practical and financial. Both the Portuguese and the Spanish had located resources and trade routes that promised vast wealth and enormous political advantage back in Europe. That being the case, the next logical step was to protect these ventures and to make them as profitable as possible, not go chasing after other finds at huge risk and vast expense. After all, fitting out ships to travel across the world was incredibly expensive, so why spend money on the search for new lands when immense opportunities were already known about and had not yet been fully exploited?

Such was the logic of the Spanish Crown and various officials in the colonial hubs of South America. Nonetheless, there were dreamers, men who fantasised about discovering new lands and prodigious sources of wealth. This should not come as a surprise, especially as the rapacious predations of the conquistadors who reived and pillaged across the empires of South America had been so successful. These military adventurers, like the Pizarro expedition discussed earlier, had not just made themselves opulently wealthy, but they had carved out small empires for themselves and been able to convince themselves they had done God's work at the same time. Such campaigns inspired a new generation of Pacific explorers to head out into the vastness of the ocean, searching for another continent, new kingdoms and people to convert to the Catholic cause.

In 1567 Álvaro de Mendaña y Nera left the Peruvian port of Callao with two ships in his command, sailing a more southerly route than the Spanish galleons usually did, in the hope of encountering new lands and starting a new phase of Spanish and Christian expansion in the Pacific. His main contact was with the people of islands to the east of New Guinea, today known as the Solomon Islands. Mendaña himself gave the islands this name, hoping he had found the outlying archipelagos of the Great Southern Land and believing he had, at the same time, encountered the fabled location of King Solomon's mines. For Mendaña and his generation of explorers their adventures in the Pacific were wrapped in Old Testament myth, as had been the exploits of the conquistadors. Mendaña's only problem was that on his return to South America no one else really shared his enthusiasm for Solomon's Islands.

(*Left*) *Nova Guinea et Insulae Salmonis*, 1602.

# Mendaña's return and Quirós's New Jerusalem

It took Mendaña almost thirty years to convince the relevant authorities to entrust him with another expedition, but when he set sail in 1595 he did so with a new pilot, Pedro Fernandes de Quirós. Mendaña and Quirós set sail in the same direction as Mendaña had done in 1567, hoping to make further contact with the islands previously encountered and eventually find the southern continent. This time they reached the Marquesas Islands, which they named in honour of the Viceroy of Peru at the time, García Hurtado de Mendoza, 5th Marquis of Cañete. Over the course of these two expeditions Mendaña and Quirós provided Europeans with their first written accounts of the Oceanian peoples who populated the smaller islands of the South Pacific. The accounts themselves were strongly biased, despite their being impressed by the martial culture of the islands, emphasising the 'heathen' nature of the people encountered and noting little of the cultural and architectural advances the of Marquesas since the first Europeans arrived.

Some of this was masked by Mendaña and Quirós's Christian fervour but it is possible that the struggles of the expedition also inhibited their perception of the cultures they encountered. The expedition continued west, reaching the Solomons again, where many of the crew, including Mendaña himself, succumbed to endemic tropical disease, most likely malaria. Quirós took over the expedition and sailed it home to friendly ports, but he too had been bitten by the bug of *Terra Australis*. Like Mendaña, Quirós believed these expeditions had been on the verge of a monumental discovery and after years of petitioning, including even travelling to Rome to make his case for the conversion of the peoples of the islands he and Mendaña had encountered, Quirós was granted another expedition, which left Callao with three ships in December 1605.

This expedition would make landfall on Espíritu Santo (Holy Spirit) Island, part of today's Vanuatu, and here all of Quirós's godly ambitions would reach a crescendo. Thinking he had made landfall on the southern continent, Quirós named the island Australia del Espíritu Santo and set about creating a colony as well as attempting to convert the indigenous Ni-Vanuatu peoples who lived around the island. Quirós's aims here were not just the construction of another trading venture and Spanish colonial fiefdom; his head was awash with ideas of Eden and of having found the site for the creation of the new Jerusalem. He named the settlement New Jerusalem and set about trying to build an ideal colony, having been heavily influenced by the ideas articulated in Thomas More's *Utopia* (1516). This dream, however, was doomed to fail. Indigenous resistance, hardship and mutiny among the sailors and colonists meant that by the end of 1606 Quirós was back in South America, the idea of New Jerusalem on Espíritu Santo now only an imagined place recorded on maps, like the copy above, secreted in Spanish archives.

Mendaña and Quirós's expeditions illustrate how trade and the realpolitik of colonial missions seen elsewhere in the history of European interest in the Pacific could become consumed by dreams and zealous religious imagination. It would not be the last time such fervour would grip Europeans in the Pacific and it would continue to change the lives of Pacific islanders.

Map of Quirós's 'Espíritu Santo', 1606, copied by William Hack, 1698.

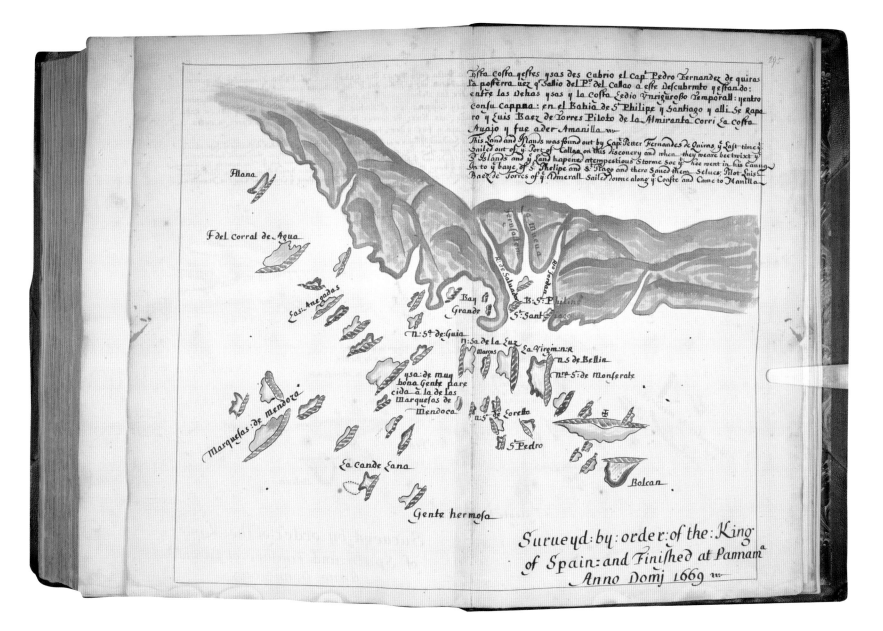

# New Guinea

The settlement and historical demography of the island of New Guinea are breathtakingly complicated. The island has been settled by human cultures for at least 40,000 years and its size and geography mean that successive waves of settlement by different cultural groups have not just arrived on the island but have also created distinct cultures with their own geographies. The possibilities for such complex settlement are underlined when one considers how big the island is: today's United Kingdom (including Northern Ireland) consists of just under 250,000 square kilometres of land, while the island of New Guinea is over 780,000 square kilometres in area. It is the second-largest island in the world (after Greenland and counting Australia as a continent) and has a geography defined by mountain ranges, complex valley systems and large waterways. As a result, it was possible for the many different cultural groups that settled the island to develop in relatively isolated ways, meaning that New Guinea maintained a huge diversity of cultures and languages within its shores.

The coast of New Guinea was still very much part of the flows and exchanges of the broader Pacific. Lapita peoples settled there, agriculture and maritime industries developed and the island became part of the trading networks of the Pacific region. One particular item from the island was famed throughout the region, and later the world, finding its way around the Pacific and becoming a highly desirable prize in the courts of various Chinese emperors: the feathers of the bird of paradise. Ceremonial dress decorated with the feathers of local bird life is encountered across the Pacific, especially in those groups broadly descending from the Lapita cultural complex, but the feathers of the bird of paradise are particularly beautiful and coveted for their value as status signifiers.

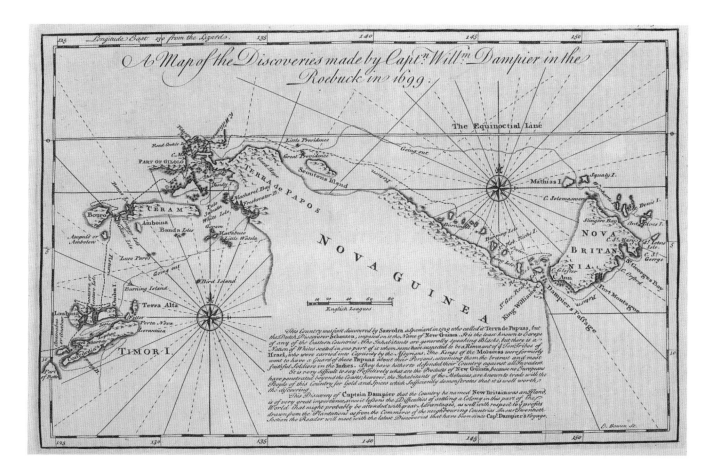

Dampier's map of Nova Guinea and Nova Britannia, from *Harris's Navigantium*, 1764.

(*Left*) Islanders of New Guinea, from *Oud en Nieuw Oost-Indien*, vol. 3.

As a result of these exchanges, the New Guinea encountered by Europeans was very much part of the networks of the western Pacific, but it was nonetheless strange to these visitors from across the oceans. New Guinean peoples first encountered Europeans in 1526–7 when the expedition of Don Jorge de Meneses arrived at the island. In 1545 Íñigo Ortiz de Retes named it 'New Guinea' as he thought the people he encountered there bore a resemblance to groups he had encountered on Africa's

Guinea Coast. The size of New Guinea led many to believe it was a part of the southern continent *Terra Australis*, but by the 1600s it was appearing on maps as an island and by 1607 a European had sailed the southern strait between New Guinea and Australia. This was Luis Váez de Torres, who had become separated from Quirós as he tried to find more evidence for the discovery of a new, provident and holy southern continent. After losing contact with Quirós, Torres had made for the friendly port of Manila, sailing

south of New Guinea and removing another piece of evidence suggesting the existence of the southern continent.

Contact with Europeans would be haphazard for New Guinea but, as the above map by William Dampier and the illustration from Dutch East India Company records suggest, it would be frequent and involve all major parties interested in the Pacific. The history of Europeans in the Pacific would not be kind to New Guinea and its peoples.

# Ports of the Pacific

Earlier discussion of the gateways to the Pacific showed that, for such a huge expanse of ocean, the main and most useful routes into the Pacific were narrow and, at least in the western Pacific, densely populated. This geography facilitated the growth of a number of principal ports, spaces where various parties interested in the development and exploitation of trade in the Pacific could enhance and defend their own interests. Such spaces existed before the arrival of Europeans in the ocean and its borders – previous discussions on the interconnectedness and rich trade networks of the Pacific prior to the sixteenth century illustrate this – but such ports took on a new phase of life after the arrival of Europeans.

Some ports, such as Malacca, were established before the arrival of Europeans while others, like Macau, took on a new lease of life after the arrival of traders and sailors from the other side of the world. Similarly, sites such as Manila and Batavia (today's Jakarta) were significantly influenced by European settlement, construction, conflict and control. In this way these points became nodes in a network of trade and exchange, with junks, ferries and ships shuttling goods between these ports and then out into the wider world, whether west to Europe via the Indian Ocean or east to South America and the cities of the growing Spanish empire.

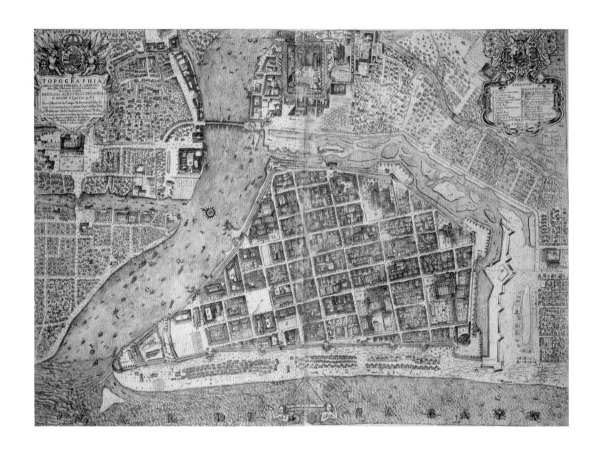

Map of Manila from *Topographia de la ciudad de Manila*, 1717.

(*Right*) Map of the Philippines with twelve marginal vignettes, 1734.

A View of the Town and Castle of Macao

On islands like the Philippines and Sumatra, these processes created diverse populations as cultures from across the Pacific were mixed together by an increasingly globalising trade network that focused on the Pacific Ocean. This would have lasting effects for the region, creating ports and cities that are still hubs of global exchange and cosmopolitan life,

located amid a geography still influenced by the histories of the colonial world. However, Europeans were not the only influencing factors. There were other forces at work too, some operating in the relatively lawless spaces of the open ocean and posing a dire threat to the traders who hoped to use the waters of the Pacific to gain opportunities and riches.

Piracy had always been an element of life on the Pacific, with bands arising and operating from various islands, especially Japan and Taiwan. As we will see, these were not just single roving ships but could be armadas of prodigious size preying on the shipping traffic, villages and major ports supporting the Pacific trade.

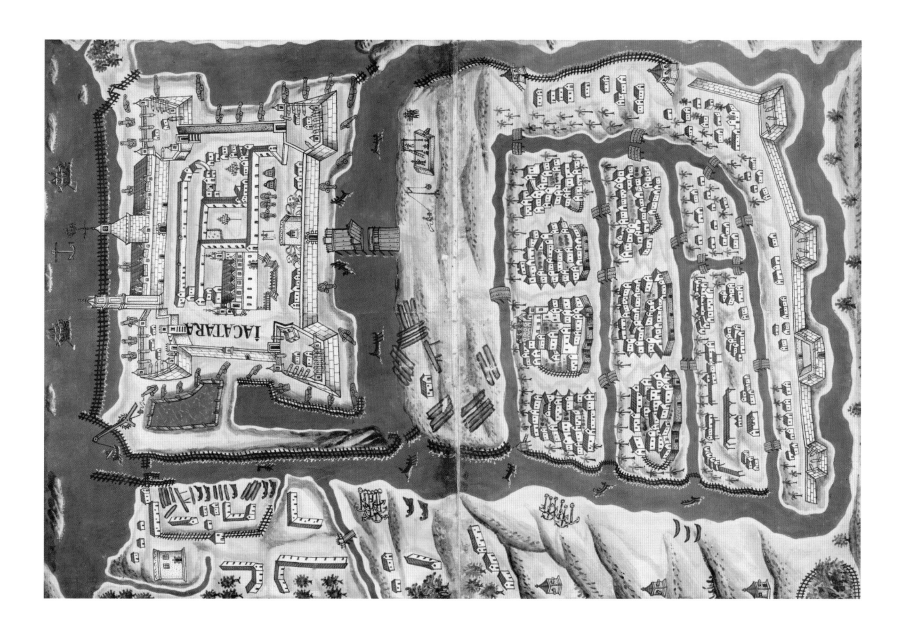

Map of 'Iacatara' (Jakarta), from the collection of
Francis Perry.

(*Left*) Illustration of Macau from George Anson's
voyage, from Harris's *Navigantium*, 1764.

I. FORMOSA .

# Pirates, exiles and the island of Taiwan

The richness of the ports and waters of the Pacific made it inevitable that some would try to profit from the ocean's networks in more illicit ways, especially through piracy and smuggling. It must be remembered that the early actions of all European nations trying to gain a foothold in the Pacific resembled, at best, privateering, as they used state-sponsored violence against indigenous and European powers to gain advantages in the region. Beyond this, though, there is a more interesting and complex history at play, one where pirates from various nations have created hybrid spaces and new oceanic routes, and shaped the relationship between Pacific islands and the rest of the world.

Piracy in the Pacific was a globalised affair and members of pirate crews came from a wide variety of backgrounds; by the sixteenth and seventeenth centuries their heritages could be mixes of Asian, European and Oceanian backgrounds, which represented the hybridising nature of the Pacific region. Others, such as Lim Ah Hong, were members of the elite of the societies they had been exiled from. Lim Ah Hong left China in 1573 and began a long campaign

of piracy around the Malay peninsula, threatening not just European shipping but the colonies as well.

Piracy was not just the domain of men and later, in the nineteenth century, a Cantonese woman, Cheng I Sao, would become the head of a pirate confederation and formidable fleet of ships. The end of Cheng's reign also shows the complex ways in which pirates in the Pacific could maintain relationships with the states and businesses operating in the

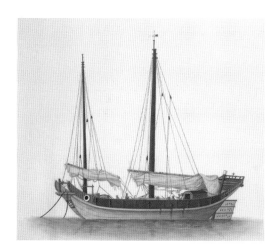

Chinese vessel with defences against pirates.

(*Left*) Dutch portolan chart of the island of Formosa (Taiwan).

ocean. Sensing that the game was up, in 1810 Cheng negotiated an amnesty for herself and many who had sailed with her. While Cheng retired, many of those directly or indirectly under her command found new work – often defending the ships they used to prey upon.

More significant, perhaps, is the career of Zheng Chenggong (also known as Koxinga). Inheriting a vast maritime network based on piracy from his father, Zheng attacked the Dutch colony on the island of Taiwan in 1662 and forced its surrender. Less than twenty years previously, control of the mainland empire of China had shifted from the Ming to the Qing Dynasty. Zheng's control of Taiwan established a Ming outpost on the doorstep of the Qing Empire.

Taiwan had long had an influential role in the Pacific, being the main site from which Lapita peoples voyaged into the Pacific and later a hub for trade in the region due to the narrow waterway between the island and mainland China. This had also made it rich ground for pirates. In setting up a site which called for the return of the Ming Dynasty, Zheng made Taiwan a thorn in the side of the ruling Chinese dynasty.

# The Sakoku Edicts and the future of Japan

The arrival of foreigners, their goods and their religions in Japan was initially welcomed after their arrival in the sixteenth century, but their presence on the islands was always contentious. Japanese rulers were happy with the arrival of certain goods and, most especially, modern projectile weapons from Europe, but increasingly influential European cultures and religions were viewed with suspicion and, at times, with overt hostility. Such indifference and suspicion of European ways was not unjustified. As discussed previously, the presence of European religions and preachers

was often the thin end of the wedge when it came to colonising spaces in the Pacific, and this was something noted by many Japanese rulers at the time. Moreover, events suggested that the Europeans had overtly hostile intentions towards Japan in the long term.

A significant moment was the wreck of the galleon *San Felipe* on the coast of Japan in 1595. The ship was carrying a number of missionaries, and they were rescued from their immediate peril, but their presence was viewed with suspicion once it became clear what else the ship was carrying. The

*San Felipe* held a large cache of weapons in its hold, raising suspicions as to the real intentions of the proselytisers who were rescued. The survivors were then killed by the Japanese and their martyrdom was highly publicised in Europe. Those who had converted to Western religions now became not just subjects of suspicion but also pawns in Japan's political games of the early seventeenth century. By 1614 the Shōgun Ieyasu was actively suppressing Christianity. His actions were easier to promote to the people of Japan because by this point both Catholic and Protestant preachers were competing against each other in the country.

The Tokugawa administration of the seventeenth century used the suppression of Christian practice as a means to enforce its own authority in a Japan still coalescing after the troubles of the previous centuries. Christians were forced to worship furtively, and in the years after 1614 possibly thousands of Japanese who had converted to the religion were killed. This came to a head in the 1630s when the Sakoku Edicts were passed. These banned not only Christian worship in Japan but all foreign incursion and influence. After a brief period of trade, preaching and

influence building, the door would be closed on Europeans who wanted to enter Japan.

This was, however, not entirely the case. Japan was still addicted to the goods that traders, especially the Dutch, brought with them, and wished to maintain a supply of manufactures into the country. A few key trading partners were therefore not entirely expelled but relocated. Mainland Nagasaki would not house the number of Europeans it had done before, but Deshima Island in the city's harbour would do so. The scene shown here is how Nagasaki and its new island of factories and traders looked less than fifty years after the passing of the Sakoku Edicts. The European presence is still strong – but elsewhere Japan's doors were closed. It was not just that outsiders could not enter the islands; the Japanese themselves were forbidden from leaving them too. Japan was an island adrift in an ocean of interconnected lands.

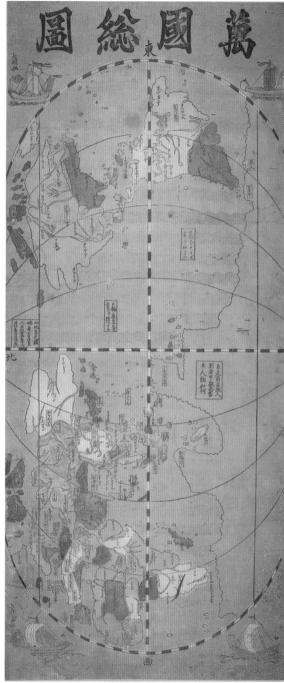

Japanese map of the world, including portraits of different peoples from around the world, 1645.

(*Left*) Map of Nagasaki from 1680 showing ships and figures of foreigners.

# The Dutch East India Company in the Pacific

The Dutch, especially through the Dutch East India Company, had a significant role in shaping the modern history of the Pacific, through Japanese trade in Nagasaki, early encounters with Australia, Aotearoa/New Zealand and Tonga, and their control of key trading nodes in the Pacific network. This history, like all colonial experiences, was a violent and exploitative network of events and begs the question of why the Dutch entered the Pacific. The answer tells us a great deal about the world beyond the Pacific and European interest in the ocean.

Until 1566 the provinces that form today's Netherlands were part of the kingdom of Spain, having passed to Philip II in 1555. At this point, Spain was a superpower in Europe, buoyed by the vast sums of silver it could pull from mines in South America and the commercial advantages of the galleon trade, and it used this hegemony to enforce religious orthodoxy on the continent. By the time Philip II took control of the Dutch territories, the Reformation had been gaining momentum for almost forty years and many in this region, especially in the more northerly provinces, were members of the emergent Protestant faith. In response Philip II used

the wealth and resulting military might at his disposal to try to enforce Catholic rule on the provinces of the Netherlands.

The result was a rebellion that stretched on for decades. The United Provinces of the north achieved some measure of independence by the end of the sixteenth century but the provinces needed to survive in a globalising world. Trade was a large part of the answer, specifically through

the establishment of an innovative, highly militarised trading body, the Dutch East India Company (VOC), which would take the fight to Spain in its colonial territories, bloodying the nose of the superpower and hopefully severing its economic umbilical cord with the Americas and the 'Spanish Lake'. So began the encroachment of the VOC into the Pacific, where it would have tremendous success over the centuries. The VOC took control of key ports and Spice

In this, the Dutch were replicating forms of exploitation mastered and used by the Portuguese and Spanish, whose vast wealth was predicated on the exploitation of the lands, resources and peoples they encountered in the Pacific and connected to its trade networks, such as the hellish, slave-worked silver mines in Potosí (in modern Bolivia). The history of European contact with the Pacific is built on such foundations, reinforced and developed by the vicious religious politics of Europe itself. For the first Europeans encountering the Pacific, the exploitation of its land and people was about thriving or perhaps just surviving back in Europe's violent kingdoms of the Reformation era.

Islands; they also sailed the wider Pacific and were the first Europeans to be encountered by Pacific peoples such as the Tongans, who met Willem Schouten in 1616.

Dutch successes in the region mounted, but they were built on the use of force, the monopolisation of resources, tactical use of environmental damage (such as the destruction of wild spice-fruiting plants), the aggressive promotion of Protestant forms of worship and the indenture and enslavement of islanders from across the Pacific.

(*Left*) *East Indian Market Stall in Batavia*, attributed to Albert Eckhout, 1640–66.

(*Above*) Map of Ambon, eastern Indonesia, including portrait of Governor Frederik de Houtman.

(*Right*) Arms of the Dutch East India Company.

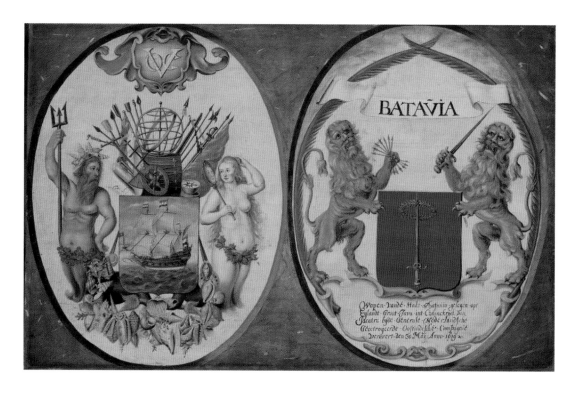

# How to break a monopoly

Jacob Le Maire and Willem Schouten set sail from the Netherlands in 1615 with a clear aim, to undermine the monopolies of the VOC and open up new trading opportunities for those who were not associated with the most profitable elements of the Company and its trade with Asia and the Pacific. As a successful venture, making profits to support the Dutch efforts against the Spanish and bloodying the kingdom's nose on its own terms, the VOC had been able to establish various rights for itself. Key among these was a monopoly of trade conducted by Dutch sailors, merchants and adventurers, and this was enforced by notional control of the established routes into the Pacific. The VOC could not effectively physically control these routes but could establish a blanket ban on all non-VOC trade through them. Crucial to this control was the idea that the known routes to the Pacific, via the Cape of Good Hope and the Strait of Magellan, were the only navigable routes into the Pacific Ocean.

For Le Maire and Schouten, then, the main aim of their expedition was clear, to find a new route into the Pacific. Their best hope lay in finding a route via South America, taking a more southerly course than the Strait of Magellan. Such routes were spoken of – Drake's circumnavigation was understood to have used such a route even if the exact details were not well known outside of England – and so Le Maire and Schouten set out to define a route that would fall beyond the control of the Company. The expedition

(*Below*) Plate showing 'Ile de Cocos' from Schouten's published account, 1619.

(*Right*) Frontispiece map from Schouten's account showing him with other navigators, including Magellan.

(*Far right*) Illustrations of conflict and trade with Pacific islanders from the same account, 1619.

was a success in this regard, encountering a passage between two landmasses on 24 January 1616 and sailing between them as the start of a route that would take them around Cape Horn and on a unique voyage to the southerly Pacific. The gap between the islands was named the Strait of Le Maire and the expedition sailed on to bring Europeans into contact with various Pacific governments, such as the Tongan maritime empire, for the first time.

Le Maire and Schouten's encounters were often aggressive, with the Europeans using their guns and technological advantages to enforce their own rules and trading patterns on communities they encountered. Despite their navigational prowess the expedition leaders were not adroit communicators across cultural boundaries. This was evidenced by their refusal to partake in kava rituals for fear the drink would be poisoned, but they nonetheless learned of new islands and resources they could base trade exchanges on.

After arriving in Dutch territories the expedition began preparing to return home, and sailed into Batavia (Jakarta) in October 1616. Here the vessels and their cargo were seized by the Regional Governor of the VOC, Jan Pieterszoon Coen, who believed the expedition had violated Company monopolies. He was not amenable to Le Maire and Schouten's arguments about their discovery of a new route. The men of the expedition were sent back to the Netherlands on VOC transports and Le Maire died en route, never having found out the fate of his attempts to break the monopoly. In the end Le Maire's father, Isaac, took the expedition's case to the Dutch legislature and they upheld the expedition's claims. Le Maire and Schouten received compensation and a new route to the Pacific officially existed.

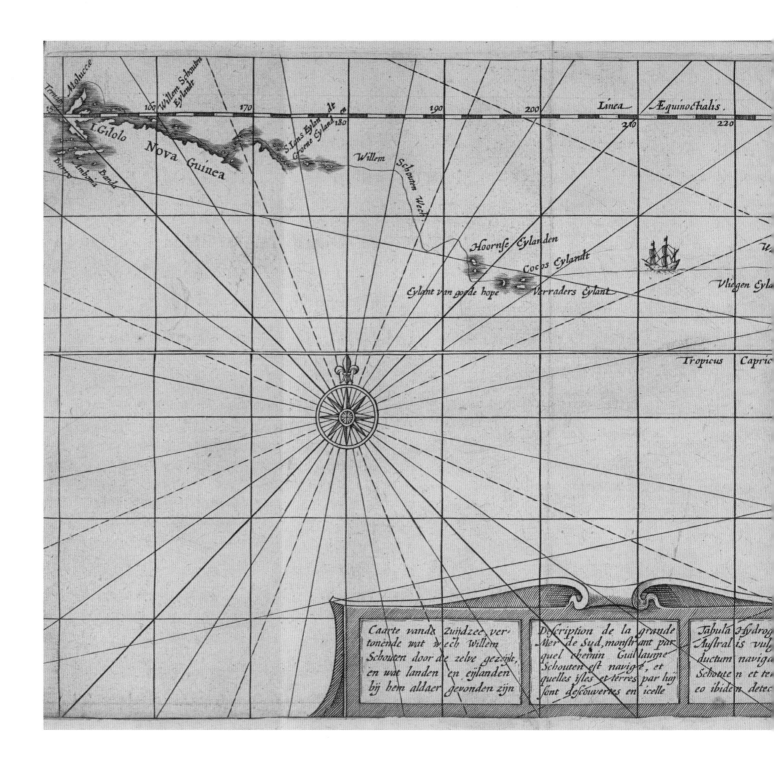

Map of Schouten's voyage
across the Pacific, 1619.

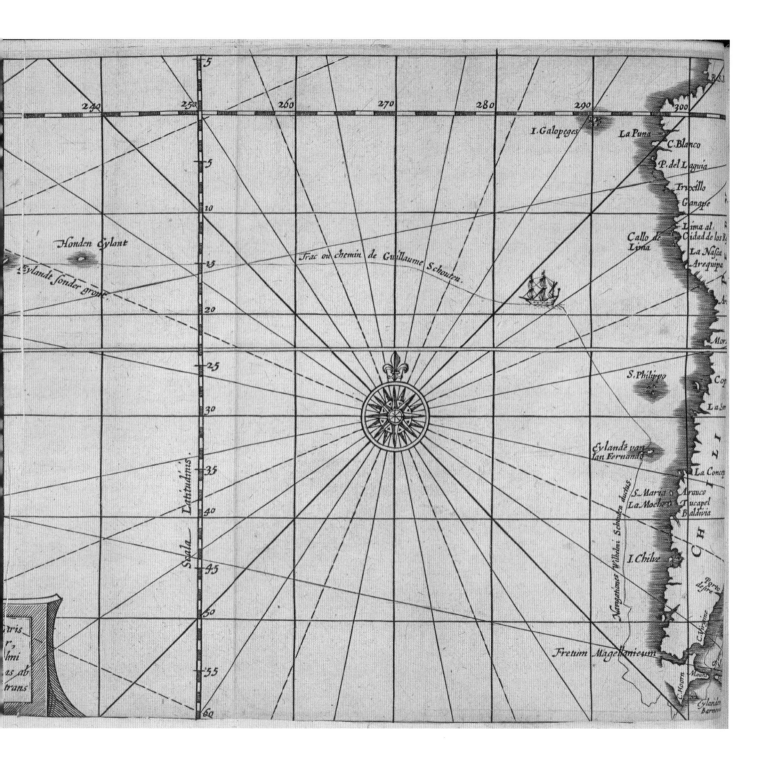

5

240    250    260    270    280    290    300

I. Galopeges                                    La Puna
                                                C. Blanco
                                                P. del Laguia
5                                               Truxillo
                                                Ganape
10                                              Lima al.
                                                Cidad de los R.
Honden Eylant                        Callo de    La Nasca
                              Lima              Arequipa
Eylande sonder grone
15    Trac ou chemin de Guillaume Schouten.

20

25                         S. Philippo

30

Scala Latitudinis.                              La Sm

35                         Eylandē van
                           Ian Fernande
                                                La Concep.
40                         S. Maria   Arauco
                           La Moebro  Tucapel
                                      Baldivia

45

I. Chilue
50

55    Fretum Magellanicum

60                                              C. Hoorn
                                                Eylanden
                                                Barnevel

# Tasman's journey to the unknown

**W**ithin the context of the religious and civil conflict underpinning Dutch interest in the Pacific it is perhaps not surprising that the Netherlands too should become involved in the search for *Terra Australis*. To those who ran the VOC, not to mention its investors, the prospect of a great, undiscovered continent which was not pockmarked with ports and strongholds under Portuguese and Spanish control was immensely appealing. Dutch adventurers had been successful in exploiting the part of the Pacific where these nations already had control; imagine what they could achieve on a continent that had not yet encountered Europeans.

These possibilities were particularly appealing to the Governor-General of the Dutch East Indies, Anthony van Diemen, and in 1642 he dispatched Abel Janzoon Tasman on an expedition to locate the great southern continent. Tasman was an accomplished navigator with an established reputation among other members of the VOC and he began his search for the continent by heading in the direction of the Pacific Ocean. Maps across the centuries had suggested that the landmass jutted far north into the wide expanse of the Pacific, making an encounter

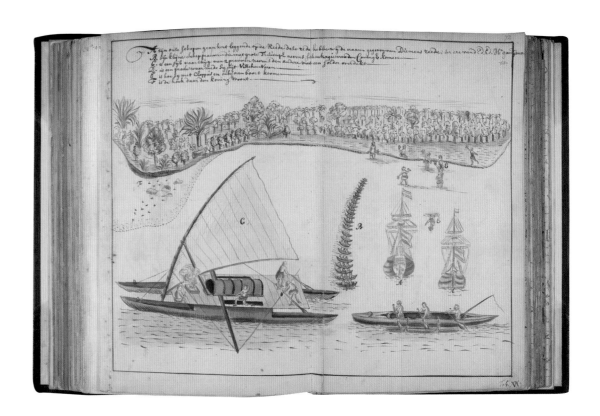

significantly more likely in this ocean. Unlike the Spanish expeditions of the previous century, Tasman approached the Pacific by rounding Africa's cape and sailing across the south of the Indian Ocean. This course brought him south of the main landmass of Australia but into contact with Tasmania,

which he named Van Diemen's Land in honour of his patron. While the locating of Van Diemen's Land was heartening to Tasman, it was troubling in terms of the search for *Terra Australis*. Dutch navigators knew of the existence of the lands that comprise Western Australia today, and it

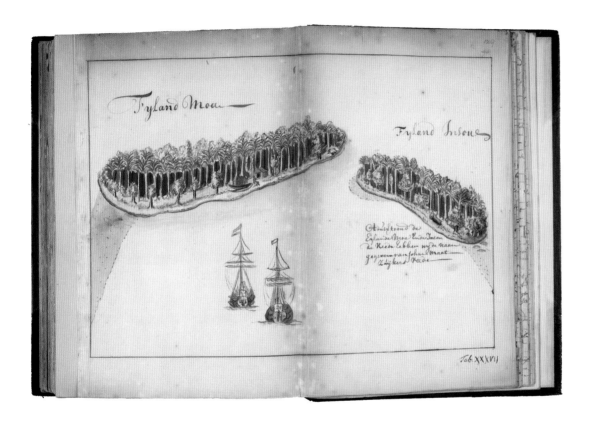

Islands and vessels depicted in a copy of Tasman's diary that belonged to Sir Joseph Banks.

Continuing on an easterly course, Tasman eventually made contact with Aotearoa/New Zealand and the Maori who inhabited the islands. The Maori were relatively recent settlers of the islands (in terms of the longer history of the settlement of the Pacific Ocean) but they had already reshaped their ecosystem: gone were many of the large species of birds that once inhabited the islands, and the Maori had built up a rich culture. This culture was indisputably a martial one and Tasman was to find his first encounter with the Maori intimidating. Arriving in the territory of the Ngāti Tumatakokiri, Tasman was hailed with challenges from Maori who rowed out to meet his ships. Simultaneously a small Dutch boat was dispatched to run a message between the ships, and this was attacked by Maori in canoes. Four Dutch sailors were killed and the body of one taken by the Maori warriors. Tasman got the message the Maori were sending, and left the islands he had just added to European maps. No other Europeans would return for almost 130 years and the VOC would eventually decide that, even if *Terra Australis* did exist, any southern continent would not be a source of profit.

must have seemed feasible to Tasman that his southerly route would bring him into contact with a great landmass before reaching the island he had named after his patron. Nonetheless, Tasman left without establishing Van Diemen's Land's status as an island. There was still hope here.

# Privateers of the Pacific

After the precedent set by Drake and others, buccaneering in the Pacific became a profitable enterprise for English mariners. The prizes brought home in the earliest days of the privateers had not just been a significant victory in English skirmishes against Spain; they had also had a dramatic effect on England's economy, providing enough profit to pay off government debts and allow investment in the state. Sending privateers to the Pacific, then, became a major enterprise for the English for over a century subsequently, with various adventurers, some successful, others less so, being sent to the 'Spanish Lake' to prey on the galleon trade and bring back any other prizes they could from the far reaches of the earth.

These were the conditions in which Captain Bartholomew Sharpe found himself in the South Pacific in command of a privateering vessel with a letter of marque (a government licence) from the Crown. He had not begun the expedition as a captain but by 1681 he was in charge of a vessel cruising the South Pacific. For various reasons, some to do with the captain's judgement, the expedition initially seemed only moderately successful, but one item taken by the crew would have a significant impact on British activities in the Pacific. Upon the taking of the Spanish ship *Rosario* the captain of the vessel was intercepted trying to dispose of various documents over the side of the ship. Once these were in the hands of Sharpe's crew it became clear the men had captured a volume of Spanish maps. This was a significant prize not just for the privateers but also for English operations in the Pacific. The Spanish Empire had been deeply protective of cartographic information it produced about the areas under its control. Maps from expeditions discussed

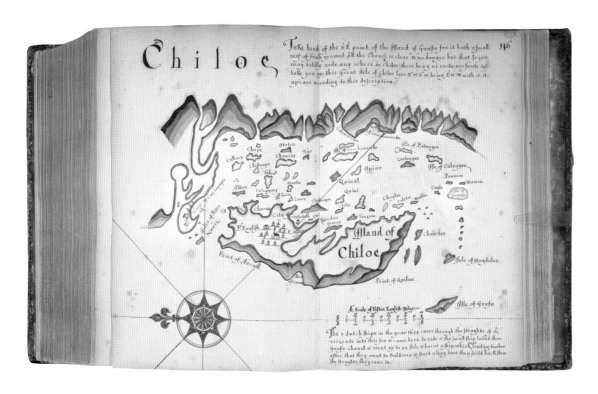

Maps by William Hack of islands in the Pacific, including the Galápagos Islands.

For Sharpe, it was lucky he had acquired the maps. Returning to England in 1682, he was put on trial for piracy, the Spanish ambassador to England having pushed for his arrest as, technically, Spain and England were at peace at the time the *Rosario* was captured. Sharpe and his men had slipped from being privateers to pirates. However, Sharpe's prize was now known and was causing much excitement back in England. Word was passed around secretly that the Crown wanted to see the maps Sharpe had returned with, and would also be keen to see the bearer of such a valuable prize set free to continue his career on the high seas. Sharpe did stand trial, ostensibly to placate the Spanish ambassador, but was acquitted on a technicality. The maps then found their way to a prominent member of the London Map School, William Hack, who produced various manuscript copies and derivative print copies of the maps. These charts, often detailed, as here, with notes on anchorages and features useful to the interests of a privateer in the Pacific, would contribute to English exploits in the Pacific for the next century and even play a role in the eighteenth-century South Sea Bubble (see p. 85).

earlier in this book disappeared into Spanish archives and only circulated among a limited number of individuals, the hope being that they would then be prevented from falling into the wrong hands. These hands were those of agents from the English Crown and the VOC, so Sharpe's capture of these maps was a significant moment.

Portrait of Hasekura, from *Relation un Grundtlicher Bericht …* (translation, 1617).

# Pacific travellers

By the time Europeans had become heavily involved in the Pacific, around the end of the seventeenth century, their activities were having a significant impact. Many networks of trade, tribute and interdependence, present in the region long before the arrival of European mariners, had evolved, modified or changed beyond all recognition. The connections the Pacific Ocean maintained with the wider world had also changed, lengthening and entangling as the world became increasingly globalised. People from different parts of the Pacific had begun to travel in and influence the world beyond their islands and regions of the ocean.

Some of them have been featured in this section of *Pacific*: people like Enrique de Malacca, possibly the first person to circumnavigate the world, and the Filipino shipwrights who voyaged around the 'Spanish Lake' in service of those who desired to make use of their skills. It is important to note that, while this world was being remoulded by the impact of Europeans, perhaps the only thing to truly change was the scale on which some of the connections across the Pacific occurred. The island communities of the Pacific had been linked by trade since the initial settlement of the islands. Especially after the coming of the Lapita cultural complex, the islands of the southwest Pacific were linked by dense trade networks that operated within the cultural boundaries of the region. As time progressed the networks in this region were distributed more widely, becoming part of the interconnected world of Southeast Asia. Feathers from New Guinea and sea cucumbers from the north coast of Australia, to name a few resources, were in demand for Chinese markets and so these parts of the Pacific Ocean became part of ever-expanding, gradually globalising trade networks. This meant that people too were circulating and mixing with new cultures as the boundaries of trade expanded.

The same was true for other areas of the Pacific, Japan being an example of another island culture bound into trade and political networks which inexorably gravitated towards the political, cultural and economic powers of the age. With the arrival of Europeans these trends continued and evolved rather than beginning for the first time. A Japanese envoy to Europe, Hasekura Tsunenga (1571–1622), is an example of the changing geography of Pacific connections. Hasekura travelled to Europe and was resident between 1613 and 1620, part of a Japanese embassy operating in Spain and the Vatican. His journey to and from Europe followed the geography of the 'Spanish Lake', using the galleon trade routes to sail from and back to Japan, and his presence in Europe was shaped by the dominant European powers in the Pacific.

Although Japan was withdrawing from European contact in this period, Hasekura was not the only islander from the Pacific to travel to Europe after the arrival of Spain and Portugal in the ocean. Nor was he the only individual to move through other global connections in the years leading up to the end of the seventeenth century. The next century would see some of the most famous travellers from the Pacific arrive in Europe, guests of expeditions led by the likes of Cook and Lapérouse, but they were going where others had travelled before; people and cultures from the Pacific were already connected to and influencing the wide world around them.

# Part 2
## Empire of Islands

三崎出船

The first section of this book has shown the interconnectedness of the Pacific Ocean, highlighting its archipelagic nature. While these connections have not always spanned the entire ocean, it is nonetheless significant that human settlement of islands in the Pacific did not generally result in the development of isolated communities but instead in the development of cultural regions where trade, resources and the exchange of traditions bound people and communities together across significant distances. Settlement of these islands also dramatically changed the way the lands and their immediate seas and parts of the ocean operated; fishing, farming, hunting, resource extraction, settlement and many other human activities significantly affected the operation of island ecosystems. The result was the creation of a very human Pacific, a settled ocean that inescapably bore the marks of human occupation and the reshaping of environments to suit people's needs.

Europeans, arriving from the late fifteenth century onwards, further precipitated the effect of human activities on Pacific landscapes. In particular, the actions of Portuguese, Spanish and, slightly later,

Dutch economic and colonial activities had wide-ranging effects, especially when driven by the desire to monopolise and exploit the financial potential of the spice trade by developing plantation monocultures on key islands in Southeast Asia. These impacts were not restricted to this one region of the Pacific. While European encounters with other islands in the Pacific were later to start and slower to gain momentum, by the end of the seventeenth century many different islands were being exposed to the various activities of representatives from European nations. In some ways the actions of Europeans only enlarged cultural processes of connection, domination and exchange that were already ongoing in the Pacific. Traders and adventurers of Dutch and Spanish origin had formidable tools at their disposal and precipitated horrendous violence on islands they came into contact with, but this had happened elsewhere too. The rise of Muslim sultans in the Malay peninsula and the warring of Shōguns on the islands of Japan are just two examples.

The change in scale of European involvement with the Pacific from the eighteenth century is undeniable. European

powers were by then actively involved with and profiteering from the resources and labour of islands in the Pacific. Some Pacific islands, such as Japan, had become aware of this and taken steps to withdraw from contact with this widening world, although they could never do so entirely. For those who could not, the increasing interest and exploitation of traders and adventurers from outside the boundaries of the Pacific Ocean would have significant, long-lasting consequences. Gone was the age of the narrow channel of the galleon trade and intermittent contact with trading companies. Globe-spanning empires were coming to the Pacific and they would attempt to carve it up between themselves, changing the geographies of interconnection, the operation of societies and ecologies of islands in ways unimaginable to those alive in the seventeenth century. In return, the Pacific and its communities would reshape the wider world too, as islanders travelled, trade developed and ideas from the Pacific inspired those explorers open-minded enough to appreciate them. The process of influence and change instigated here may not have been balanced but it at least flowed both ways.

# A heritage of exploration

**B**artholomew Sharpe was not the only English privateer to have made his way into the Pacific. By the late seventeenth century a number of vessels from England were preying upon Spanish trade in the Pacific and making their presence known. Another who was involved in these pursuits was William Dampier, who entered the Pacific via Cape Horn in 1683 before setting out to cross it in 1686 as a member of the crew of the ship *Cygnet*. Dampier would claim he was not involved in any effective piracy during his initial time in the Pacific, although the lie is given to this by the time he spent in command of a Manila galleon captured in 1687.

Dampier's account of his time in the Pacific, *A New Voyage Around the World*, was published in 1697 and was a financial success for both publisher and author. So vivid was the account and so widely did it circulate that it attracted the interest of the Admiralty, especially because of Dampier's notes about contact with the west coast of Australia. Western Australia had been known of by Europeans since Dutch and English contact with its shores in the early seventeenth century, but Dampier was able to interest

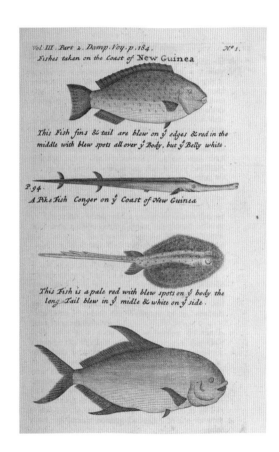

the Admiralty in the idea that the shores he visited could have been part of *Terra Australis*. He was entrusted with the fifth-rate ship HMS *Roebuck* and departed on his expedition in 1699. Dampier's expedition made little progress on answering the

Plants and fish encountered around New Guinea, as depicted in Dampier's published account, 1729.

(*Opposite*) Map of Dampier's 1699 voyage, published in 1729.

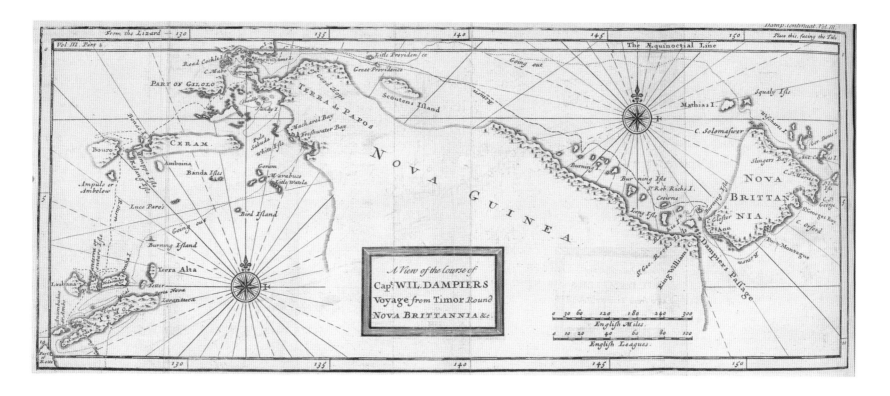

question of *Terra Australis* but the voyage is significant nonetheless. It represents a shift in the Admiralty's interest in the Pacific, to one which was more formal and undertook exploration for the sake of exploration and the improvement of English knowledge of this part of the world. Dampier himself also brought new and influential perspectives to the English practice of exploration.

Explorers associated with the VOC had historically taken an interest in the landscapes, flora and fauna they encountered, with an eye to finding resources which could be harvested at a profit. English sailors in the Pacific, however, had been involved more often in privateering and loose trading expeditions than in the exacting business of exploration and chart-making, which was why Sharpe's capture of Spanish maps (pp. 74–75) was such a coup. Dampier brought a keen eye to the Pacific in his privateering voyage and the 1699 expedition. He produced maps, took notes on the cultures he encountered and made detailed observations, with accompanying rudimentary illustrations, of the flora and fauna he encountered. To modern eyes the work Dampier produced has much scope for improvement, but it was the idea of recording these plants and animals in extensive detail as part of an expedition that was revelatory to English minds.

Dampier was to inspire a future generation of explorers and naturalists with his actions and his publications, as evidenced by the illustrations shown here. These are from a copy of Dampier's *Collection of Voyages* (1729) which formed part of the collection of Sir Joseph Banks and accompanied him on the *Endeavour* voyage with Captain Cook. The map and illustrations shown here would have been used for reference by Banks and the naturalists who accompanied him; they also, perhaps more importantly, inspired Banks to take part in a scientific expedition the scale of which had not been seen before.

(*Left*) Herman Moll, 'A New and Exact Map of the Coast Countries and Islands within the Limits of the South Sea Company'.

(*Above*) 'Lucipher's New Row-Barge', a satirical print of Robert Knight.

# The South Sea Company

Despite privateering and other forms of piracy being officially off the table for English sailors from the end of the seventeenth century to the beginning of the eighteenth century, English mariners still chafed at the idea of Spanish control of the Pacific still chafed at English mariners. Figures like Dampier frequently argued against Spanish control, asserting that the empire of Spain used little of the ocean and controlled more territory than it knew what to do with. At the start of the eighteenth century such arguments increasingly aligned with shifting power dynamics in Europe. The newly unified kingdom of Great Britain was beginning to take a more belligerent stance with its European neighbours, which placed Spain firmly in its sights.

With Britain already established as a maritime power, the oceanic realms of the Spanish Empire were a prime target in conflicts like the War of Spanish Succession (1701–13). Success in the conflict brought increasing confidence and demands for the redistribution of trade access in the Americas and the Pacific. Prior to the end of the war,

British confidence was so high that the South Sea Company was set up, a venture like the East India Companies of previous centuries which aimed to control trading opportunities in various parts of the globe. The map shown here was published around 1720 by the mapmaker Herman Moll and showed the purported sphere of influence of the South Sea Company. Inset maps depicting key island territories covered by the Company are significant not just because they suggest British claims over islands in the 'Spanish Lake', but also because they have a notable provenance. The representations of the Galápagos Islands and other features of the insets are copies from Sharpe's *Waggoner* (pp. 74–75), which was captured as part of unofficial privateering ventures in the Pacific during the previous century. Two points arising from the presence of these maps are worth noting. Firstly, the desire to keep the information they contain secret has clearly not succeeded. Secondly, their presence on the Moll map also shows the continuing significance of Sharpe's find and its role in undermining the Spanish monopoly on knowledge of the Pacific.

All the impressive maps in the world could not make the South Sea Company a success, however. By the time Moll's map was published in 1720 it was part of widespread and feverish interest in the Company which had gripped British society. Investors piled money into the Company but its only assets were based on paper; no ships were charted, no crews instructed and no significant expeditions had yet been sent out. Nor would they ever be, in fact. In the end, the South Sea Bubble burst, causing a catastrophic financial crash that affected not just the British economy but also investors across Europe who were connected to the Company. The Pacific was becoming increasingly entangled in the political and economic dynamics of the wider world and this entanglement had now reached a point where the idea of the Pacific could have a profound effect on European economies. The South Sea Company may never have launched a consequential venture to the ocean but it did represent a changing relationship between Europe and the Pacific, as well as the erosion of Spanish power there.

# The figures of Rapa Nui

Contact between Rapa Nui (Easter Island) and the rest of the Pacific was less common than elsewhere but not unheard of in the centuries after its settlement. The island formed part of trading circulations across the ocean and assimilated cultural practices from the broader Pacific, such as the Polynesian pantheon of gods. Contact with Europeans, however, was fleeting and did not occur until some time after the first European incursions into the ocean. Inevitably, it was the continuing search for the fabled continent of *Terra Australis* that drew the first Europeans to Rapa Nui's shores, with Jacob Roggeveen and his crew encountering the island in 1722. Roggeveen had set out in 1721 on yet another expedition to try to undermine the monopolies of the VOC by finding the theorised southern land and continuing work to find an unclaimed westerly route to the Malay peninsula.

Roggeveen recounts that when he arrived at Rapa Nui in April 1722 he was greeted by a significant population of islanders but that they lived on an island stripped of resources and seemed to possess no ocean-going craft. He was also the first European to be overawed by the gigantic mo'ai statues arrayed across the landscape. Roggeveen spent a single day on the island but he created its most enduring European legacy by renaming it Easter Island, after the day he and his crew arrived. Subsequent European visitors would be infrequent but they would continue to be struck by the same details Roggeveen and his crew noted. In particular the majestic mo'ai loomed large in the few published accounts detailing the island, with Lapérouse's later voyage, shown here, not just illustrating the mo'ai but ruminating on their geometry and architecture as well. Europeans who followed would also be struck by the seeming precariousness of the existence of those on Rapa Nui, and the decline in the number of people living there became increasingly clear.

Europeans would have a hand in this, as later discussions of 'blackbirding' will show, but between Roggeveen's expedition and those of later explorers it is apparent the island was wracked by conflict. This was precipitated by the environmental catastrophe unfolding on the island. Put simply, the large number of people were placing too great a strain on the ecosystem of the island. It has long been suspected that the erecting of the mo'ai led to the deforestation of the island, but the complete story of ecological collapse is more complicated. Pollen samples and archaeological evidence (such as bone heaps) suggest declining wildlife populations, with significant extinctions by the fifteenth century, no doubt as a result of over-hunting.

Human settlement of islands like Rapa Nui also occasioned indirect ecological changes, as introduced animals, especially rats, made their mark on the new ecosystems they encountered. In Rapa Nui's case it is likely these introductions, along with the stresses caused by human habitation, were major factors in the ecological erosion of the island. Furthermore, the island's relative isolation meant that the population based there had to be more self-sufficient than most, exacerbating the demands they placed on the island. Rapa Nui reminds us all of the dangers posed by living beyond the means of the natural world that surrounds us.

Mo'ai figures, as depicted in the account of the voyage of Lapérouse.

# El Niño

*El Niño*, the change to wind and oceanic current patterns in the southern Pacific which alters the climate across the Pacific region and often the globe, was officially defined in the twentieth century, but its effects have been perceived for centuries. The early use of the name *El Niño* refers to a regular change in water flows and temperatures that affects the southern Pacific and is most noted by fishermen, who initially assigned the moniker, around the Christmas period. Today we understand it to mean a more significant and complex series of climatological dynamics that cause the western part of the Pacific to experience less rainfall than normal, and parts of the eastern Pacific to experience more than normal.

While this contemporary definition is relatively recent, it is clear from paleoclimatic techniques, such as the growth rings of coral affected by *El Niño* events, that the event has occurred regularly for thousands of years. It has also had a demonstrable impact on human history, especially in and around the Pacific. One such example is the settlement of Rapa Nui (Easter Island) by groups originating from the westerly Polynesian islands sailing there no later than 1200 CE. The current chart here shows that this should be impossible, as the prevailing winds and currents for that part of the Pacific Ocean would preclude Polynesian groups from the western Pacific being able to reach the islands. They would always be pushed back – unless they set sail during an *El Niño* event. In these years the winds and currents would facilitate travel to the islands. The settlement of Rapa Nui is testament to the knowledge of the ocean these navigators and wayfinders built up over the centuries, as it required careful planning, which suggests a knowledge and desire to take advantage of the effects of an *El Niño* series.

*El Niño* reminds us that humans did not shape this ocean of islands in isolation. Instead, the ingenuity of ancestors from these islands was facilitated by the ebbs and flows of the ocean, as well as by other climatological events. The action of the Pacific and its *El Niño* flows through the societies of the Pacific and has shaped their history and the history of the world.

Alexander Johnston's 'Physical Chart of the Pacific Ocean', showing the currents and trade routes of the ocean, 1856.

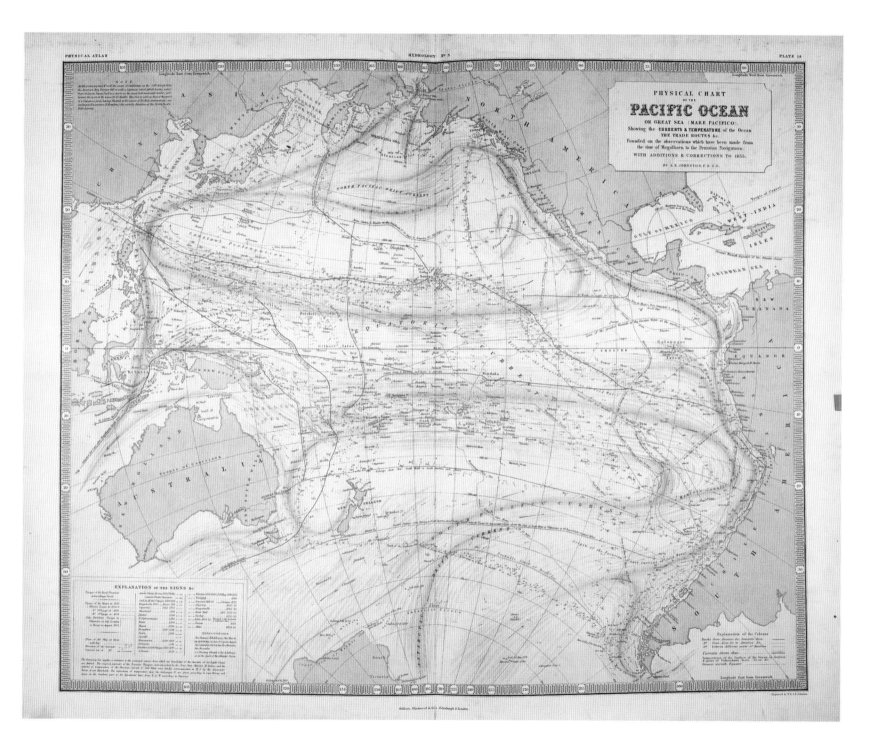

PHYSICAL CHART
OF THE
**PACIFIC OCEAN**
OR GREAT SEA (MARE PACIFICO).
Showing the **CURRENTS & TEMPERATURE** of the Ocean
**THE TRADE ROUTES &c.**
Founded on the observations which have been made from
the time of Magalhaen to the Prussian Navigators.
WITH ADDITIONS & CORRECTIONS TO 1855.

BY A.K. JOHNSTON, F.R.S.E.

EMPIRE OF ISLANDS

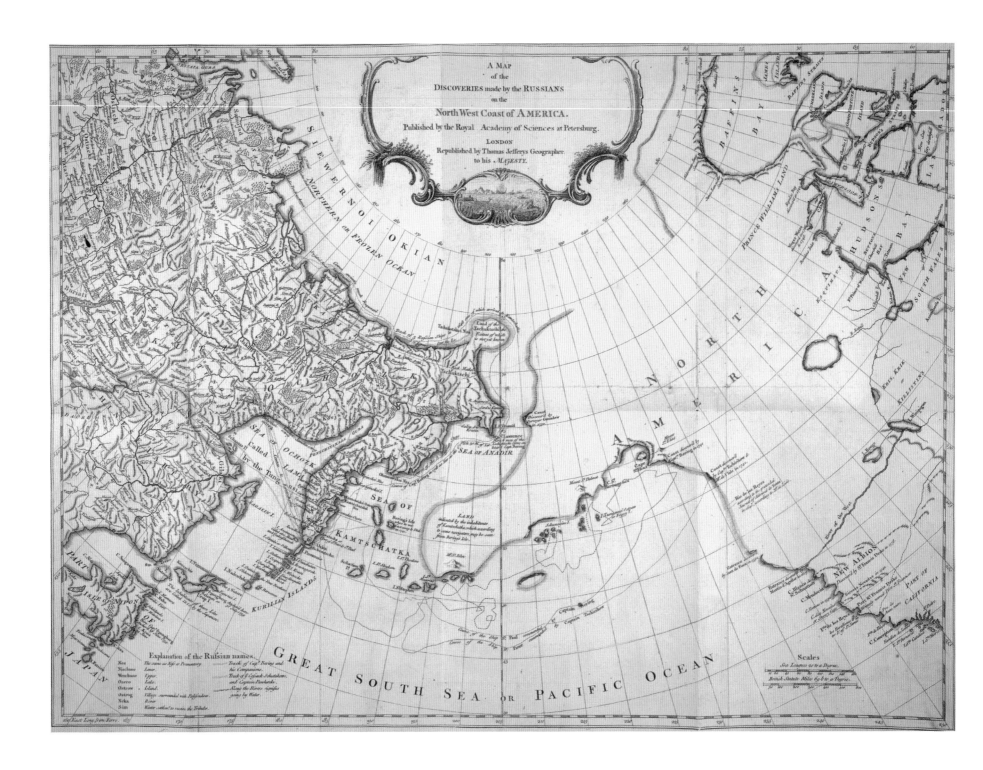

A MAP of the DISCOVERIES made by the RUSSIANS on the North West Coast of AMERICA. Published by the Royal Academy of Sciences at Petersburg.

LONDON Republished by Thomas Jefferys Geographer to his MAJESTY.

# Russia and the North Pacific

The peoples and cultures of the North Pacific have so far had less attention in this volume, but the island populations of the Aleutian Islands and archipelagos in the most northerly parts of the Pacific maintain complex oceanic connections like those discussed previously. The Aleut peoples who make up a substantial population of these islands are related to the Inuit who reside in much of the North American Arctic. Their lives on the islands revolve around the seas, with their *bidarka* (kayak) vessels allowing communication and exchange between groups as well as hunting and harvesting from the northerly waters of the Pacific Ocean. The islands themselves are possibly the conduit through which the Americas were settled by the earliest human migrations, so we see here further examples of the Pacific islands as parts of a dense web of interconnections across the ocean and the wider world.

Nonetheless, these islands were relatively untouched by the processes discussed earlier, be this the extending trade and tribute networks of early powers around the Pacific, like China, or the incursion of European traders like the Spanish and the Dutch.

Undoubtedly there were trade and exchange connections between the Aleutian Islands and these southern networks, especially as commodities from the Arctic such as amber, ivory and furs were always in demand in more southerly cultures, but there was not extensive contact between these islands and the wider world. This changed in the eighteenth century, as Russian ambitions spread into the North Pacific.

Russia had watched the searches of other nations for northerly trade routes to Asia with interest, especially as the growing nation extended its sphere of influence further and further east. This necessitated the discovery of overland and Arctic sea routes that could help connect the growing land empire together and perhaps provide it with commercial outlets into the Pacific Ocean and Asian markets. Tsar Peter the Great instituted a great exploratory push to determine if such routes to Asia could be found and, if not, whether Asia was connected to North America. Either discovery would have significant implications for Russian trade and expansion. Appointed to the task in 1724 was the Danish navigator Vitus Jonassen Bering, and his subsequent expeditions would chart the strait that lay between mainland Asia and North America.

Bering's expeditions also began to uncover the valuable commodities of the North American Arctic, especially the rich furs that could be obtained from sea otters. Maps like this are not only the result of the formal expeditions of men like Bering (although it reflects his expeditions and notes significant events, like the island location of Bering's death in 1741), but they also contain the finds of various fur trading expeditions to the Aleutian Islands and beyond. This trade was responsible for much of the detailed early mapping of the North Pacific, even if the results were looked down on by many other explorers in Europe. Nonetheless, the trade would have significant impacts on the islanders of the North Pacific and it drove continued Russian interest in the region.

Map of the North Pacific, including notes on the site of Bering's death, 1758.

# The 'Oro cult

It was not only goods and settlers that travelled around the Pacific; cultural practices and religious ideas circulated widely in these networks too. The dissemination of cultural objects and practices, as evidenced by the wide spread of Lapita pottery across the southern Pacific, has already been illustrated, as has the interaction of some of the world's major religions with the island populations of the ocean. Even before the arrival of Christians on the ocean and its margins, Buddhism, Confucianism and Islam had become the significant religious beliefs in many areas of the western Pacific, underpinning daily life and political power on islands where these religions were dominant.

Not all religions developed from outside the Pacific, however. The indigenous peoples of North American islands were part of a complex web of religious beliefs that were tied to their lives on and their relationship with the ocean. Elsewhere the very geography of the Pacific influenced the development of particular religious practices. Initially developing on the island of Ra'iātea, the worship of the war god 'Oro would become a defining feature of many Polynesian islands by the seventeenth century. Spreading to neighbouring islands like Tahiti, the system of worship worked its way along trade and communication networks that existed among the islands in this region of the Pacific. Key to the worship and success of 'Oro was a culture of learning that codified forms of knowledge and heraldry, meaning it also became an important factor in strengthening chiefly power on islands where it became the dominant religion. After originating on Ra'iātea it radiated out across the Polynesian Pacific, reaching Rapa Nui, Hawai'i and Aotearoa/New Zealand. The worship of 'Oro was by no means homogeneous in this region. There were a number of gods in the Polynesian pantheon and each could be used to underpin chiefly power and social practices, but by the time Europeans reached this part of the Pacific 'Oro was dominant.

By the time Captain Cook first reached Tahiti, in 1769, 'Oro was the religion of the dominant chiefs in Tahiti and had a substantial influence on Cook's encounter with the island, especially due to the work of Tupaia. Tupaia was an 'Oro priest who had been forced to abandon Ra'iātea when it was attacked by rival islanders. Meeting Cook and his expedition on Tahiti, he came to act as a translator and cultural mediator, providing the expedition with significant information on the island, Polynesian culture and the geography of the region Tahiti was part of. The illustration seen here is one of Tupaia's many works that became part of the collection of Sir Joseph Banks, and it depicts one of Tahiti's religious monuments.

Europeans arrived here to find cultures underpinned by 'Oro and the other gods of the Polynesian pantheon. They were significant not just for the practice of religious worship but also for people's day-to-day lives and for sustaining the political power balance of islands and the region. However, the arrival of Europeans and their competing empires would, as seen in the Malay peninsula and Japan, throw new and competing religious beliefs into this cultural mix. This would have a lasting impact on the 'Oro-worshipping cultures and the region surrounding Ra'iātea.

Tupaia's illustrations of a marae: front (*left*) and side (*right*) elevations, 1769.

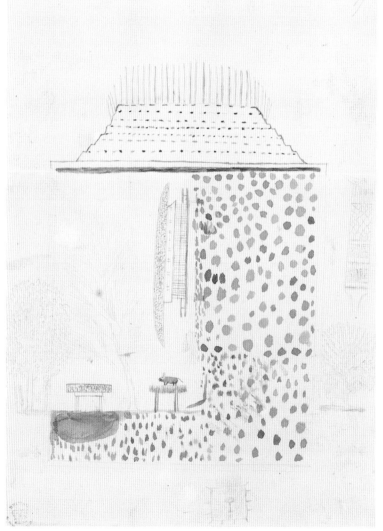

# The Transit of Venus

The arrival of Lieutenant (acting Captain) Cook and the *Endeavour* expedition is regarded as one of the seminal moments in European contact with the Pacific, but it is often forgotten exactly why his first expedition was sent there. The year 1769 was a rare moment when the place of the earth in the solar system could be mapped and other questions about the cosmos quantified and possibly answered. That year the planet Venus would make a visible transit across the face of the sun, allowing the speed of its journey to be measured and, as a result, the distance of the Earth from the sun to be calculated. To get an accurate result, readings had to be gathered from across the world and so began one of the greatest scientific expeditions ever undertaken at that point. Teams of observers from a plethora of nations were dispatched with the single task of observing the event and reporting their findings. Cook and his expedition were to view the transit from Tahiti, thus connecting the Pacific as a node in a vast scientific network that spanned the globe.

*Endeavour* and its crew departed London in 1768 with other instructions than to participate in the observation of the Transit of Venus. Tahiti and the surrounding region of the Pacific were becoming important locations in an ocean where a growing number of European nations had interests. The British and the French were developing spheres of influence in the southern Pacific, joining the Dutch, Spanish and Portuguese activities of the previous centuries, and as a result locations like Tahiti were becoming nodes and potential spheres of influence. As a result, Cook was provided with instructions to chart the area around Tahiti, building British influence and shoring up potential future claims to the islands and resources he encountered. Even by the mid-eighteenth century the search for *Terra Australis* was not complete either. As well as conducting his observation and learning more about the island groups around Tahiti, Cook had specific instructions to look for the southern continent.

While Cook was dubious as to the existence of the continent it was, nonetheless, his acting on these instructions that would bring the *Endeavour* into contact with Aotearoa/ New Zealand, the east coast of Australia and, very directly, the Great Barrier Reef. Cook would fill in the gaps in European knowledge about Aotearoa that had been left by Tasman's abortive contact with the islands and the resident Maori, establishing authoritatively that it was not part of any southern continent. The exploring and charting Cook conducted would have far-reaching implications for the islands and peoples he encountered. The success of the expedition, coupled with the ever-growing ambitions of European powers to increase their strength in the Pacific, meant that an intermittent train of explorers, followed by whalers, traders and missionaries, would begin to encroach further and further into the Pacific. These actions were supported by the, admittedly erratic and indecisive, actions of the administrators of empires back in European metropoles. The whole Pacific was now being drawn inexorably, irrevocably into the political, economic, scientific and cultural currents of empires half a world away.

Illustrations of Fort Venus, by Spöring.

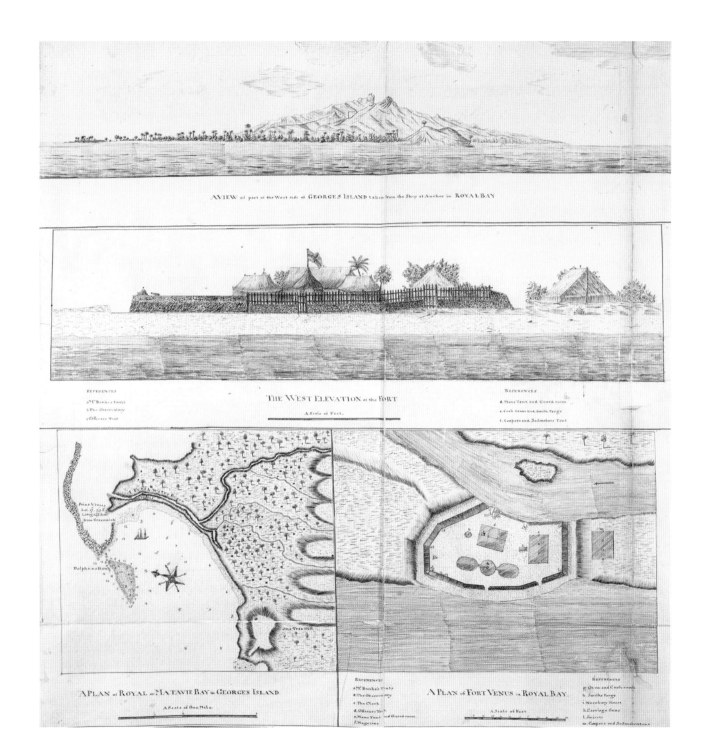

A VIEW of part of the West side of GEORGES ISLAND taken from the Ship at Anchor in ROYAL BAY

THE WEST ELEVATION of the FORT

A Scale of Feet.

REFERENCES

a Mr Banks's Tents
b The Observatory
c Officers Tent

REFERENCES

d Mens Tent and Guard room
e Cook room and Smith Forge
f Coopers and Sailmakers Tent

A PLAN of ROYAL or MATAVIE BAY in GEORGES ISLAND

A Scale of One Mile.

A PLAN of FORT VENUS in ROYAL BAY.

A Scale of Feet

REFERENCES

a Mr Banks's Tents
b The Observatory
c The Clock
d Officers Tent
e Mens Tent and Guard room
f Magazine

REFERENCES

g Oven and Cook room
h Smiths Forge
i Necessary House
k Carriage Guns
l Swivels
m Coopers and Sailmakers tent

# Collecting the Pacific, influencing Europe

Travelling with Cook was a team of naturalists assembled by the young Sir Joseph Banks, a scholar of natural philosophy who had already conducted his own personal expedition to North America, specifically Newfoundland and Labrador. Banks had been nominated to accompany the expedition as part of the broader scientific

mandate the *Endeavour* was tasked with, and he and his team were driven to create a natural history of a scope previously unseen. The young naturalist was inspired by previous journeys of exploration that had paid overt attention to the geography and natural history of the places they encountered, with accounts like William Dampier's having a formative effect on his approach. However, Banks believed that few, if any, expeditions undertaken before had approached this subject on anything like the right scale. He wanted to look comprehensively at the geography, flora, fauna and peoples the *Endeavour* encountered, and so took with him a team of naturalists – such as Daniel Solander and H. D. Spöring – and draughtsmen, including Sydney Parkinson. These individuals, supported by Banks's resources, on-board library and various pieces of technical equipment, had the sole aim of observing and recording what the *Endeavour* encountered in the Pacific and the rest of its journey around the world.

Banks and his team recorded in detail much of what they encountered in the Pacific, recording the peoples and cultures encountered by the expedition. Much of this

was aided a Ra'iātean priest the expedition met on Tahiti, Tupaia, and indeed the detail and insight achieved would not have been possible without his assistance. As a result of the scope of the *Endeavour* expedition, Banks's ambition, the insightful work of team members like Solander and Parkinson and the input of Tupaia, not to mention the welcome of many Pacific islanders encountered by the ship, the record produced would have a lasting impact on European views of the world. After arriving in Batavia (Jakarta), Cook's expedition would endure tremendous sickness and hardship, losing many members of the crew and Banks's team, but nonetheless it returned with and disseminating this view from the other side of the world.

It was not just the wonders of natural history that grabbed people's attention, but also the cultural insights from the Pacific. This is similar to the enthusiasm which accompanied the publication of Dampier's account of his seventeenth-century voyages in the Pacific and his display of his Indonesian slave, Jeoly, who was of popular interest on account of his tattoos. Benjamin West's portrait of Banks, seen here, shows how Banks attempted to communicate the

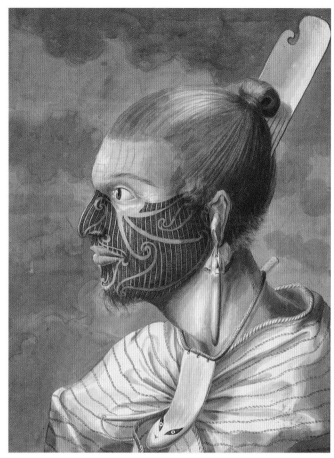

Two of Parkinson's portraits of Maori sitters.

(*Left*) Mezzotint of Benjamin West's portrait of Sir Joseph Banks.

natural history and cultural legacy of the expedition. Banks stands clothed in a Maori gown and surrounded by Maori weapons, a Tahitian headdress and various other items collected during the expedition. For him, these objects and the insights they would provide to Europeans were the legacy of the *Endeavour* expedition and, in many ways, Banks's collections are the legacy of the expedition. John Hawkesworth's official account of the expedition, published in

1773, is a poor description of the work of Cook and those who accompanied him, and other publications associated with the expedition were plagued by disputes. Banks's collections, though, were open to scholars at his Soho Square residence and went on to form a cornerstone of the collections of the British Museum, Natural History Museum and British Library. As a result, they still contribute to our framework for understanding the Pacific today.

21.593. C.

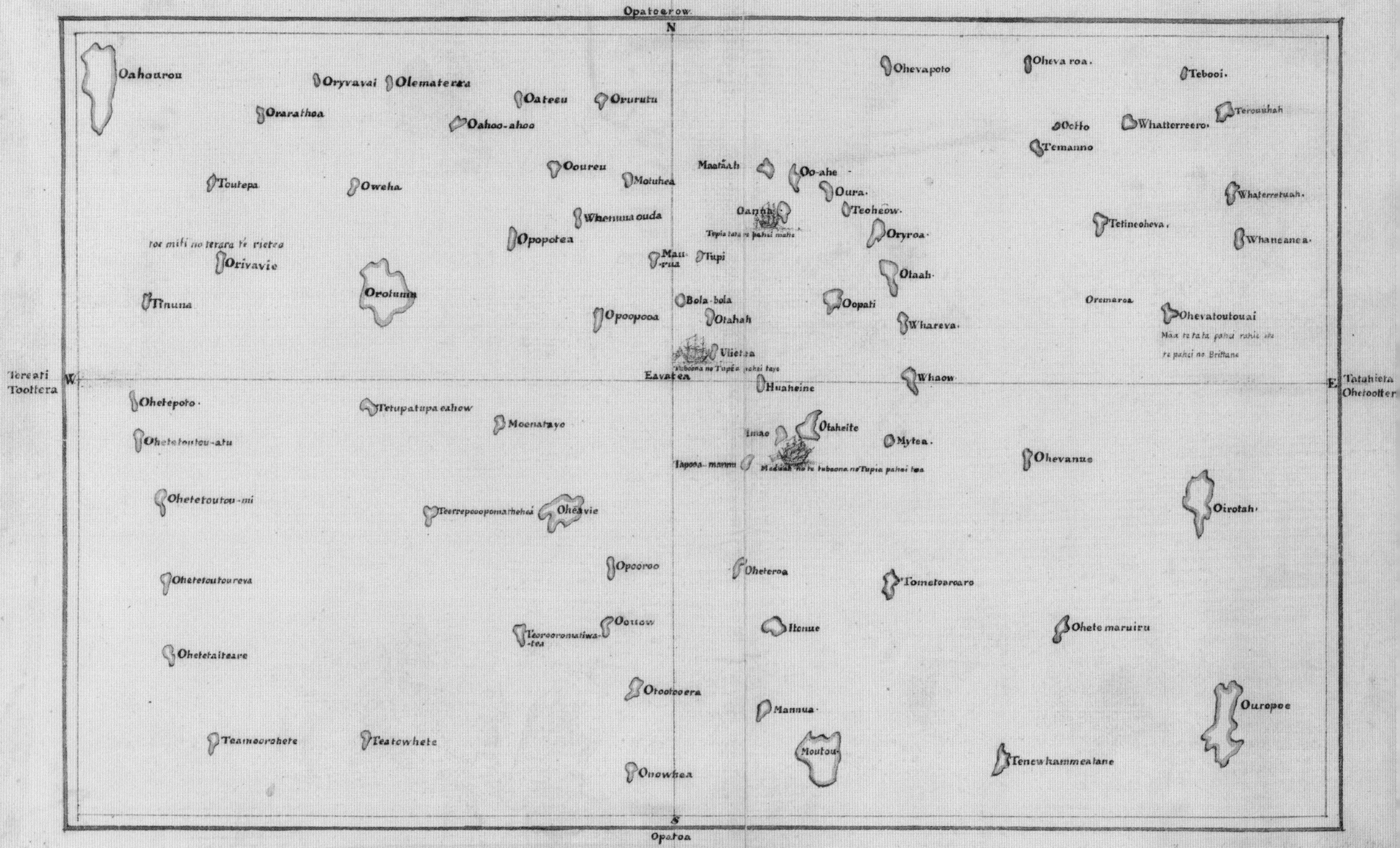

Opatoerow.

N

Oahourou

Oryvavai  Olematerxa

Orarathoa

Oateeu  Orurutu

Oahoo-ahoo

Ohevapoto  Oheva roa.  Tebooi.

Ocito  Whatterreero.  Terouuhah

Temanno

Ooureu  Maataah  Oo-ahe

Toutepa  Oweha.  Motuhea  Oura.

Teoheow.  Whaterretuah.

Whenuua ouda  Oanuu  Oryroa  Tetineoheva.

Tupia tata ra pahei matte  Whangana ea.

toe miti no terara te rietea

Opopotea  Mau-  Tupi  Otaah.

Orivavie  rua

Tinuna  Orotunu  Bola-bola  Oopati  Oremaroa

Opoopooa  Otahah  Whareva.  Ohevatoutouai

Vlietea  Max te tata pahei rahie ate

Teboona ne Tupia pahei tayo  ra pahei no Brittane

Tereati  W.  Eavatea  Whaow  E.  Tatahieta

Toottera  Huaheine  Oheteotter

Ohetepoto.  Tetupatupa eahow

Moenatayo  Imao  Otaheite  Mytea.  Ohevanus

Ohetetoutou-atu  Tapooa-manuu  Meduah no te teboona ne Tupia pahei tea

Ohetetoutou-mi  Teerrepooopomathehei  Oheavie  Oirotah

Opoorao  Oheteroa  Tometoaroaro

Ohetetoutoureva

Oottow  Itenue  Ohete maruiru

Ohetetaiteare  Teoroaronatiwa-  
tea

Otootooera  Ouropoe

Teamoorohete  Teatowhete  Mannua.

Tenewhammeatane

Onowhea  Moutou

S

Opatoa

# Pacific perspectives

The collections of Sir Joseph Banks that made their way to the British Library contain many of the insights the Ra'iātean priest Tupaia provided to the expedition. Tupaia and the members of the *Endeavour* expedition met on Tahiti, where Tupaia was resident after being displaced by religious and political strife on his home island. The Ra'iātean quickly became indispensable to Cook, Banks and the rest of the expedition, not just as a translator but also as a source of information about the region of the Pacific surrounding Tahiti. Banks's collections contain numerous sketches by Tupaia that denote key elements of Tahitian culture. His representations of religious figures and his depiction of the island's landscape seem to have formed part of helping Banks and others understand the society they found themselves in. Further, his later illustrations and interpretations of other Polynesian and South Pacific societies the *Endeavour* encountered provide non-European insights into these moments of initial contact.

Such a perspective forms an invaluable part of the historical record not just of Pacific cultures but also of how those cultures mixed and intermingled, especially during the period of European expansion and the increased attention of empires such as Britain and France. A key item in this regard is the chart of the 'Society Islands' (Tahiti and surrounding islands) which Cook copied from a chart provided by Tupaia. The information contained in the chart is a record of the indigenous names of various islands in the region, preserving this heritage in a period where European explorers would overwrite and rename many of the islands and landscape features they came into contact with. Even more significant is the geography conveyed by Tupaia's chart. It is not orientated around the geospatial projections familiar to Western cartographers either then or now. Instead the chart has its own spatial logic. It conveys relative distances from Tahiti as a series of concentric rings which represent sailing time from the island. The chart, therefore, is a representation of how Polynesians understood and imagined the interconnections that existed between islands across the Pacific Ocean; it is the pre-European geography of this part of the world.

In many ways Tupaia's chart is a fascinating historical record that pre-empts Epeli Hau'ofa's idea of a 'Sea of Islands', the Pacific as a distinct, culturally interconnected region where the sea is a framework of conduits rather than a barrier between islands. Modern scholarship suggests such networks were in decline at the time Europeans arrived in the Pacific, that Rapa Nui was not the only island increasingly disconnected from the 'Sea of Islands'. Tupaia's chart, and life, however, suggest these networks endured in the cultural imagination and the life-geography of Pacific figures.

The contribution Tupaia made to the *Endeavour* expedition and the historiography of the Pacific was, sadly, truncated. His curiosity had led him to join the expedition and provide us with his insights into Maori and Aboriginal Australian cultures, but he was one of the many who fell sick and died in Batavia (Jakarta). The susceptibility of Pacific islanders to continental disease was an increasingly serious issue as outsiders travelled further and for longer across the ocean, and it robbed history of Tupaia's further insights about the world.

Tupaia's chart of the islands surrounding Tahiti, copied by Captain Cook, 1769.

# Strained contacts

By the time Cook's ships visited Tahiti, contact between islanders from the South Pacific and European explorers was becoming increasingly common. Ships from many different nations now looked for new islands and opportunities, particularly with an eye to settlement and trade. This would prove to be a dangerous shift in the dynamics of contact. While expeditions like the *Endeavour* showed how much Europeans could learn about Polynesian culture, and that sustained contact was possible, it also showed how stresses and strains developed between Europeans and the communities that they insisted host them. Even the most well-meaning of crews over-stepped social boundaries, misinterpreted local cultural norms and transgressed the spiritual laws governed by *tapu*, the system of prohibitions surrounding particular sites, objects and foods associated with spiritual or chiefly power.

This was the cause of much friction between Cook's crew and the Tahitians around Fort Venus, the location from which Cook's crew observed the Transit of Venus, with tensions occasionally boiling over into violence, both threatened and actual. Another example of the strains of prolonged contact comes from the expedition of Marc-Joseph Marion du Fresne, the French explorer who sailed the *Mascarin* and the *Marquis de Castries* to the Pacific in 1771. By March 1772 du Fresne had reached Aotearoa/New Zealand and begun making contact with local Maori while refreshing his stocks and harvesting timber to resupply the ships. Du Fresne was of the same frame of mind as Captain Cook, interested in indigenous cultures and keen to develop friendly relationships with those his crew came into contact with. Indeed, du Fresne could perhaps be regarded as being even more determined to engage with the indigenous communities he encountered, having developed an enthusiasm for the eighteenth-century theory of the 'noble savage'.

The expedition spent over five weeks in and around the Bay of Islands, later to become a site of intense interest for the United States, making contact with the local Ngare who had made the area their home. It seems that at first relations between the expedition and the Ngare were friendly, the crew managing to converse through the Tahitian vocabulary previously established by Louis de Bougainville, a French contemporary of Cook and du Fresne. They were being welcomed to local ceremonies by 8 June that year. However, by 12 June relations between du Fresne's expedition and the Ngare had soured and du Fresne was killed, along with a party of his men, while out on a fishing expedition. A violent cycle of reprisals then began which lasted over a month before the remaining French expeditionaries sailed out into the Pacific. By then, more than 250 Ngare had been killed.

Accounts from the expedition are too sparse to account for exactly what went wrong and changed the relationship between du Fresne's men and the Ngare so dramatically. Perhaps it was miscommunications driven by the use of a Tahitian vocabulary for communication; it could also have been frustration with the length of time du Fresne and his crew were staying. It would not be the last time European explorers would mistake a ceremony for friendly welcoming when instead the message was more akin to, 'please leave'. It is most likely that the crew, or perhaps even du Fresne himself, transgressed a number of local laws regarding *tapu* (sacred spaces or foods) and, eventually, the slights became too much for the Ngare to bear. We will never know if this was the cause, but later events with other expeditions suggest it is possible.

Dramatised depiction of the death of du Fresne.

# THE
# INJURED ISLANDERS;

## OR,

## THE INFLUENCE OF ART

### UPON

## THE HAPPINESS OF NATURE.

W. Hamilton del.                                                    Isaac Taylor sculp.

*New wonder rose, when ranged around for Thee,*
*Attendant Virgins danc'd the* TIMRODEE.

## LONDON,

PRINTED FOR J. MURRAY, No. 32, OPPOSITE ST. DUNSTAN'S CHURCH,
FLEET-STREET; AND W. CREECH, EDINBURGH.

MDCCLXXIX.

# Bearers of pestilence

As well as new sources of trade and conflict, the arrival of Europeans in the Pacific brought hitchhikers carrying diseases from the other side of the world that could cause tragic levels of human suffering across the ocean's islands. By the time Europeans were reaching deeper into the Pacific and contacting islands such as Tahiti, Hawai'i and Rapa Nui, the effects of European disease on indigenous communities had already been seen elsewhere. Introduced diseases such as smallpox, measles, influenza and possibly even malaria had decimated indigenous populations across the Americas since the arrival of Columbus. While they were still rife and damaging in Europe, many Europeans had developed some sort of inherited resistance to these diseases. Pandemics would occur and large numbers died each year from infections but they rarely cut through entire populations and nations in the way they did in the Pacific islands.

Some islands in the Pacific, such as Japan, Taiwan and the Spice Islands, maintained close enough contact with the continental mainland, its cycles of trade and systems of agriculture that their populations too developed some resistance to diseases from Eurasia and Africa. Further out into the Pacific, however, it was a different story. Moreover, ships were extremely effective vectors for the circulation and transmission of disease. Cramped conditions on board vessels made the trans'mission of contagious diseases between crew members possible, while those who recovered could still act as carriers once they came into contact with communities and people on shore. There was also the matter of how sailors behaved when they were given shore leave on the islands.

As seen during Captain Cook's first expedition to Tahiti and the wider Pacific, sailors granted shore leave found it impossible not to develop intimate relationships with the islanders they met. These relationships could be mutual and reciprocal but there was also often coercion and aggression involved. These physical relations developed, they provided the ideal conditions for the transmission of respiratory diseases and diseases such as measles and, most devastatingly, the introduction of numerous sexually transmitted infections to the islands.

Shown here is the frontispiece to *The Injured Islanders*, an unusually uncompromising work attacking the effects on islanders of European expansion into the Pacific. While condemning many of the cultural effects introduced by Europeans, the poem also referes to the effects of venereal disease on the culture of islands like Tahiti. Contact with outsiders would only increase for islanders across the Pacific as the eighteenth and nineteenth centuries progressed. Explorers, missionaries, traders, whalers, colonial officials and many others would come in increasing numbers, introducing and nurturing diseases that would rampage across islands. The arrival of Europeans in the Pacific had created profound social, economic and political changes on the islands of the Pacific, but the changes paled in comparison to the profound effects of introduced diseases and the consequences of the death and destruction they brought.

Title page of the poem *The Injured Islanders*, 1779.

# The missionary endeavour

Around the world, where explorers from Europe and the Americas have gone, representatives of the Christian faith have been sure to follow, and the islands of the Pacific were no exception. Indeed, the enthusiasm generated by Cook's Pacific expeditions coincided with a marked rise in the public's willingness, especially those who were members of evangelical Anglican churches, to participate in and support missionary endeavours. Combined with the British enthusiasm to promote Protestant values to peoples in the Pacific, as a counter-pressure to the Catholic missionary work that was already common in the area, it is no surprise that the Pacific islands became a focus for British missionary activity from the end of the eighteenth century.

This work was led by members of the London Missionary Society, originally the Mission Society, who undertook the conversion of the peoples of the Pacific islands. The first works of the Society were established in Tahiti, with missionaries being transported for free by Captain James Wilson on his ship *Duff*. During this voyage missionaries were also placed on nearby islands. Everywhere they found themselves in a rapidly evolving social, cultural and political situation. Rather than arriving in communities that had little contact with Europeans and other outsiders, it rapidly became apparent to the missionaries that these islands were very much connected to the outside world. Explorers from various nations, early traders and men of many nationalities left behind by their ships – the iconic 'beachcombers' – were already affecting the societies missionaries encountered.

As a result missionaries found that many islanders whom they encountered already had preconceptions of who they were, the benefits they could bring and the role they would play in local societies. However, the refusal of Society missionaries to aid in the resolution of local feuds made it difficult for them to win the trust of chiefs with whom they were resident and gain influence with them. Perhaps most importantly, evangelical Anglicans mostly abstained from taking part in kava bowl ceremonies because of their belief in the evils of alcohol. Avoiding such ceremonies, which were important at community and individual levels, meant that missionaries situated themselves apart from local people, making it harder to influence them and begin any process of conversion. *A Missionary Voyage* is, in many ways, a record of these early problems with the missions. During the eighteenth century the Society and other missions in the Pacific would begin to drive significant changes in the region, especially as islanders began to take on the role of missionaries themselves.

From the eighteenth century onwards missionary groups in the Pacific would become involved in indigenous politics, record languages and histories, and markedly change the structure of belief and religious celebration in the Pacific islands. Not all of this work was conducted by evangelical Anglicans, however, and, as will be shown later, missionaries were inextricably linked to the local and global politics of religious belief and practice in a world of globalising empires.

Scenes from *A Missionary Voyage to the Southern Pacific Ocean*, 1799: (*top left*) 'Missionary House and Environs in the Island of Otaheite'; (*top right*) 'Great Morai of Temarre in Pappare in Otaheite'; (*bottom left*) 'Morai and Altar at Attahooro with the Eatooa and Teees'; (*bottom right*) 'The Afiatookas of Futtafaihe at Mooa in Tongataboo'.

# Pacific visitors

As illustrated by the voyages of earlier travellers such as Enrique de Malacca and Hasekura Tsunenga, by the eighteenth century islanders from the Pacific region had already travelled significantly in Europe and the Americas. They had not only forged cross-cultural connections at the highest level but they had also been involved in, and at the forefront of, significant events in world history. In the late eighteenth century, Polynesian voyagers became bound up in this network as part of the expeditions of voyagers such as Cook or the activities of traders making journeys deeper into the Pacific.

Travellers from the southern Pacific arrived in this network and became part of European discourses at a unique moment in European intellectual history. While not all, like the voyager Tupaia, completed their journey and arrived in Europe, these individuals too had a profound impact on how Europeans encountered new regions of the Pacific. They also continue to influence how we see and understand the world around us, as the continuing fascination with Tupaia's chart of the islands of the South Pacific reminds us. Within this exchange there was also a significant cohort of travellers who came into

direct contact with the lands and cultures of the Americas and Europe during the late eighteenth and early nineteenth centuries. Many of these individuals were travelling and working with whalers and traders seeking to make fortunes from various Pacific trades. For these individuals, ports across the Pacific and islands in other oceans, most notably the Atlantic island of Nantucket, would become significant sites of contact.

Of the Pacific islanders who became bound up in the activities of the increasing number of European explorers travelling the Pacific, the Ra'iatean Mai is one of the best known. He met Cook and his expedition during their time spent on Tahiti observing the transit of Venus and four years later (in 1773) he travelled to London on the ship HMS *Adventure*, under Commander Tobias Furneaux. The portrait shown here is one of a large number produced of Mai (known as 'Omai' in European circles) during his two years in Europe. Mai was a subject of intense fascination in European society of the time, not only because of the desire to experience and celebrate the exotic but also because he quickly became known for his wit and charm. By the time Mai arrived in

London the tone for Polynesian visitors to Europe had been set by Ahutoru, a Tahitian who travelled with Bougainville. Ahutoru had participated in the salon scene of Paris, meeting figures from across the upper echelons of French society. His influence here is seen in the writings of Jean-Jacques Rousseau and other eighteenth-century thinkers who developed ideas of the 'noble savage', arguing that civilisation had a corrupting influence from which peoples such as the Tahitians were, so far, largely free. These ideas would frame much European engagement with the Pacific for generations.

Mai followed a similar circuit in London, meeting luminaries such as Sir Joseph Banks as well as having an audience with King George III, whom he referred to as 'King Tosh'. The result of this was a sphere of influence similar to Ahutoru's and an extensive body of artistic work in which he is the subject and focus. Unlike earlier travellers, such as Tupaia, Mai was destined to see his home again, being repatriated by Captain Cook during his third voyage of exploration to the Pacific. Indeed, a sign of how engrained Mai, Tahiti's people and the islands of the Pacific more generally were becoming in the global politicking of European nations is provided by his return. Cook's stated aim on this voyage was specifically to return Mai to Tahiti but, in fact, he sailed with a set of secret instructions ordering him to find a way home through the fabled Northwest Passage. Mai's homecoming, then, was a significant sleight of hand in a game of geopolitics that was centuries old.

Portrait of Mai from Cook's *A Voyage towards the South Pole, and Round the World*.

# Encountering Hawai'i

Until the late eighteenth century Europeans had no awareness of the islands that today comprise Hawai'i. The circulation of Pacific currents and the networks established by Europeans, such as the galleon trade, meant that, despite centuries of involvement in the Pacific, European vessels had spent all of this time navigating around the islands. It is possible that the galleons of Juan Gaytan stopped at the islands in 1542 but, even if this fleeting contact did occur, the beginning of European contact with Hawai'i was not until 1778 and the arrival of James Cook.

Until this time Hawai'i remained a distinctly Polynesian culture, consisting of various kingdoms arranged across the islands. The islands themselves were directly linked to Polynesian voyaging culture, having originally been populated some time before the eleventh century CE and settled by Tahitian voyagers around 1200 CE. It was these Tahitians who would establish a dominant culture on the islands that would endure to the arrival of Cook and his expedition. This culture bore many of the hallmarks of Polynesian culture discussed earlier, with authority wielded by a network of chiefs who drew their status from complex networks of genealogy and the *mana* that this imparted. *Kahuna* priests were repositories of knowledge regarding arts and medicine, while the general body of society adhered to rules defined by networks of *kapu* (*tapu*) similar to those found on other Polynesian islands.

Such was the world encountered by Cook, who by now had experience of first encounters with Polynesian communities. The fascination of his crew with Hawai'i is illustrated by accounts from the expedition such as that by the surgeon's mate from HMS *Discovery*, William Wade Ellis, but the significance of the location of Hawai'i is illustrated by the role it played in the remainder of Cook's third voyage. Cook eventually set sail for the west coast of North America and in search of the Northwest Passage on his way home. The voyage was fraught with ill luck and was eventually forced to return south by the onset of winter and the development of significant amounts of ice in the Passage. As a result of damage to the ships and with supplies running low, Cook decided to set a course for a return to Hawai'i, thinking to resource his needs from a well-placed (and warm) location.

(*Above*) Illustrations of Hawai'ian artefacts by Louis Choris, 1822.

(*Right*) 'A View of Morai on O'Whyhee', from Ellis, 1782.

What is crucial here is not the death of Cook but the choice of Hawaiʻi as a resourcing point. The islands were well located, and had a population amenable to engage in trade, suitable harbours and significant resources of use to those on long expeditions. Cook was one of the first to use the Hawaiʻian Islands in this way but he would be far from the last. Whalers and traders would soon resort to Hawaiʻi's various islands safe harbours and restocking locations, while for others it became a point of exchange as goods shipped from North America were passed on for sale in Chinese markets. The arrival of Europeans would have dramatic consequences for the islanders Cook encountered, as illustrated by King Kamehameha's dramatic unification of the islands a short number of years after, using European weapons. Subsequent changes brought about by the work of missionaries and the virulent effects of European diseases wrought continuing dramatic changes on the islands. Their strategic role in the heart of the Pacific would only grow, and was to shape the globalisation of Hawaiʻi in the nineteenth and twentieth centuries.

# The Nuu-chah-nulth
# meet James Cook

Cook's third journey to the Pacific led him to the west coast and islands of North America. After returning Mai to Tahiti, Cook's instructions were to turn his attention to the search for the Northwest Passage and a route home. It is important here to reiterate the disdain many European nations felt for Russian mapping, as discussed earlier. In spite of the well-developed Russian charts of the period, which illustrated the narrow channel that exists between Kamkatchka and today's Alaska, the British Admiralty was inspired to engage Cook on this expedition by something altogether more spurious. A series of speculative charts circulated by armchair geographers, in particular France's Philippe Buache, had gained acclaim and generated renewed interest in the Northwest Passage. These charts showed the North American coast falling away steeply and drawing a direct southerly line almost from Banks Island in the Arctic to the shores of California.

View of Nuu-chah-nulth settlement in Nootka Sound, by Webber, 1778.

Therefore when the expedition arrived at 'Nootka' Sound on Vancouver Island, Cook and his crew must have believed that the entrance to the Northwest Passage was near. Instead, what lay ahead was an arduous and disappointing journey all the way around the coasts of Alaska before they had to turn back for Hawai'i. This search for the Northwest Passage, as with many more attempts to come, was a failure, but the arrival of the expedition on Vancouver Island was historic. It began a series of sustained contacts between the Nuu-chah-nulth and various European groups, and instigated a new trade route across the Pacific Ocean. The heart of this trade was a fur picked up by Cook's crew and greatly desired by the Russian trappers whose maps many ill-informed European nations ignored.

During the now common process of barter that accompanied European contacts with Pacific islands, some of Cook's crew picked up a number of sea otter pelts in exchange for European goods. The quality of the furs was clear but the crew did not yet know the exact value of what they had acquired. Many months later, after the failure to find the Passage and the fateful return to the islands

of Hawai'i, some of the surviving members of the expedition traded the sea otter pelts in Canton for fantastic profits. Fantastic may, in fact, be an understatement, as some of the expedition members managed to trade single furs, bartered in exchange for items such as belt buckles, for hundreds of Spanish dollars.

When there was sufficient demand, high-quality pelts were worth more money than a barrel of high-grade whale oil, and they were less dangerous to acquire. For Cook's crew this was a silver lining to a journey that had ended in disaster; to those who heard of their trades it was a route to new fortunes. The result was the exploitation of an animal population that already inhabited a precarious niche, and a new network of exchange across the Pacific. Cook's third voyage would, as a consequence, have rapid and lasting consequences for two islands he came into contact with, as the lands of the Nuu-chah-nulth and the islands of Hawai'i became hubs in a trade taking sea otter pelts to Canton and other Chinese markets. As a result, the Nuu-chah-nulth would have to manage their place and their islands' ecology in a rapidly changing world.

# Trees, fruits and mutiny

Sir Joseph Banks understood the economic potential of what he had seen on his voyage with James Cook, especially with regard to the various uses of the botanical species he saw and collected. One particular fruit, encountered in Tahiti, stood out above all others: the breadfruit. In breadfruit Banks saw a highly productive plant that yielded a high-energy foodstuff cheaply, and could thus be useful elsewhere in the British Empire. Specifically, the fruit would become important in the slave economies of the Caribbean.

By the late eighteenth century the islands of the Caribbean were ecologically barren monocultures given over almost completely to the production of sugar. This sugar was produced using the labour of large numbers of enslaved people who needed to be fed on islands that produced little or no staple food, a problem under normal conditions and a significant issue during times of war, when food supplies could be cut off. To men like Banks the breadfruit was a potential solution to one of the Empire's food security problems, and articulating its potential to Parliament became one of his many projects. In 1787 Banks's lobbying, and the lure of a financial reward and gold

medal from the Royal Society, resulted in the outfitting of an expedition on HMS *Bounty*, led by commanding officer Lieutenant William Bligh.

Bligh had experience of the Pacific, having been granted the position of ship's master under Captain Cook during his third and final expedition to the ocean. He had continued to serve in the Navy during the intervening years, seeing action relating to the

Fourth Anglo-Dutch War and the American War of Independence, as well as working as a captain in the merchant service. As a result Bligh would have been familiar with the type of his new vessel, HMS *Bounty*, originally a merchant ship refitted for the task of carrying breadfruit. The main focus of this refit was to construct a cargo area suitable for the transport of the breadfruit trees, illustrated here. The design of the ship (top right) shows a great deal of care and attention, with trees

on the desert island. While castaways were nothing new – Gulliver, after all, was one – accounts by those who had been shipwrecked and who had ended up living out months and years on various islands in the Pacific were received with great enthusiasm when printed in newspapers and journals for metropolitan audiences. The account of Alexander Selkirk, stranded for four years on Más a Tierra, just off the Pacific coast of Chile, formed the foundation of the novel *Robinson Crusoe* (1719), even though this was set in the Caribbean. This did not stop Más a Tierra being renamed Robinson Crusoe Island in the mid-twentieth century, creating an odd hybrid where the island of Selkirk's isolation has been overlaid with the name of a character who had never set foot in the Pacific.

During the nineteenth century a large body of popular works such as *Coral Island* developed, using the deserted Pacific island as their core theme. Other novels, such as *The Swiss Family Robinson*, drew inspiration from the reports of Pacific islands and the wider canon of writing around them, while other works that fed off them, including the 'sequel' to *The Swiss Family Robinson*, *Willis the Pilot*, were located

explicitly in the ocean. The use of Pacific islands as locations for the development of fictional tales continued throughout the twentieth century, with novels like *Lord of the Flies* and films such as *Cast Away* continuing to use and re-popularise the trope for subsequent generations. Furthermore, the Pacific island was not the only space of the ocean that inspired great works of literature, particularly in the anglophone canon. The ocean itself, its vastness and the effect it has on the minds of the men who sail it, has given rise to great works of fiction, among them a novel many regard as one of the greatest works of American literature, *Moby-Dick*. Here we see another example of how those who were drawn to the Pacific – through the promise of profit or the glory of exploration – would inspire works of fiction that still allow us to look critically at ourselves and the world around us to this day.

Attacked by a shark in *The Coral Island*.

# Maquinna and the Nootka Crisis

While the value of sea otter pelts had been unknown to all but a few Russian traders prior to Cook's final voyage, this soon changed. The results of the trades by former members of Cook's crew were so striking that, within a few years, British ships such as *Nootka* and *Sea Otter*, were ranging the Pacific with names that evoked the riches to be found in the region.

A leading figure in these expeditions was the former Royal Navy officer and trader John Meares, who would cruise the Pacific in ships under various flags trading sea otter pelts to Chinese markets. It was this trade that brought Meares to today's Vancouver Island and put him into contact with a local chief, Maquinna. Maquinna's rule was characterised by European contact. Evidence suggests that he came to power in the year of Cook's arrival (1778) and that he would play a leading role in framing his territory's early engagement with European powers. Meares believed, or at least argued, that he had purchased land on the island from Maquinna, a source of contention as Spain attempted to reassert its control on the west coast of North America, in reaction to increasing British and Russian trading interests in the area.

This led to the so-called 'Nootka Crisis'. Spain's attempt to dispossess British traders such as Meares almost brought the two nations to war, as well as leading to the occupation of Maquinna's territory at Yuquot (part of Nootka Island, which lies within Nootka Sound). The situation was broadly resolved by 1790 with the passing of the Nootka Conventions, but Spain

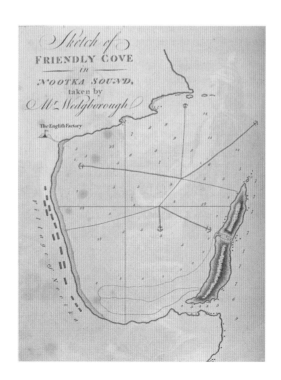

and Britain both sent official expeditions to Nootka Sound in order to resolve the territorial dispute. By the summer of 1792 both Juan Francisco de la Bodega y Quadra and George Vancouver had arrived at the island to chart the landmass and seaways for their respective empires and flesh out the details of the accords. Despite the background of the Conventions being set out in Europe and the arrival of these two well-armed antagonists, Maquinna did not allow himself to be sidelined. Instead, he took an active role in negotiating between the two parties, who spent much of their time on the island feting Maquinna.

Bodega's expedition departed the island with Spain still in control of the area of Yuquot, but within a few years this had been ceded and Maquinna's people returned, removing Spanish infrastructure in the process. Individuals like Maquinna were significant actors in the period of empires in the Pacific. Not only did they have significant roles in brokering agreements between imperial powers, but they also used these newcomers to solidify their own power bases. Further, they used competition between empires and the traders who associated with them

to generate greater profits from their interactions with Europeans. Competing interests for resources, like sea otter furs, could be used by Maquinna and others to increase their own profits and solidify their power base. Over subsequent decades the

pressures of empires, colonists and disease would dramatically reduce the agency of indigenous leaders in these islands' spheres, but their significant role in shaping how different locations engaged with a globalising Pacific should not be underestimated.

'The Launch of the North West America at Nootka Sound. Being the first Vessel ever built in that part of the Globe', from Meares's *Voyages Made in the Years 1788–89*.

(*Left*) Sketch of 'Friendly Cove', from Meares's *Voyages Made in the Years 1788–89*.

# Bad partners: Russia and the Aleutian Islanders

Russia's interest in the North Pacific continued to grow after the expeditions of Vitus Bering (see p. 91). The trading possibilities presented by fur trapping in the area, as well as the suggestion that a route to China and Japan was still possible via a Northeast Passage, led to a succession of expeditions by hunters, traders and explorers into the North Pacific. The map shown here, from Gavril Sarychev's account of the Russian government expedition led by Englishman Joseph Billings in 1785–94, speaks to much of what was learned of the North Pacific between Bering's expeditions and the end of the Billing expedition. The geography of various coastlines, not least the Alaskan coast, has come into sharper focus, and such maps were fundamental to a greater understanding of the geography, people and resources in these lands, which would gradually be annexed by the Russian Empire. In short, Sarychev's maps illustrate how Russia had developed into a truly Pacific power.

The expansion of Russia into the Pacific would not just be catastrophic for sea otters and other fur-bearing animals resident in the North Pacific; it would be disastrous for many islanders too. Of these groups the Aleutian Islanders bore the brunt of Russia's Pacific expansion. Fur traders working in the area quickly realised that Aleutian hunters were able to track and hunt sea otters more effectively than they or any other indigenous group could. As a result, they were soon brought into the employ of Russian traders and quickly bound into systems of indenture and slavery in all but name. Working for Russian traders and the trading companies that followed them was not optional: violent reprisals resulted for any individual or group who refused to hunt for Russian traders. Even the local extinction of sea otter populations was not enough to save Aleutian communities from the predations of Russian interests.

Sea otter populations have never been large at any point in history, largely because of the peculiar ecological niche they inhabit. Cold-water living, a high metabolic rate, high rates of calorie burn and a low birth rate mean that the entire North Pacific region never contained a large population of sea otters. However, the extinction of a local population merely led Russian traders to kidnap Aleutian hunters and their families (female Aleuts were equally important for their work skinning animals and preparing furs). These individuals, sometimes most of a community, were then taken around various parts of the

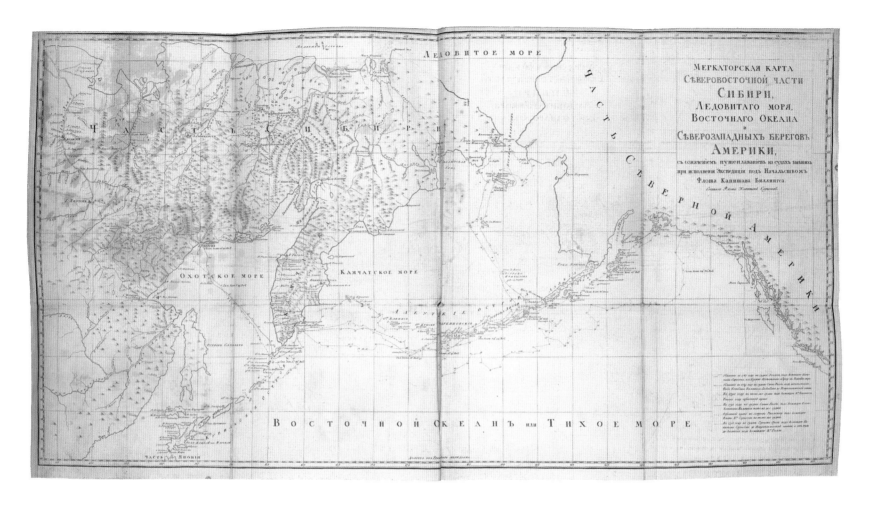

North Pacific in order to continue hunting local sea otter populations. Aleutian Islanders were taken around Alaska, Vancouver Island and well down the California coast as Russian fur traders continually moved in search of new sea otter populations.

The results were as catastrophic for Aleutian Islanders as they were for sea otters, with violence, social dislocation and exposure to new diseases wreaking a terrible toll on the population and social structures of Aleut communities. The expedition of Billings and Sarychev did attempt to do something about the exploitation of Aleut communities by trappers and traders by conducting a census and reporting their findings back to the Russian government. Aleut communities also attempted sporadic resistance and rebellions against various local traders and companies. However, fur traders were too well organised to be controlled by the government and too well armed to be resisted by Aleut communities. Ultimately, all that could check the activities of the traders was the near extinction of the sea otters and other animals they sought to profit from; only then would the predation of the northern Pacific decline.

Map of the Bering Strait, from Sarychev's account of the 1785–93 voyage.

(*Left*) Illustrations of Aleutian Islanders.

121

# Lapérouse in the Pacific

The work of Captain James Cook inspired an intensification not just of British but also of wider European interest in the Pacific. By the later eighteenth century the great maritime powers of the age were taking a distinct interest in the areas of the Pacific which Cook had encountered in his first expedition. Commercial opportunities and the diplomatic soft power that came with filling in blank spaces on European maps were the aim of many expeditions that set out after Cook. One of the most famous was that of Jean François de Galaup, comte de Lapérouse, who was appointed in 1785 to sail around the world on a voyage of discovery akin to those already sailed by Captain Cook.

French interest in Lapérouse's voyage ran deep, with King Louis XVI taking a personal interest in the expedition and its possible outcomes. This map shows the scale and scope of Lapérouse's expedition, sailing to Hawai'i, Alaska, Japan, Rapa Nui, Australia and numerous other locations on a route that held few surprises for late eighteenth-century explorers. Indeed, what is notable about the reporting of the early stages of Lapérouse's voyage is that the places visited, Pacific

features marked and the views depicted for readers back home had become almost standardised. Visits to Hawai'i, views of mo'ai, and depictions of Pacific material culture were to be expected in the accounts of explorers to the region. In this regard, the desire to explore and find new opportunities for empires became consumed by what were now strongly

'View of the Anchorage of the Vessles at the island of Mowee', from the posthumously published account of the expedition, 1798.

(*Right*) Map of the voyage of Lapérouse, from the posthumously published account of the expedition, 1798.

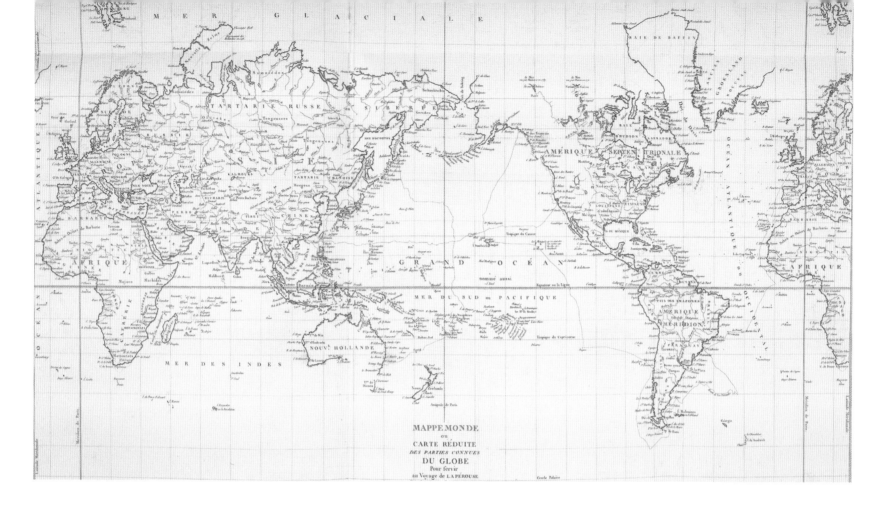

MAPPEMONDE
ou
CARTE RÉDUITE
DES PARTIES CONNUES
DU GLOBE
Pour servir
au Voyage de LA PÉROUSE

developed narratives of the exotic and the perceived paradise of the more southerly Pacific islands.

The early stages of the expedition were successful, but the situation would change after the departure of Lapérouse from Australia. He sent his most up-to-date papers back to France and sailed out of Botany Bay in March 1788 after overwintering in Australia. He and his crew were never heard from again. Only the disappearance of the later Arctic explorer, Sir John Franklin, would excite as much interest as to the fate of an expedition as did the disappearance of Lapérouse, the ships *La Boussole* and *L'Astrolabe*, and all hands in 1788. Despite huge interest in the fate of the expedition – Louis XVI is reputed to have asked, 'What news of Lapérouse?' on his way to the gallows – and the despatch of relief expeditions, no trace of the captain, ships or crew were found that century (although HMS *Pandora* ignored signs that could have led to survivors in 1791). Evidence of the fate of the expedition was not found until 1826, when Captain Peter Dillon acquired artefacts and information suggesting that the expedition had disappeared while trying to get away from the island of Vanikoro, part of the Santa Cruz Islands in the Solomon Islands.

For Lapérouse, then, there would be no garlanded welcome back to Europe or feting of the discoveries of his expedition. Instead, as Cook had learned on his first expedition by running aground on the Great Barrier Reef, Lapérouse's fate reminded Europe that paradise had teeth.

# The unification of Hawai'i

The unification of the islands of Hawai'i, led by King Kamehameha I, was a monumental moment in the history of the Polynesian islands and established one of the longest-running dynasties in the history of the Hawai'ian island chain. Kamehameha's rise to prominence accelerated in 1790, when the British-American ship *Fair American* was attacked by Kamehameha and a party of men in reprisal for the beatings and murders enacted by an earlier visiting ship, the *Eleanor*. Over the next twenty years successive campaigns and acts of diplomacy would result in the unification of Hawai'i's islands under the single kingship of Kamehameha I and his descendants.

Much has been written about the achievements of Kamehameha's reign, especially in the areas of society and law. He prohibited ritual sacrifice and made it compulsory for travellers to be treated with respect and care. Kamehameha also understood that the ocean around Hawai'i was changing and that the Europeans who visited and often acted with impunity needed to be controlled. If this could be achieved, Hawai'i and its people might prosper in this changing world. The vast stands of sandalwood on the island were attractive to European traders, who would eventually strip many islands around the ocean of this valuable resource. Kamehameha instituted a government monopoly over the trees, controlling their felling and sale.

Attention was also paid to the coming and going of ships from the islands. For European sailors on the Pacific, Hawai'i held a central location in the ocean, which meant that, as well as vast and potentially profitable resources of its own, it was a useful stopover, trading and resourcing point for traders, merchants, whalers, military ships and other American and European vessels plying the Pacific in the early nineteenth century. The management of the visits of ships and, in particular, the imposition of port duties on them added to the significant incomes being derived from the sandalwood trade on the islands, developing a strong economic base for the government led by Kamehameha. The profits generated from these administrative structures would only increase as the century progressed, particularly as the activities of whalers and pelt traders in the ocean

King Kamehameha I (*above*) and Queen Ka'ahumanu (*right*), by Choris, 1822.

increased. As a result, Hawai'i and its rulers would spend a portion of the nineteenth century in the ascendant.

In spite of these achievements and the political and administrative abilities of Kamehameha I, the islands of Hawai'i did not completely control the influx and actions of white sailors, traders and potential colonisers who would arrive over the century. The geographical location of the islands was just too significant, especially as networks of trade and the logistical needs of new technologies became apparent as the nineteenth century wore on. As a result, imperial and colonial pressures continued to mount on the islands, and the rapidly changing world around the Pacific meant that the people of Hawai'i needed to adapt to frequent changes and challenges. Their success could offer a model to islands across the ocean for how to develop and maintain their independence in an ocean of growing empires; failure would suggest that few others stood a chance of staying afloat in a tempest of change.

# Ocean of global wars

For many the concept of global war is synonymous with the world wars of the twentieth century. While these were truly global conflicts with, as we shall see later, significant theatres in the Pacific, they were not the first conflicts to range across the globe. The Seven Years' War (1756–63) was a truly global clash between Britain and France, while the American War of Independence and the War of 1812 both had theatres a world away from the main battlegrounds. In all these cases one of the sites of conflict outside the main spaces of engagement was the Pacific Ocean, largely because of the valuable resources Europeans and Americans were extracting from the region from the eighteenth century onwards. It is worth noting that the seeping of these conflicts into the ocean was not completely indiscriminate: the exploring expeditions of Cook, for example, were considered off limits to the Americans and French during the War of Independence. By and large, however, these conflicts turned the Pacific into an ocean of raiding and privateering that sought to exert an influence on wider conflicts.

This was not new: the Pacific had been seen as a source of soft, valuable targets during the period of the 'Spanish Lake'. Even during periods where European nations were not at war, privateers could prowl the ocean hunting for galleons making the run between Manila and the Americas. War merely raised the stakes. The War of 1812 saw Captain David Porter of the US Navy commissioned to sail into the Pacific with the aim of hunting down British whaling vessels working in the ocean. For a United States still in the early phases of nationhood this could be an invaluable strategy. Britain was dependent upon whale oil to keep its manufacturing economy moving and to light the streets of its rapidly growing urban areas. Whale ships taken in the Pacific in large enough numbers could therefore impact on the operation of the British economy. Even if this could not be achieved, the captured oil could be sold upon return to the United States, a potential financial windfall for a nation facing the might of the British war machine.

Porter set out in the ship *Essex* in 1812 and over the course of the conflict took twelve whale ships. His tactics were underhand but effective: he would often run up a British flag while approaching a potential target and then make his true allegiance known

Portrait of Captain David Porter.

(*Right*) A view of 'Madisonville', from *A Voyage to the South Seas*, 1823.

once it was too late for the whaling captain to oppose the *Essex*. More importantly, Porter's work captured the imagination of the American press and public. News articles celebrated his successes and his work in the Pacific was a propaganda coup in a conflict where the United States was believed to be outmatched at sea. This meant that, even when the British turned their attention to the *Essex* and disabled her in an engagement

off the Chilean port of Valparaiso, in 1814, it was reported as a heroic and defiant action to the public back in the United States. The work of the *Essex* was a significant moment in the history of the US Navy in the Pacific. She was the first US Navy ship to round Cape Horn and enter the ocean; she won great acclaim for the victories and defeats there, and Porter even attempted to lay claim to America's first colony in the ocean, when

he annexed the Marquesas Islands in 1813. The claim was never ratified by Congress but Porter had made an impression on the Pacific that set the tone there and in the minds of the American public in decades to come. The work of the *Essex* reasserted the potential of the Pacific as a space of global conflict and privateering. It also marked a turning point in America's relationship with the ocean.

# A pan-Pacific trade

Of all the tradable commodities driving the globalisation of the Pacific during the late eighteenth and early nineteenth centuries, the trade in sea otter pelts was potentially the most lucrative. As a result, the trade provides one of the more detailed insights into how the actions of Americans and Europeans chasing profits were changing commercial networks across the ocean and reworking the relationships various islands had with the rest of the world. Earlier sections of this book on the encounter between the Nuu-chah-nulth and James Cook, as well as the later role of Maquinna, have detailed the beginnings of this trade and hinted at the desire for profits that drove traders to undertake journeys to sea otter territories, particularly Vancouver Island, and then across the Pacific Ocean.

The value of these pelts was such that by the late eighteenth century traders descended on these areas in vast numbers. Russian traders carved out their own niche with an exploitative way of acquiring pelts but American and British traders also travelled to the west coast of North America in increasing numbers. Once the sea otter furs were acquired, the vast Pacific Ocean lay

between them and the generation of profits in the Chinese markets that so desired access to the lustrous furs. Given the huge distances involved, a well-placed midway point could be particularly valuable to fur traders, providing an opportunity to resupply, repair ships that had been pushed to their breaking point or perhaps even barter pelts to a middleman so traders could return to source a new cargo of furs more quickly.

Of all the islands scattered across the Pacific none fit the bill like those of Hawai'i,

recently brought under the sole rule of Kamehameha and organised to provide the facilities and market required by the growing volume of traders plying the Pacific Ocean. Geography played a key role here: Hawai'i was centrally located in the ocean, provided large harbours and could also locally produce a significant amount of the supplies needed by traders when they came into port. The organisation of the government of the islands was undoubtedly key, providing reliable facilities on a scale required by the

significant volume of ships that crossed the Pacific each year. This was crucial, as Hawai'i was not just the hub of the sea otter trade: many other commodity traders relied on it and its unique location. For whalers the islands were an invaluable location for supplies and shore leave after months at sea searching for sperm whales and other cetaceans. Sandalwood traders would use the islands as a place to gain stock and supplies, as would a growing number of traders interested in a variety of commodities that

could be sourced from islands across the ocean. The scale of growth is illustrated by the port of Honolulu, which even by 1824 was seeing 105 ships dock in the year. By 1850 this number had risen to 476.

Hawai'i, then, was a hub of the Pacific Ocean and emblematic of the developing trade networks of nineteenth-century empires and capitalism. Under strong and insightful leadership, like that of Kamehameha I, the governments of Pacific islands could play

a significant role in this trade, using their unique locations and attributes to develop a place in this globalised world. The challenge would be capitalising on these flows while maintaining the independence of islanders and their islands.

(*Left*) A view of Russian–American Company trading post Novo Arkhangelsk (present-day Sitka). 'Vue du Port Hanarourou', by Choris, 1822.

129

# The closed islands

As the pace of contact heated up around the Pacific Ocean, drawing its islands and their peoples ever deeper into the destructive cycles of imperial and colonial globalism, one group of islands remained largely detached from the process: those that comprised the nation of Japan. Since the Sakoku Edicts of 1635, Japan had remained isolated from the wider world, especially those portions of it that fell under the influence of the expanding European powers. The isolation was not total: shipwrecked mariners would occasionally wash up on Japanese shores, and Japanese fishermen were sometimes rescued from alien lands by foreign ships, only to find it almost impossible to regain access to the islands they called home. This was the fate of the shipwrecked Japanese sailors whom a group of missionaries tried to return home in 1837; their ship was fired upon and the sailors had to make new lives in Macau, Singapore and elsewhere. There were also infrequent attempts by adventurers, possibly more from a desire for profit than for self-preservation, to re-establish trade with a group of islands that had once again become shrouded in mystery.

The nineteenth century witnessed European powers again turning their attention to Japan as their global empires and sphere of influence in the Pacific Ocean coalesced. Russia's expansion into the North Pacific made it in some ways inevitable that the empire would attempt to establish a trading relationship with the markets of Japan and China. In 1803 Adam Johann von Krusenstern was commissioned by Tsar Alexander I to undertake a mission of exploration that sought to establish the viability of trading with China, Japan and East Asia by using sea routes via the Cape of Good Hope and Cape Horn. Departing with two ships, Krusenstern's three-year voyage made a number of significant additions to the cartography of the Pacific and he also completed Russia's first circumnavigation of the world. His attempts to open up trade with Japan met with little success, however.

Not much later, in 1818, a British merchant vessel, the *Brothers*, arrived at the Japanese port of Uraga. The crew of the *Brothers* were also determined to open up trade with Japan, cornering new markets and opportunities for themselves. While Krusenstern's voyage left us with Russian perspectives of Japan, the voyage of the *Brothers* generated an insightful account detailing Japanese responses to European visitors during this period. The work not only illustrates the ship itself but also many of the items of paraphernalia on board. Pistols, rifles and swords are, perhaps understandably, given attention, but so too are tables, anchors, compasses and umbrellas, along with a number of other items stored on the ship.

Despite the fascination the *Brothers* stimulated, the crew of the ship were no more successful than Krusenstern's earlier expedition. Japan was still locked in its isolation and it would take a more forceful approach to bring the islands into the globalising fold. The fact that traders were once again arriving in Japan, however, illustrated that the nineteenth century would see Pacific islands being drawn into new, intense trade networks involving a different cast of actors.

A view of Nagasaki, from the published account of Krusenstern's voyage, 1813.

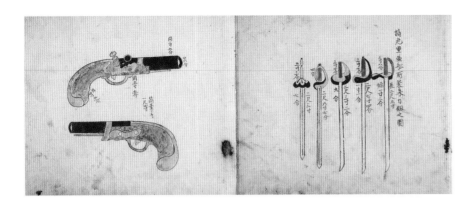

Japanese illustrations of the ship *Brothers*, its crew
and various objects, 1818.

# Outcast islands

From early on, European empires used faraway lands under their control as a place to deposit convicted criminals. Until the American War of Independence, North America was frequently used by the British Empire, and after this the lands Cook and others encountered in Australia and other parts of the Pacific seemed fit to take over the process, at least as far as metropolitan administrators were concerned. To these locations were sent vast numbers of individuals, some guilty of horrific crimes, some, such as forgers, guilty of defrauding the state, and others guilty of being little more than poor and hungry.

Despite the emphasis placed on these colonies being spaces of isolation, they had a deep impact on the islands of the Pacific, sometimes solely as a result of their location and other times as a result of the complex interconnections they forged in order to survive. These colonies and their prisoners would not exist adrift from the ocean of

Map of Van Diemen's Land, with insets showing Hobart and Launceston, 1838.

(*Right*) *Hobart Town*, by W. J. Huggins, 1830.

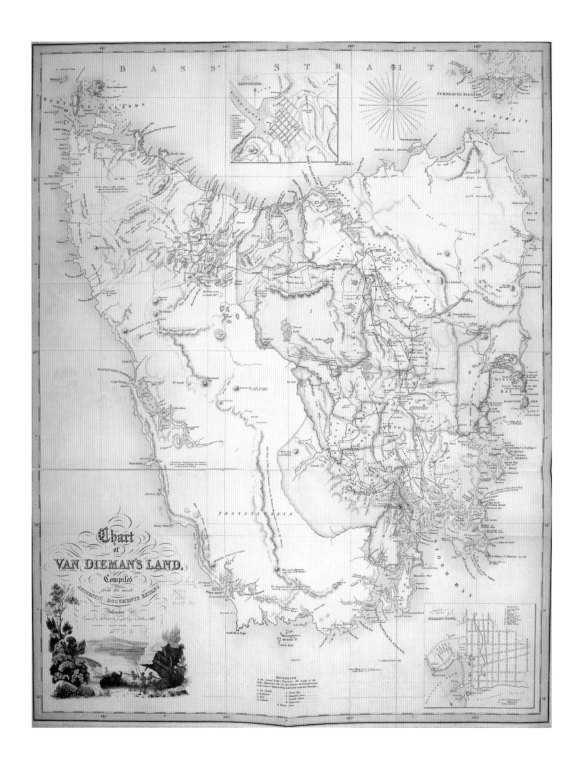

islands around them. Some islands, such as Van Diemen's Land (today's Tasmania) experienced the impact of penal colonies as they were selected to house significant numbers of those being transported from Britain or other European nations. From the early 1800s to the abolishment of penal transportation in 1853, Van Diemen's Land was the primary destination for convicts sent to the Antipodes. As a result, by 1853 more than 70,000 convicts had been transported to the island. During this time there were also attempts to send colonists to the island. Those arriving spent their time surrounded by convicts and former convicts who were also contracted to improve the land, construct buildings and facilitate the development of the colony.

Penal colonies, especially those such as Norfolk Island, between Australia and Aotearoa/ New Zealand, were often infamous for their brutality and have left dark histories behind them. It was not just those incarcerated in the colonies who suffered because of them, either. The penal colony and ongoing settlement of Van Diemen's Land led to conflict with the indigenous Palawa over food resources, and the expansion of the settlement created an environment where further conflict and disease could decimate Aboriginal numbers. Before transportation ended there were fewer than fifty individuals of solely Aboriginal descent remaining on the island.

Van Diemen's Land was not the only island where the penal colonies harmed the communities around them. Colonies across the ocean relied on trade with islanders, particularly for foodstuffs, to keep them going, creating networks of intense dependence between the penal colonies and the islands that surrounded them. This could place tremendous stress on those whom the colonies came to rely on, as the experience of French penal colonists in New Caledonia illustrated. Here, pressures in Europe led to the foundation of a colony in an area unable to support the tremendous food and supply needs it would generate. This in turn led to reliance upon and conflict with the local Kanak populations who surrounded the settlement.

For some Pacific islander groups the presence of penal colonies meant competition for resources, conflict and the decimation of populations as the colonies grew and expanded. For others it meant becoming bound up in networks of exchange and dependency that

had profound impacts on their social and economic structures. Crucially, the penal colonies of European empires were not spaces to which convicts were shipped off to live in complete isolation from the world around them. Instead, they were transported to a part of the world where they were embedded in the networks of the Pacific and could only ever be someone else's problem.

Illustrations from *Picturesque Atlas of Australasia*, 1886: (*left*) prison interior in New Caledonia; (*right*) convicts making roads in New Caledonia.

# From slave trading to drug dealing

In the early nineteenth century, the search for goods to trade with China was still prompting many American, European and Russian voyages to the Pacific. To many merchants China was the source of products such as tea and silk that could be acquired and resold in home markets for significant sums. The problem for these traders, as it had been for centuries, was that the Chinese market did not want many of their trade goods. Resourceful merchants had located products like sea otter furs and sandalwood, but these were hard to acquire and strictly limited resources that could only be obtained at great cost and risk. In the absence of these few consumer items, Chinese traders wanted only one thing in return for their wares: silver.

For nations hoping to trade with China this meant huge volumes of precious metals leaving their economies and so some, like Britain, decided an alternative must be found. Opium, an effective and deeply addictive narcotic, was illegal in Qing Dynasty China outside of a medicinal context, but this did not stop the East India Company from smuggling it into the country. Once in the country it was sold only for silver, which in turn could be used to buy tea and other products from Chinese traders. The opioid addiction crisis that resulted prompted the Qing government to act, and in 1839 they forced the British Chief Superintendent for Trade in Guangzhou (Canton) to hand over stocks of opium for disposal.

Many in Britain railed against the Chinese resistance to trade and the restrictions placed on British traders. For them this was a chance to lobby the government to secure a better trade relationship with the Chinese government. This was a euphemism for forcing them to trade more openly through gunboat diplomacy. Between 1839 and 1860 there were two Opium Wars in which British forces rained destruction on China, its lands

Signatories of peace accords: Prince Kung (Yixin) (*left*); Sir James Hope Grant (*right*).

and seas. Illustrative of the technological one-sidedness of the conflict was an engagement in November 1839 where HMS *Voltage* and HMS *Hyacinth* defeated twenty-nine Chinese vessels while evacuating British refugees from Guangzhou. The result of the conflicts would be greater British access to Chinese ports, including the island port of Xiamen, and 'free trade' for British merchants in the country. During the peace accords, where photographs like those seen here were produced, China would also cede the island of Hong Kong and Kowloon peninsula to Britain.

While the Opium Wars were essentially of marginal importance to the islands of the Pacific, they spoke to the still-changing political and economic context of the ocean. Adventurers, explorers and merchants who had been plying the ocean for centuries, trying to gain access to Chinese and other Asian markets, increasingly had the upper hand. A period of foreign empires in the ocean was at hand. The globe-spanning activities of these empires also opened up some glaring ethical contradictions. Britain in 1839 was riding a wave of moral superiority resulting from the abolition of plantation slavery in the Caribbean. However, its activities in the Opium Wars show that the British Empire had merely replaced its role as slave trader with that of international drug dealer.

'The East India Company's Iron Steamship *Nemesis* Destroying Chinese War Junks in Anson's Bay, January 7th 1841', coloured aquatint by and after E. Duncan, 1843.

# Another ocean's island

Whaling in the Pacific Ocean has given us one of the quintessential literary depictions of the vast expanse of the ocean and of the people who live on and around it, in the pages of Herman Melville's novel *Moby-Dick* (1851). The book shows us how one of the islands that had the most significant impact on the eighteenth- and nineteenth-century Pacific actually belonged to another ocean: the Atlantic. Nantucket is a low, sandy bar lying just off the coast of Cape Cod. For over a century it was also the heart of the American whaling industry. Once the crews of ships setting out from the island, charted here in 1775, had exhausted the stocks of the Atlantic, their eyes turned west, to the Pacific, which explorers and privateers reported was full of whales.

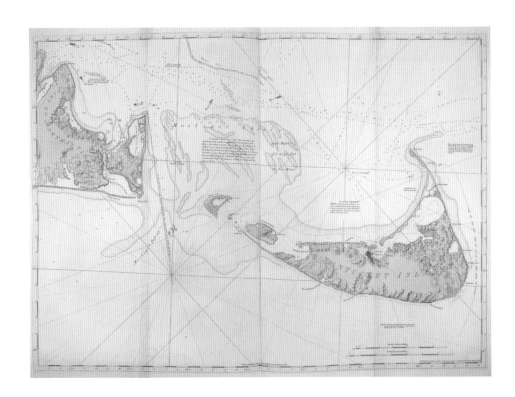

Into the ocean they pursued the sperm whale, butchering these creatures in order to render them down into a profitable collection of oils. The effects of this on the ecology of the Pacific are discussed below, but it is worth first noting the effect of this trade on the islands of the Pacific. Nantucket and its whalers represent the beginning of American influence in the Pacific. Ships set out for voyages lasting years and so needed to make land and to resupply regularly during their hunts across the ocean. As a result, islands such as those of Hawai'i and Aotearoa/New Zealand saw growing numbers of whalers making land as the profits that could be derived from whales in the ocean were better understood. As they traded, resupplied and took shore leave, the whalers had profound impacts on the islands they encountered. At the very least, their trading for food and other supplies altered the economies of the islands they visited. The whalers also brought disease to the islanders they visited, including sexually transmitted infections, in spite of the captains and many of their crews hailing from a particularly God-fearing island in the Atlantic.

Such interactions were not one-way, however. A significant number of Polynesians found work on whaling boats, sailing the ocean and the world with their new employers. *Moby-Dick* gives us such a character in Queequeg, the adventurous former chieftain who works as a harpooner and is a respected member of the crew of the *Pequod*. In reality many Polynesian sailors and whalers experienced a reality more akin to indenture and suffered great abuse at the hands of the captains and their crew-mates.

The whaling industry, and Nantucket in particular, also led to some of America's earliest colonial ventures in the Pacific. As a result of the actions of Nantucket interests, James R. Clendon was assigned, from 1838 to 1841, as the US Consul in the Bay of Islands in Aotearoa/New Zealand. The Bay of Islands quickly established a reputation as one of the most unlawful ports in the Pacific, largely through the efforts of Nantucket whalers. Abuse of the Maori population was rampant and the administration of the port was famously corrupt. Despite, or perhaps because of, this, the Bay of Islands was a site of intense speculation by Massachussets whalers, traders and politcians, who hoped the port could become a toehold for the creation of an American colony (and profitable whaling interest) in the southern Pacific Ocean. Nantucket has the distinction, therefore, of not only propelling the dramatic impact the whaling industry had on the islands of the Pacific Ocean, but also instigating some of the early experiments in American colonialism and empire.

Entry to the Bay of Islands, with the American consul James Reddy Clendon's flag flying.

(*Left*) 'A Chart of Nantucket Island and Part of Martha's Vineyard', 1775.

# Bleeding an ocean dry

Whaling in the Pacific was big business, not just for American whaling crews but also for ships from a number of European nations. In the eighteenth and nineteenth centuries the industry and factories of these nations ran off whale oil, which acted as a lubricant for the growing number of machines being developed to produce manufactured goods. Whale oil also provided light during the night, and the finest types, such as spermaceti, were highly valued in the cosmetics industry. The properties of each oil were unique to different species of whale and the use a whale made of the waxy fluid in its body; for example, spermaceti acted as the focusing medium for the echolocation of the sperm whale. As a result, different whales were hunted for different products and needed to be chased across whichever ocean where they could be found in significant numbers.

The near extirpation of various species of whales in the Atlantic is illustrated in these whale encounter charts from the US Bureau of Ordnance and Hydrography, published in 1852. They show little activity in the Atlantic but still significant numbers of encounters in the Pacific Ocean. Knowledge of the numbers of whales in the Pacific was originally gleaned from the accounts of explorers, as the charting of unknown spaces opened them up to the capitalist exploitation of the European world. Once the significant hunting grounds were known, whalers set off in growing numbers, particularly from Nantucket and other parts of the eastern seaboard of the United States.

Whaling was far from easy. Whales were dangerous quarry, easily capable of stoving in the smaller boats in which crews chased their prey and even sinking a ship, as in the case of the *Essex*, which was sunk by a sperm whale in 1820. Furthermore, the Pacific Ocean itself was a hazardous place. Disease, justifiably hostile islanders and privateers from enemy nations were just a few of the dangers faced by whaling crews. The potential profits, however, were enormous. Charts like these illustrate the results of this profitable hunt, clearly showing the progress towards extinction of various whale species across the Pacific. The hunt would continue until it was no longer financially viable. Ultimately, only cheaper oil extracted from the ground of the continental United States would save many species of whale in the Pacific.

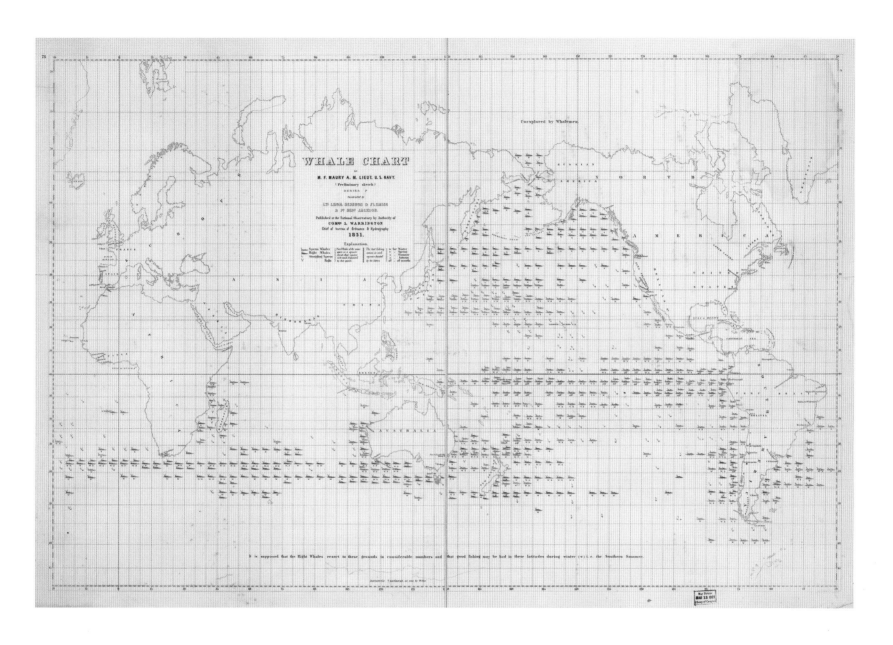

(*Left*) Sperm whale being harpooned, from
Robert Hamilton, *The Natural History of the
Ordinary Cetacea or Whales*, 1843.

American chart of whale numbers in
the Pacific, US Office of Ordnance and
Hydrography, 1852.

# A theory of the Pacific

**D**uring the nineteenth century there was continued British interest in exploring and surveying lands in and around the Pacific Ocean. Generally this went hand in hand with the interests of the British Empire, as illustrated by the voyage of HMS *Beagle*. The *Beagle* left England at the end of 1831 to survey the coast of South America, an area of speculation for British interests as the territories of Spain and Portugal began to fray and fracture. The voyage also included a circumnavigation of the world that would take the ship's crew not only around South America but also across the Pacific to Australia and beyond. The journey of the *Beagle* would take five years.

While the survey work of the expedition was its primary focus, and of most obvious benefit to various elements of the British Empire, this is not why the expedition is remembered. Instead, it was the presence of a twenty-two-year-old geologist, Charles Darwin, that would set the voyage of the *Beagle* apart from its chart-making peers. Darwin would spend almost three and a half of the next five years on shore in various parts of the Americas and the Pacific. His observations on the geology of the Andes and other parts of South America would connect him to the work of the Prussian scientist Alexander von Humboldt and, later, James Dwight Dana of the United States Exploring Expedition. Geology may have been Darwin's primary focus at this time but it was his wider observations during the expedition that made their most lasting impression. As he encountered the biodiversity of the Amazon, trailed nets from the *Beagle*, took observations of Australian fauna and travelled to the islands in the Pacific, Darwin made wildlife observations that were to form the focus of his thinking for much of the rest of his life.

Much of the biodiversity of the Pacific islands had dissipated by the nineteenth century, with species forced into extreme isolation or extinction by successive waves of human settlement and modification of their environments. There were some locations, however, of such extreme isolation or with such abundant diversity of life where peopling and later colonising of the Pacific had not been able to completely diminish their natural diversity. The Galápagos Islands were not totally protected by their isolation – they had long been an invaluable site for sailors and privateers to resupply – but their unique situation in the Pacific Ocean meant that life continued to thrive on and around the islands. As a result, Darwin was still able to encounter a location that highlighted the effect of islands on the development of differentiation across species. His observations of the finches of the Galápagos

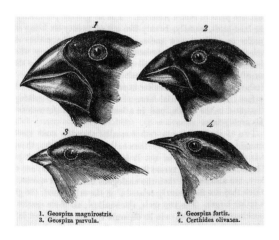

1. Geospiza magnirostris.
2. Geospiza fortis.
3. Geospiza parvula.
4. Certhidea olivasea.

are a famous cornerstone of his theory on the evolution of species, and influenced his thinking on the decades between his voyage on the *Beagle* and the publication of *On the Origin of Species* (1859).

The unique geography and ecology of Pacific islands provided a rare opportunity for Darwin to observe essential patterns in nature, and his resulting theory influences our thinking about the natural world to this day. However, Darwin's work is only one example of how the exploration of the Pacific has influenced a global understanding of the world. Such insights had arisen (and would continue to arise) from Pacific island cultures, as well as the voyages of Cook and others. As the nineteenth century unfolded, there was also more to come.

(*Left*) Examples of finch beaks from Darwin's account of the *Beagle* voyage, 1860.

(*Left above*) Galápagos marine iguana, from *The Zoology of the Voyage of HMS Beagle*, part 5, 1843.

(*Right*) Finches, from *The Zoology of the Voyage of HMS Beagle*, part 3, 1841.

# Charting the 'American Lake'

Almost from the moment of the United States' independence, whaling, business and political interests around the coast of New England talked of the nation's destiny to become a power in the Pacific. To them it seemed that the creation of an 'American Lake', as twentieth-century theoreticians would later call it, was the most financially and geopolitically profitable enterprise the federal government could undertake. While such an endeavour would have various facets – for example, installing a consul on some islands with a view to strengthening American administrative influence there – by the nineteenth century it was clear that any American imperialism in the Pacific would begin with one crucial element: a voyage of exploration. The works of Cook and the many others who had followed in his wake had illustrated the importance of sending explorers to chart spaces and fly the flag for a developing empire. In the context of the Pacific, not only would an American expedition fulfil this function, but it could also open up new financial opportunities (new whaling grounds always being good news), and, by mapping the dangerous shoals off Pacific islands, make the eking out of profit from the region safer and easier.

Despite what whalers and others with a financial interest in the Pacific saw as the undeniable good sense of these arguments, the US government spent decades prevaricating. It was not until 1838 that the grand United States Exploring Expedition, known as the 'Ex. Ex.', set out with a complement of two sloops of war, one ship, one brig and two schooners under the overall command of Lieutenant (not Captain, much to his chagrin) Charles Wilkes. Wilkes was faced with a gargantuan task: heading south

Map of the Oregon Territory, from *Narrative of the United States Exploring Expedition*, 1850.

to investigate the possibility of land in the Antarctic; charting various Pacific islands; and then heading to the western coast of North America to chart the lands around the Columbia River. This left the expedition with at least three major objectives: to create charts that could secure the western seaboard for the federal government and bring a continental nation closer to being; to generate imperial glory by finding land in the Antarctic; and to protect traders, such as those looking for sandalwood, by charting the dangerous shoals around islands such as Fiji.

Added to this was Wilkes's responsibility for a large scientific corps and ships, especially the supply vessel *Relief*, that were unfit for their role in the expedition. In spite of the fundamental challenges faced by the expedition, the ongoing disagreements between Wilkes and his crew and Wilkes's ability to embroil himself in violent conflicts with the islanders he encountered, the expedition laid down a number of milestones contributing to American influence in the Pacific. The charting of the Columbia contributed to the nation's development of a Pacific coastline, while the charts developed of islands like Fiji, gained through significant conflict and loss of Fijian life, protected American ships trading in these parts of the Pacific. Wilkes also made a number of observations about locations in the Pacific that would be significant for generations to come. While in Hawai'i Wilkes charted and sounded what he called 'Pearl Harbor' (known then as Wai Momi), noting that it

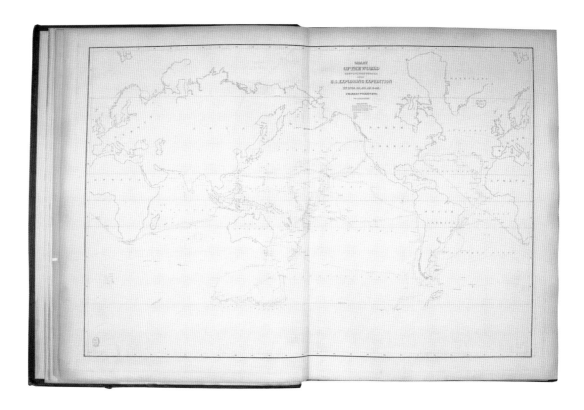

was so capacious as to warrant becoming the most significant port in the Pacific in coming decades. Between the financial interest of Nantucket whalers and the geopolitical observations of men like Wilkes, many in the United States were becoming increasingly aware of the strategic importance of Hawai'i and its potential role as the lynchpin of an American Pacific.

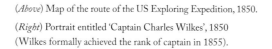

(*Above*) Map of the route of the US Exploring Expedition, 1850.

(*Right*) Portrait entitled 'Captain Charles Wilkes', 1850 (Wilkes formally achieved the rank of captain in 1855).

# A map bought with blood

Sandalwood was what brought the Fijian islands to the attention of colonial traders in the nineteenth century. Since Tasman's expeditions Fiji had been largely avoided by European and other explorers, who knew of the islanders' reputation for violence and cannibalism. As a result, a procession of explorers in varying degrees of splendour or humiliation (Bligh sailed among the islands while adrift after the *Bounty* mutiny)

sailed close to but avoided prolonged contact with the islands. That changed with the fever for sandalwood that gripped colonial traders in the early nineteenth century. In 1800 members of the American brig *Argo* found themselves among the Fijian people after being shipwrecked in surrounding waters. Two years later, on leaving the islands, they took valuable knowledge with them. There were large stands of sandalwood on this group of islands.

The financial imperative that underpinned the sandalwood boom lay in the Chinese market. Here was one of the limited group of commodities that traders from Europe and the Americas could import into China and use to generate a large profit. As a result it joined the ranks of sea otter furs and that most sinister trade item entering the Chinese market, opium. Harvesting sandalwood could therefore be profitable business, and traders and their cutting teams began to descend on any island known to contain stands of the tree. Fiji's isolation from those encroaching on the Pacific was about to come to an abrupt end.

The feared aggression of Fijian islanders was not the only concern for traders attempting to harvest sandalwood from the archipelago. The coral shoals of the islands quickly became infamous, combining with the lack of proper charts of the area to claim many ships and lives. While the sandalwood boom on Fiji was largely over by 1815, as a result of the stands of easily harvested wood running out, by the time Wilkes and his Exploring Expedition departed the ports of the United States there was still a desire that these dangerous shoals should be mapped.

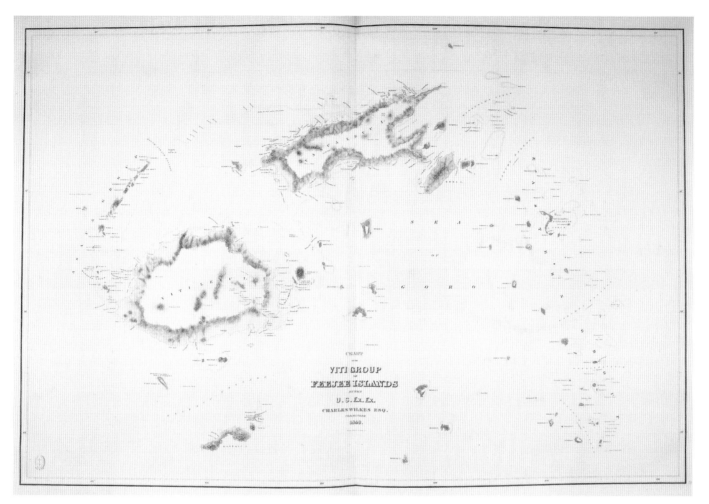

'Chart of the Viti Group or Feejee Islands', produced by Wilkes from the survey conducted by the expedition.

(*Left*) 'Club Dance, Feejee', from the account of the US Exploring Expedition.

Wilkes and his crew arrived in the islands well into their arduous expedition and full of the fractious conflict that defined the voyage. As a result, when tempers frayed between Wilkes's crew and the islanders surrounding them during their survey work, the lieutenant's temper was a tinderbox waiting to ignite. In a show of force Wilkes took to shore with a mind to assault any Fijian warriors, villagers, women and children who crossed his path, irrespective of whether they had been involved in the original assault or not. The lieutenant eventually agreed to peace, although only after insisting that a large group of islanders present themselves to him and offer their apologies. Wilkes also took prisoner the chief he held responsible for the attack on his men, Veidovi (recorded by Wilkes as Vendovi), and insisted he accompany the expedition back to America. The Exploring Expedition would leave the islands with a complete chart, literally placing Fiji and its people at a fixed point on the map. The chart, as with many other Pacific maps, was paid for with violence and bloodshed.

# An influential collection

By the nineteenth century the presence of natural historians and scientists was understood to be an essential part of any voyage of exploration, not least one to the Pacific. Sir Joseph Banks and the long train of inquiring minds who sailed on voyages before and after him established a pattern through which enquiry into the natural world helped to promote the work of any expedition and build the imperial and colonial case that followed. Comprehending the world was an integral part of laying claim to it.

Wilkes's United States Exploring Expedition, then, needed a team to develop this arm of the expedition, and it needed to be on a scale appropriate to a vast, ambitious exploring expedition. This did not stop Wilkes paring back the scientific corps when he took over the troubled expedition and assuming a number of responsibilities himself. While Wilkes covered surveying, meteorology and astronomy, he still needed to fill a number of other specialisms. Here he made strong appointments: Titan Peale (naturalist), William Rich (botanist), Charles Pickering (naturalist), Joseph Couthouy (conchologist), William Brackenbridge (horticulturalist) and James Dwight Dana (geologist). These men

would develop significant insights into the history and culture of the Pacific, as well as contributing to our broader understanding of the wider natural world, in spite of the near-constant aggravation visited on them by their commanding officer. While the attitude of their commanding officer was a hindrance, Wilkes did comprehend the importance of the scientific arm of the expedition and his men wanted for little in terms of equipment. This no doubt helped people like Dana considerably in developing the insights they published on their return.

During the course of the expedition Dana collected thousands of samples, many relating to his chosen field of geology, though he also made inroads into Couthouy's specialism and collected samples of corals and molluscs. On his return he published his findings in conchology (producing insights that would support the work of another scientist who had already travelled to the Pacific, Charles Darwin) and in his home field of geology. In particular, Dana's work on Hawai'i and around the ocean helped him to develop insights into the workings of volcanoes and their relationship to the movement of tectonic plates over the surface of the earth.

He put forward the theory that volcanoes and mountains were caused by the impacting of plates on the earth's surface, regarding them as wrinkles on the earth's surface – which is close to today's understanding of subduction zones and their resulting volcanic activity.

Dana's work therefore laid the groundwork for understanding the Pacific as one enormous ring of volcanic activity, with the west coast of the United States forming part of the geological activity of the wider ocean. This and other ideas of the connectedness of the United States to the wider Pacific would inform dramatic American expansion into the region over the next century. After a protracted and painful process the collections of the Exploring Expedition eventually became a founding cornerstone of the Smithsonian Institution collection in Washington, DC. The work of Wilkes and his team in exploring and collecting in the Pacific therefore still exerts a profound influence on how Americans see and understand the world today.

Natural history illustrations, including Dana's corals, from the atlas that accompanied the United States Exploring Expedition's *Narrative*.

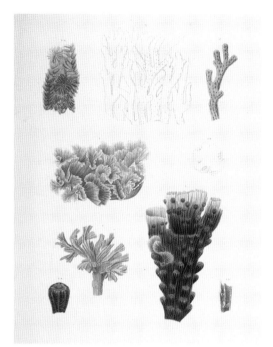

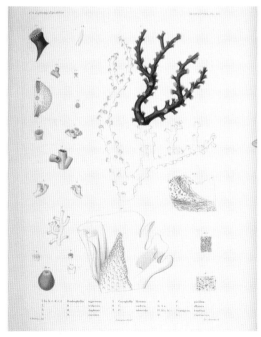

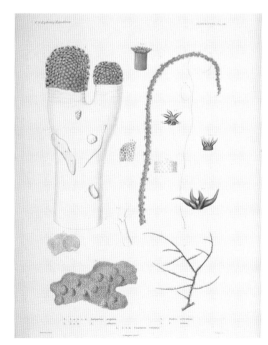

# Slavers of the Pacific

That the economic interconnection of the Pacific islands with the financial networks of outsiders, as driven by fur traders, whalers and others, should have a dark underbelly was immediately obvious. Violence, drinking and a proliferation of sex work on islands entwined with these trades were just some of the destructive exchanges brought about by the actions of sailors from outside the Pacific. By middle of the nineteenth century the colonisation of the wider Pacific, especially the eastern Australian coast, and the economic development and technological modernisation of part of Latin America, had created a new need for manpower that many traders were keen to fill. Sugar plantations, guano extraction operations and other developing economic ventures needed constant supplies of human labour in order to operate, and these industries were unscrupulous as to where the labour came from. The solution, as far as a number of unethical capitalists were concerned, was to turn to the kidnapping and enslavement of Pacific islanders.

Such activity was known as blackbirding, and those involved in the transportation argued that they were providing opportunities to Pacific islanders, as the 'indenture' they offered would bring money and the chance to travel. In reality, those involved in the practice would depart from ports in Chile or New South Wales, travel to lesser contacted islands in the Pacific and lure groups of people onto a beach, before moving to capture them, transport them across the ocean and sell them to those

(*Below*) Sketch showing the forced recruitment of South Sea Islander labourers in the New Hebrides, 1892.

(*Left*) Labourers from Pacific islands planting sugar cane at a plantation in Mackay, Queensland, in the 1870s.

(*Left*) Forced recruitment of South Sea Islanders to work on plantations in Queensland, 1893.

(*Above*) Seizure of the schooner *Daphne* by HMS *Rosario*.

in need of labour around the ocean's periphery. The practice, which ran from the 1840s until the early twentieth century, was slavery in all but name, and the individuals caught up in it found themselves toiling in the same dangerous, back-breaking conditions that enslaved individuals in the Caribbean had endured for centuries. A particularly corrosive aspect of blackbirding was how susceptible Pacific islands were to the population decline instigated by the systematic removal of men who were in the prime of their health from a small society and population base. Rapa Nui was already struggling as a result of introduced disease and the impact of environmental degradation on the island, but the arrival of blackbirders in the 1860s meant that the population would collapse to just over a hundred individuals in the coming decades.

By the 1860s, attempts were being made to control the practice of blackbirding. Ships such as HMS *Rosario* (illustrated here) were on patrol to look for ships carrying islanders forced into indenture, but the practice was difficult to police. Some ships moved Pacific island labourers around the ocean quite legitimately, even if this still brought with it extreme and abusive treatment. Despite the clear parallels with slavery, therefore, blackbirding inhabited an area of just enough uncertainty to ensure that, even with the increasing oversight of various colonies and empires, the practice would endure as long as it was financially profitable. Tragically, even when intervention was made on the part of those who were kidnapped

and enslaved, the consequences could be catastrophic in different ways. An attempt to repatriate kidnapped labourers from Lima to Nuku Hiva ended in disaster when those who returned brought smallpox with them. More than 1,500 people on the island died. Rapa Nui too was further ravaged by diseases introduced by those who were kidnapped and returned. The blackbirders exacted a devastating price from the islands of the Pacific.

Islanders on the deck of a ship arriving at Bundaberg, 1895.

# Colonising Pacific histories

Since the earliest arrivals of Europeans in the Pacific, rudimentary attempts at anthropological study of the peoples inhabiting islands had been attempted. The arrival of expeditions like that led by Cook and the growing activities of missionaries in the Pacific increased the scope and reach of this anthropological work. Some of this was driven by a spirit of enquiry, a desire to understand more about the world, its peoples and their societies. Much was driven by a desire to record the cultures of various groups so this understanding could be used to proselytise more effectively to indigenous populations. The practice of anthropological study also went hand in hand with the development of collections of cultural and spiritual objects from Pacific island communities. From a colonial and evangelical point of view, this had the dual benefit of developing the scope of museum and private collections in the metropole and of removing significant objects from island society in order to replace them with Christian idols.

These activities went hand in hand with a growing body of works that attempted to record islander traditions and histories from the Pacific. Such works were compiled from anthropological studies made across the ocean, from New Guinea to Aotearoa/New Zealand, to Hawai'i, to Vancouver Island and on and on. The account seen here, *Polynesian Mythology*, was compiled by the British soldier and colonial administrator Sir George Grey, and published by John Murray in 1855. There was a strong relationship between colonialism, its administration and the practice of anthropology that is similar to that seen with missionary practices. As colonial administrators attempted to 'civilise' the world of the Pacific islands, they believed it was inevitable that the cultures they currently governed would disappear, with indigenous peoples adopting colonial cultures, manners and religions. Despite this being seen as a favourable outcome, there was still a strong desire among many colonial figures to record the cultures and traditions they sought to supplant. Sir George Grey was a man in this mould.

*Polynesian Mythology* is an unusual work in this canon, however, as it draws directly from the knowledge of Aotearoa Maori who surrounded Grey, particularly Te Rangikaheke (baptised as Wiremu Maihi or William Marsh). Te Rangikaheke worked as a colonial public servant and was a scholar of Maori history, compiling numerous manuscripts detailing Maori traditions, language, genealogy, legends and history. Grey used these accounts to compile *Polynesian Mythology*, giving Te Rangikaheke no credit and introducing numerous errors in the process. Colonial anthropological publications were common throughout the nineteenth century and cover a spectrum of intellectual robustness that runs from the ridiculous to the significant. *Polynesian Mythology* is, in many ways, illustrative of many texts produced by colonial figures but it is elevated by the anonymised work and scholarship of Te Rangikaheke.

Frontispiece and title page of Grey's *Polynesian Mythology*, 1855.

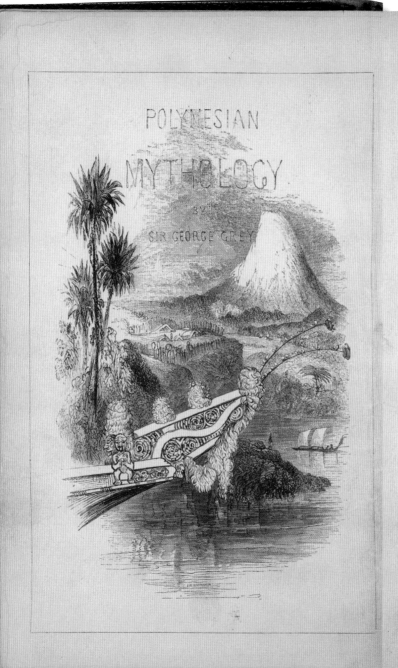

# POLYNESIAN MYTHOLOGY,

AND

## ANCIENT TRADITIONAL HISTORY

OF THE

### NEW ZEALAND RACE,

AS FURNISHED BY THEIR PRIESTS AND CHIEFS.

BY SIR GEORGE GREY,
LATE GOVERNOR-IN-CHIEF OF NEW ZEALAND.

LONDON:
JOHN MURRAY, ALBEMARLE STREET.
1855.

# Dark shapes on the horizon

The ambitions of the United States in the Pacific were not limited to those islands approached by Wilkes during the Exploring Expedition of 1838–42. American commercial interests, driven by belief in the nation's Manifest Destiny in the Pacific, would continue to develop throughout the nineteenth century, in some places with direct political and military help from the federal government. The most significant intervention of the US government in the Pacific during this period is possibly that led by Commodore Matthew Perry during the years 1852–5. During this period Perry led a growing expedition of US Navy ships to the islands of Japan in an attempt to force the isolated kingdom to open its ports and markets to foreign trade.

Traders from Britain, Russia and other empires had been consistently trying their luck with Japan during the early part of the nineteenth century, but by the middle of the century the political and economic pressures driving the competition between empires in the Pacific were building to a head. The expanding manufacturing base in many industrial nations, in parallel with the growing colonial and imperial spheres of empires invested in the Pacific, meant that by mid-century all known economic opportunities in the Pacific Ocean were being exploited. Japan may not have represented the same scale of market as China but it was still a large kingdom that had been largely cut off from outside influences for centuries. As a result, there were significant opportunities

to develop new financial markets and spheres of geopolitical influence. The continued technological ascendancy of those nations involved in nineteenth-century empire building also meant a period had arrived where Japan could be dominated through strength of arms.

Perry's approach to his diplomatic and military expedition to Japan exploited the possibilities of the military technology available to him at this time. Taking the steam paddle-wheeled frigate *Mississippi* as a flagship, and modern armaments, including cannons capable of firing explosive shells, Perry sailed into Edo Bay in July 1853. He quickly engaged in a textbook exercise in gunboat diplomacy: surveying the bay in spite of official objections, firing blank rounds

from the cannons and issuing notices that any resistance would result in direct assault. Perry's demands were deceptively simple, the opening of Japan to trade, and he soon departed, promising to return for answers in one year. This was a misleading promise and Perry returned in six months, having bolstered his squadron to ten ships, to apply pressure on the Japanese administration. The fear and confusion sowed by Perry is evidenced in Japanese accounts of the expedition, which emphasise the threat posed by the ships and exaggerate the features of the Americans represented. The imposing ships and grotesque figures are illustrated in the account shown here.

In the end, Perry sailed away believing he had opened Japan to American trade. The reality was more complex, primarily because of the way the officials he dealt with related to the Shōgun and because of other intricacies of the Japanese administration. Nonetheless, he had established rights of access for US ships in Japanese waters, safety and good treatment for stranded sailors, the opportunity for the federal government to send consuls to open up Japanese ports and, crucially, a most-favoured-nation clause that granted any concessions Japan made to other nations to the United States as well. America's belief in Manifest Destiny and practice of gunboat diplomacy were paying dividends in the Pacific.

(*Left*) Untitled Japanese scroll depicting the arrival of Commodore Perry's ships at Uraga Bay, 1853.

(*Right*) Hiroshige print showing a Japanese man and boy standing on the shore of a harbour in which an American steamship is docked.

159

# Wars of Manifest Destiny

The expansion of American geopolitical interests into the Pacific made it almost inevitable that some form of conflict would unfold on the islands around the ocean. Periods of expansion and contraction for empires are often marked by conflict as different spheres of influence overlap and become spaces of competition. In the context of the belief of many Americans in the nation's Manifest Destiny in the Pacific, conflict was made even more likely by the belligerent approach taken by the United States and its representatives on the ocean, as illustrated by Perry's dealings with Japan and the actions of other commanders like Wilkes. Some of the conflicts that arose from American expansion in the Pacific and its surrounding seas, however, verged on the ridiculous. The 'Pig War' of 1859 unfolded on the San Juan Islands which sit between Vancouver Island and the continental United States. Relatively recently the expedition of George Vancouver had charted the islands and their location in the strait but the placement, illustrated in the expedition atlas and shown here, was imprecise. Vancouver's expedition was not the only one to place the islands and the strait between them incorrectly; Wilkes made a similar error

Chart of Vancouver Island produced from surveys during Vancouver's expedition.

during his survey of the Columbia River region. It is easy to understand why mistakes were made, as the challenging climate and geology of the strait combine with the world's strongest tidal flow to make the task of surveying here extremely difficult.

The problem caused by these cartographical errors arises from the quirk of the US–Canadian (then British North America) border around Vancouver Island. Much of the western border between the nations is marked by the 49th northern parallel, but this dips through the strait in order to leave Vancouver Island on the Canadian side. This created a dispute over what side of the strait the islands were on. It is worth remembering that tensions between the British Empire and the United States ran high during the nineteenth century: war broke out between the two in 1812, the Oregon Treaty was deeply contentious and Britain interfered in the Civil War later in the century, so any conflict over these islands was potentially explosive and threatened to open up broader conflict between the nations.

When conflict did arise it began with the killing of a pig. An American settler on the islands killed a pig belonging to a Hudson's Bay Company employee and this, although it may seem hard to believe, led to the dispatch of small military forces from both the American and the British sides. While the commanders and troops on both sides refused to let the mobilisation stray into overt conflict, the situation was undoubtedly

dangerous. In the end it was in the interests of both nations to stand down and mediate the situation. Nonetheless, the ambiguity of the border would remain, along with military occupation of the islands by both sides, until 1871, when the dispute was resolved by international arbitration and the border placed firmly to the west of the islands. America had won another tussle over islands in and around the Pacific, but not all of its geopolitical actions against other Pacific empires would be resolved so bloodlessly. The Spanish-American war of 1898 would lead

the United States to send a significant fleet and put 11,000 marines on the ground in the Philippines. While victory here against the Spanish was relatively swift, the resulting conflict between US forces and Filipino resistance would last for over three years and claim the lives of more than 200,000 civilians. America's Pacific destiny, then, would develop at the great expense of many who lived on islands across the ocean.

Illustration of 'English Camp', San Juan Island.  161

# Splitting an ocean

Despite the Pacific Ocean taking up more space on the surface of this planet than all of the landmasses combined, it is unusual, especially for Europeans, to be able to picture it as a holistic space. Instead, it is splintered into fragments, the east Pacific forming the west of many Mercator-projection global maps while the west forms the eastern side of these maps. This occurs across the ocean, as various imagined and cultural borders carve this huge body of water up into chunks. There is one other human construct overlaid on the Pacific that impacts our everyday lives and how we understand the geography of the ocean: the International Date Line, the demarcation line separating one day from another. This spatial delimiter of time is important not only for understanding what day it is; for mariners it has a fundamental impact on their ability to comprehend their longitudinal distance from another fixed point of reference, now usually the Greenwich meridian. Since the earliest days of European exploration in the Pacific Ocean, the line of demarcation has been placed somewhere in the ocean, helping navigators keep track of days during their journey. However, the line is a flexible construct.

During the centuries of the Spanish treasure fleets, the date-line geography of the Pacific was markedly different from today's. At one point the east coast of the Philippines, now significantly to the west of the Date Line, fell on the American side, effectively keeping it behind the time in Spanish America. In the north of the Pacific, the Date Line has moved east and west as the boundaries of the Russian Empire expanded and contracted during the fur-trading period. Similarly, the Meridian Conference of 1884 influenced the geography of the Date Line by establishing the prime meridian in Greenwich, England. This not only established the geographical centre of many map projections, but also fixed the point from which midday can be articulated. For a ship needing to measure longitude, the distance east or west on the Earth's surface is conveyed in degrees, minutes and seconds from the prime meridian. Further, if Greenwich is understood to represent a fixed point from which time and distance are articulated, the 180-degree meridian falls through the Pacific.

During the 1884 Meridian Conference, which set the prime meridian but explicitly avoided fixing the International Date Line, it was nonetheless remarked that a 180-degree point that fell through the Pacific was ideal as it covered little land and made decisions about who went on which side of the Date Line easier. However, in over 130 years since the Meridian Conference there has been a significant amount of horse trading over which side of the Date Line various territories fall on. Just as the line shifted with the sale of Alaska from Russia to the United States (driven by the collapse of animal populations and rapidly diminishing profits for Russian trading operations), the colonisation and independence of various Pacific territories also led them to move from one side to the other. Kwajalein Atoll is an example of that, as it has passed between Spanish, German, Japanese and American influence, moved to different sides of the Date Line and established new working patterns to bring it into line with the economies it is most closely integrated with. These details help us understand the significance of a human construct that divides the Pacific Ocean not just temporally but in our imaginations as well.

US Air Force map showing time zones and International Date Line, 1947.

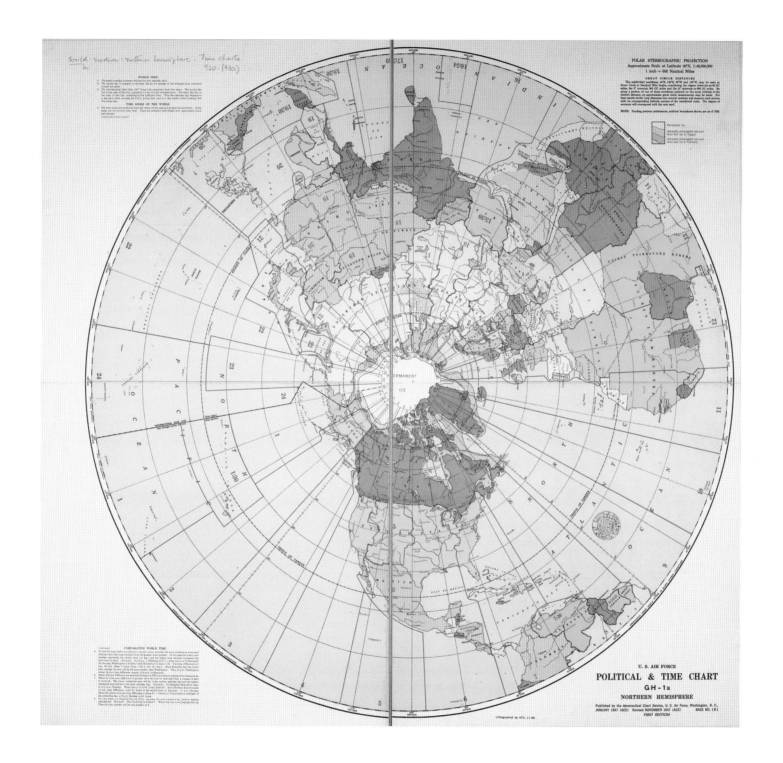

EMPIRE OF ISLANDS

163

# The Polynesian Confederacy

The reign of the Kamehameha Dynasty came to an end in 1872, when Kamehameha V died without naming a successor. During the years of Kamehameha reign Hawai'i's prosperity and political interconnectedness with the world had grown. This network would have to be taken over and further developed by whichever dynasty took the place of the Kamehameha lineage. The Hawai'ian constitution was clear that if no successor

was established by a reigning monarch, the legislature of the islands would elect a new monarch and dynasty to take over. What followed was a fierce contest, which took place over fourteen months, and eventually Kalākaua was elected to succeed the Kamehameha Dynasty.

Kalākaua's reign did not start auspiciously: he needed British and American aid to suppress dissent arising from his election over Queen Emma (the widow of Kamehameha IV). This did not impede his ambition for what he hoped to achieve during his reign or Hawai'i's growing place in the world. Kalākaua planned to leverage Hawai'i's interconnectedness with the wider world of nations and empires to develop a political structure that would improve the status of Polynesian islands in the wider world. Of particular concern to Kalākaua was the ability of colonial powers like Britain, not to mention the rapidly developing influence of the United States, to manipulate and overpower smaller, and particularly Polynesian, islands around the rest of the Pacific. Kalākaua saw this as unjust, and was keen to create a political system that would give smaller nations greater influence on the international stage.

In 1881 Kalākaua left Hawai'i on a series of official visits that would see him become the first Hawai'ian to officially circumnavigate the globe. During the resulting diplomatic meetings, Kalākaua's thought about how to develop the role of Hawai'i and the other Polynesian islands in the world. His visit to Japan, which was rapidly moving out of isolation and developing a significant presence on the world stage, highlighted to Kalākaua how a nation could embrace elements of westernisation in technology, governance and economics while retaining that which made its people unique and culturally distinct. During the voyage Kalākaua also developed a strong sense that the only way to deflect the attentions of foreign powers and maintain a strong, independent presence in the wider world was by confederating smaller states into a larger, federalised organisation.

Achieving this would not be easy. By the late nineteenth century various European powers and the United States were politicking across the ocean, manipulating island governments and each other in order to increase their presence in the ocean at large. Efforts to build the Confederacy started

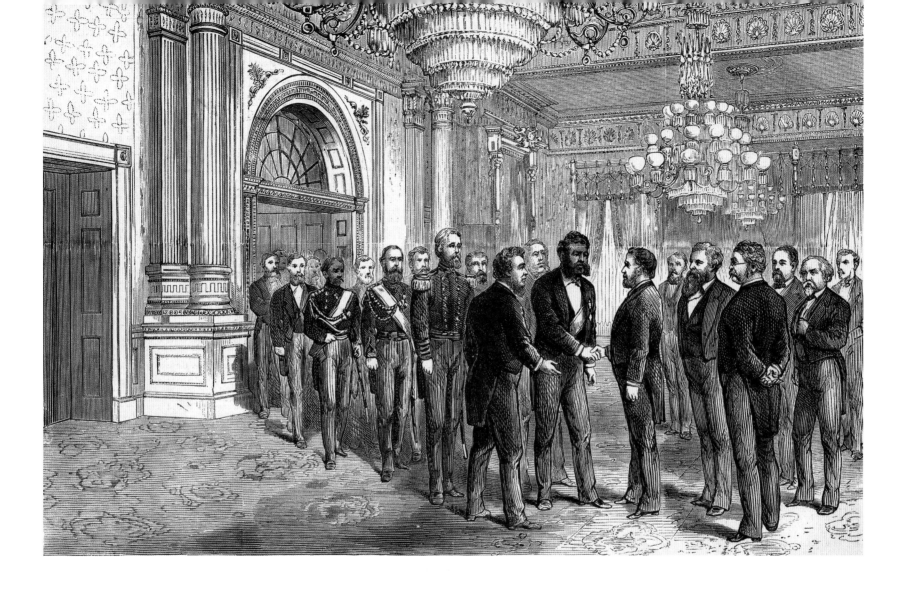

On Kalākaua's state visit to the United States, President Grant hosted the first modern state dinner in his honour, 1874.

(*Left*) King Kalākaua.

with complex problems of organising each island's priorities and developing a coherent sense of what federation would involve, while also fending off the machinations of imperial and colonial powers. In spite of the grand vision of the Confederacy and its lofty actions (Japan was even sounded out about becoming a member), in the end the idea was too ambitious to execute with

so many disruptive foreign actors already working against it and its geopolitical ambitions. Kalākaua's philosophical mind and determination to preserve Polynesian independence may also have emboldened his enemies in their plans to undermine the government of the Hawaiʻian islands. The end of the nineteenth century would bring fundamental change here.

# The annexation of Hawai'i

For much of the nineteenth century Hawai'i had seemed to American interests a source of opportunity and anxiety. It provided an invaluable hub in the Pacific for American whalers, was a focus of evangelical missionary work from the United States, and opened up a number of agricultural opportunities, especially with regard to the growing of sugar cane. At the same time, Hawai'ian independence, as well as the threat that a European nation, perhaps Britain or France, might come to hold sway over the islands was a source of anxiety for the United States. In short, the islands could either encourage the development of American Manifest Destiny in the Pacific, or significantly hinder it. The main reason for this was the same as it had been throughout the century, and is simply illustrated by the maps shown here: Hawai'i was at the geographical and strategic heart of the Pacific Ocean. The winds of the ocean may have kept European sailors away for centuries, but the nineteenth century and the advent of steam power, with its associated need for coaling stations, made Hawai'i a key location in an ocean of changing currents.

This strategic importance is, in large part, why the publication this map accompanied – *A Handbook on the Annexation of Hawaii* (1898) – came to be printed. The reign of Kalākaua made it clear that Hawai'ian monarchs intended on keeping the islands independent and strengthening this independence in

*Puck* magazine satirises the actions of Sanford B. Dole.

the century to come. However, the latter years of his reign and those of his successor, Queen Lili'uokalani, saw waves of agitation from members of the Hawai'ian legislature, who accused Kalākaua and his legislature of corruption and bribery. Between 1887, notably not long after ideas of the Pacific Confederation began to be explored, and 1898, there were waves of agitation, articulated by the likes of Sanford Ballard Dole, a lawyer of American descent who advocated westernisation. This unrest eroded the power of Kalākaua and Lili'oukalani.

In 1893 a coup was staged, overthrowing the monarchy. The new government began working closely with the US Minister to Hawai'i, John L. Stevens, in order to begin a process whereby Hawai'i would be assimilated as a territory of the United States. While initial overtures were well received, a change of president, to Grover Cleveland, meant that the delegation Sanford Dole sent to the United States in 1894 met with limited enthusiasm. Indeed, Cleveland attempted to reinstate Lili'uokalani, a move that prompted Dole to declare Hawai'i an independent republic. The situation changed rapidly when the United

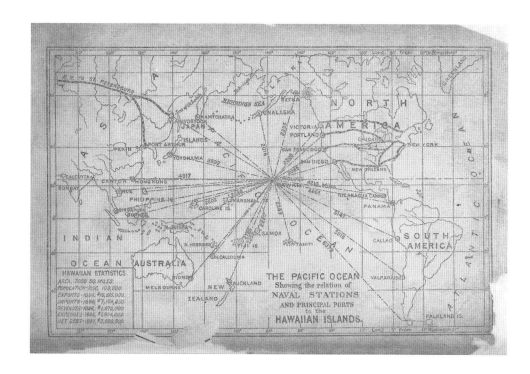

States went to war with Spain in 1898 and a wave of nationalism, as well as realisation of the strategic military importance of the islands, led another president, William McKinley, to annex the Hawai'ian islands. They became a US territory in 1900. Hawai'i's experience of American colonialism and, later, imperialism, illustrates the situation Pacific island nations found themselves in. They were forced to navigate a world of geopolitical, military, economic and colonial intrigue where agents of various nations could work at cross purposes or in concert (as illustrated by the chaos of Hawai'i's coup and later annexation) but ultimately to the detriment of an islander government. Maintaining order and a stable place in the world under such circumstances was increasingly difficult. This was especially the case as conflicts from across the ocean, such as the Spanish-American war and hostilities in the Philippines, could rapidly change the political context in which islanders were working. America's growing influence in the Pacific was destabilising and chaotic, but not all islands faced the fate of Hawai'i. Japan, for one, navigated the nineteenth- and twentieth-century world of empires very differently.

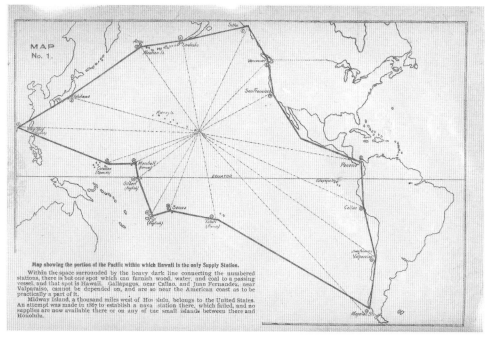

# Islands against the bear

For much of the twentieth century the Pacific would have a different political and economic balance compared to the centuries past. In many ways this is encapsulated by the decline of China and the rise of Japan. The ascent of the kingdom of the Japanese islands seems remarkable, especially in light of the events that occurred around the arrival of Perry's 'Black Ships' in the mid-nineteenth century. The two events are subtly linked, however. By the time Perry arrived, the Tokugawa Shōgunate had ruled Japan for over two centuries, dividing the country into areas of feudal control and isolating it from foreign influence. The system had been largely successful – peace and stability were the norm – but the nineteenth century made it clear that such social structures were no longer useful for a modern Japan. Growing populations, technological developments elsewhere and the dramatic expansion of foreign empires in the Pacific made it increasingly clear that Japan needed to change its social and political outlook. For any who still doubted this, the arrival of Perry's ships and the Opium Wars Britain fought against China made abundantly clear what could happen to Japan if the islands did not put themselves on a more equal footing with the wider world.

These factors, and others, combined to facilitate the fall of the Tokugawa Shōgunate, which resulted in the restoration of an emperor, Emperor Meiji, as the figurehead of a centralised government that ruled over all of Japan. The Meiji Restoration did not bring back power to the Emperor; instead the Emperor ruled under the direction of a centralised Japanese legislature. This group perceived the wider world in the same way as the Hawai'ian King Kalākaua: only political cohesion and modernisation would strengthen Japan's position in a Pacific Ocean increasingly crowded by foreign empires. Japan may have opted out of joining Kalākaua's Pacific confederacy, but understood the philosophy that underpinned it: Japan must be united to stand on its own terms and, ideally, develop its own sphere of influence and empire in the Pacific.

While the idea of a Japanese empire would be contentious within Japan and its government for decades, momentum quickly developed, assisted by a rhetoric of cultural supremacy, behind plans to take advantage of the weakened states of China and Korea. During the end of the nineteenth century Japan undertook military campaigns and clandestine operations in both nations, leading to an expansion of Japanese influence in the region and on the world stage. For many in Europe this was a threat not only to the ascendency of European empires but also to the racist ideologies that underpinned the logic of empire in the period. The ascendency of an Asian empire was anathema to many leaders of Europe, including Tsar Nicholas II. For the Tsar, Japan's rise threatened Russia's sphere of influence in the northern Pacific. Tensions between the two nations rose steadily until, in February 1904, Japan stunned Russia by declaring war and attacking the Russian fleet at Port Arthur. What followed was a campaign that would shock Western empires. Russia struggled with the logistics of fighting a war at the far side of its empire, while

Japan's rapid modernisation and bureaucratic centralisation had resulted in an effective military machine. When peace, moderated by the United States, was declared, Japan emerged victorious and annexed the Korean peninsula; Russia was left to deal with the internal recriminations of a humiliating defeat. Of the three parties that negotiated the peace of the Russo-Japanese War, it was Japan and the United States who would most dramatically influence the twentieth-century Pacific.

(*Left*) Kisaburo Ohara's map articulating Russia's growing global influence, 1904.

(*Above*) A Russian illustration of the Battle of Chemulpo, 1904.

(*Right*) The Emperor Meiji (1867–1912).

KOI GAWA

YAMATE

NE FUKUSH

TEMMA GAWA

OTA GAWA

MOTOYASU GAWA

HIROSHIMA AIRPORT

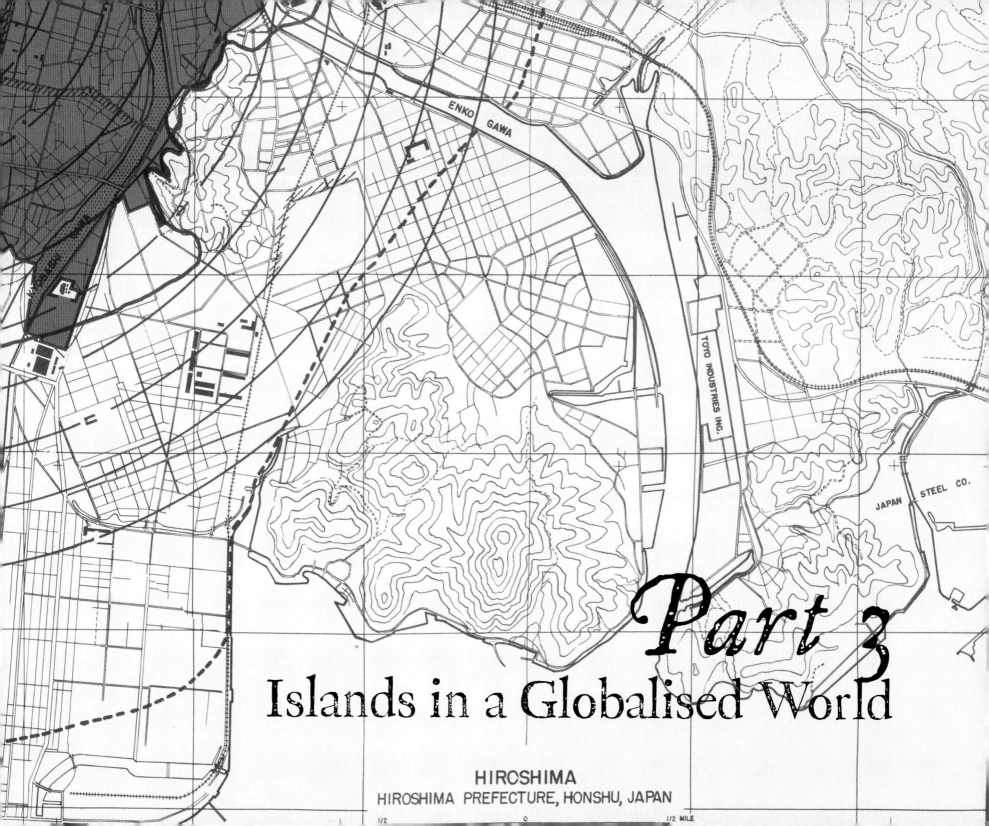

ENKO GAWA

TOYO INDUSTRIES INC.

JAPAN STEEL CO.

# Part 3

## Islands in a Globalised World

HIROSHIMA
HIROSHIMA PREFECTURE, HONSHU, JAPAN

1/2                    0                    1/2 MILE

The Pacific had evolved significantly over the course of the four centuries before 1900. Much of this had been driven by the encroachment of outsiders, in particular Americans, Europeans and Russians who sought to bend the ocean and its islands to their will and their needs. However, to assert that all change had been driven by this influx of new influences would be incorrect. On many Pacific islands a wave of change was already sweeping societies, governments and economies before the arrival of any Europeans. More to the point, even when encounters with outsiders did drive islanders to change, a large number of these developments were self-motivated and went beyond what was required merely to deal with arrivals from outside the ocean. Japan's Meiji Restoration and Kalākaua's vision of a Polynesian confederacy were driven by complex processes and philosophical imaginations that reached well beyond the contact zones that existed between Pacific islands and the Western world.

Furthermore, the Pacific had changed those who had come into contact with it. The observations of Banks and others shaped European thinking about the world throughout the Enlightenment period. Meanwhile, researchers who travelled to the Pacific – Darwin and Dana loom large here – developed theories from their observations of the ocean's islands that still shape how we understand and perceive the world today. The Pacific was also shaping day-to-day economies around the world. Whale oil from the Pacific kept the industry of the world moving, furs from the Pacific defined global fashions, sandalwood decorated drawing rooms across Eurasia and innumerable other products were essential or highly desired commodities around the world. What happened (or did not happen) in the Pacific and on its islands could make or break local, regional and international economies, as illustrated by the South Sea Bubble economic crash.

During the twentieth century the patterns seen previously – resource exploitation, changing patterns of interconnection, the expansion and contraction of foreign empires – continued. As before, the islands of the Pacific were the stage for events, astounding as well as horrifying, that defined the century and how we understand the world around us to this day. Some of the events discussed here, not least the dropping of nuclear weapons on Japan, are etched in a global social consciousness; many are part of our day-to-day understanding of the world and we do not always remember their Pacific origins. From the ban on whale-hunting to the founding of Greenpeace, the birth of surfing as a global way of life and beyond, many developments of the twentieth century occurred in or originated from the Pacific Ocean and its islands.

The islands of the Pacific continue to provide a lens through which to view the ebb and flow of global geopolitics. Most importantly, the Pacific in the twentieth and twenty-first centuries is a constant reminder of the effects humans and our societies have on the planet we inhabit, especially as it shows us how our politicking and environmental impacts are linked. Such a vast oceanic space, flecked with small but significant points of land, is a perfect prism through which to view the toll we exact from the world and the challenges we will need to address in the coming century.

# Japan's pelagic empire

During the twentieth century Japan continued to develop into a maritime power, building on the success of the Russo-Japanese War at the start of the century. Japan's relationship with the ocean, however, was somewhat different from that of other global powers. It also relied on the Pacific as a vast network of interconnected resources. Japan's military, political and economic expansion during the late nineteenth and early twentieth centuries was focused on developing these networks, and it created something unique, what the American historian William Tsutsui has called the 'pelagic empire'.

Japan's development of this new kind of empire began relatively quickly after the arrival of Perry's ships. The end of policies of seclusion led to Japanese fishing vessels ranging ever further from the islands, and the embrace of rapid technological modernisation also led to significant development of the fishing industry. It is easy to think of Japan's technological innovation in this period as being driven directly by military aims, an attempt to place the nation on an equal footing with aggressive maritime empires encroaching on the Pacific. Japan's administrators and planners were keenly aware, however, that modernising the military alone would not be enough. How the nation fed, governed and conducted itself in the global sphere would all need developing.

The pelagic empire was therefore not just underpinned by the adventurous spirit of Japanese fishermen who felt able to range further than before; the administration also negotiated improved fishing rights in the waters of minor and major powers who controlled territory around the Pacific. Once these rights were negotiated, Japanese businesses wasted no time in growing their use of oceanic resources and developing this exploitation over the decades to come. As a result, Japanese vessels came to dominate the waters of foreign fisheries, as illustrated in the northwest Pacific, where Japanese vessels quickly dominated Russian vessels and continued to increase in number while Russian use of the fishery remained static.

Growing Japanese control over the western Pacific Ocean was also linked to the development of a Japanese empire in eastern Asia. In spite of various conflicts, such as the Russo-Japanese war (1904–5), the population of Japan was to grow steadily during the early twentieth century. More of this population would be involved in the military and manufacturing, and there was also the matter of feeding populations now forced to be part of the Japanese Empire. This required further growth of the fisheries sector and more development of the technologies of fishing; the pelagic empire was intimately linked to Japan's conquest of and expansion into mainland Asia.

The horrors of the Japanese empire would become all too apparent across the Pacific during the twentieth century, but it is worth noting that the development of the pelagic empire was a distinctly Pacific phenomenon. A network of waterways, islands and coastal mainland areas that stretched across vast distances, the pelagic empire was reminiscent of the trading networks of Pacific islanders that had existed for centuries and of the later theoretical constructs of Pacific scholars such as Epeli Hau'ofa; this was no ocean of isolated islands but a network of lands interconnected by valuable oceanic spaces.

Map of the Japanese Empire, 1919.

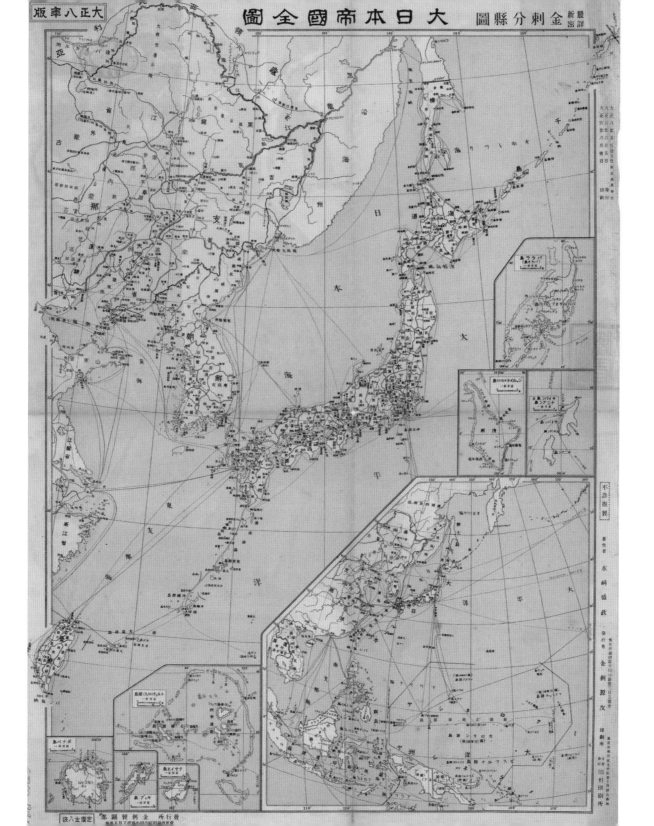

# The First World War and the Pacific

Europe's descent into war in 1914 made it inevitable that the Pacific, by now an ocean containing significant colonial interests of all parties involved in the First World War, would become a theatre of conflict. While the European side of the war, and the theatre most often discussed, was defined by trench warfare, attrition and the vast loss of human life, the Pacific theatre was different. Significant battles were fought at sea, as a result of the squadrons all colonial powers had in the Pacific and the neighbouring Indian Oceans, and the Entente forces gradually attacked various German-controlled islands in the Pacific. Many of these islands fell with little bloodshed, a market contrast to the European fronts of the war.

The war also provided a theatre where scores that had arisen over decades could be settled. The interests of empires had created points of conflict that had nearly bubbled over into war in the nineteenth century. The Samoan Civil War of the 1890s, among other issues, had almost led to open war between Britain, Germany and the United States. Now the First World War provided an opportunity to revisit some of these conflicts and redraw the lines on the map established during

the flashpoints of the nineteenth century. German Samoa was occupied by forces from Aotearoa/New Zealand in August 1914. Japan's role in the war was particularly notable, and not only because the war saw it take on a major role in an alliance which also included its opponent in the war of 1904–5, Russia. For the Entente powers Japan was an invaluable partner, securing shipping lanes in the Pacific and occupying German-controlled islands in the western Pacific. For Japan the

war was an opportunity to expand its sphere of influence in mainland Asia and among the islands of the western Pacific. The pelagic empire would grow in scale significantly during the conflict.

Perhaps most notably, Japan also saw the war as an opportunity to further develop its influence on the world stage. During treaty negotiations at Versailles Japan sat amongst the delegations from the major Entente powers and won significant concessions for the Japanese Empire. Japan also secured a seat at the League of Nations; the country's achievements were similar to those Kalākaua had sought for Hawai'i a century before. Not all went according to Japan's plan, however. The nation and its empire benefited hugely from the geopolitical gains it made during war and the peace negotiations that followed, and they were no doubt closer to the top table of international politics. Nonetheless they were still treated as outsiders who were racially inferior to their European and American counterparts, a fact most strongly illustrated by the rejection of their desired Racial Equality Clause of 1919. This would have seen all members of the League of Nations treated as equals in subsequent meetings. The Japanese desire to achieve this is depicted by documents such as the map shown here. The rejection of this clause, and the refusal to treat with Japan as equals, sowed the seeds of resentment and conflict that would grow into Japan's role in the Second World War. The Japanese delegation in Versailles were not the only Pacific islanders to come to Europe as a result of the conflict. During the war itself Maori, like those detailed in the publication *Maoris at War*, and other Pacific islanders travelled to Europe to fight on behalf of the empires that controlled their islands.

So it is important to remember that the conflict in Europe was far from a European war; it also illustrated how enmeshed many Pacific island societies had become in a globalised world and its spheres of conflict.

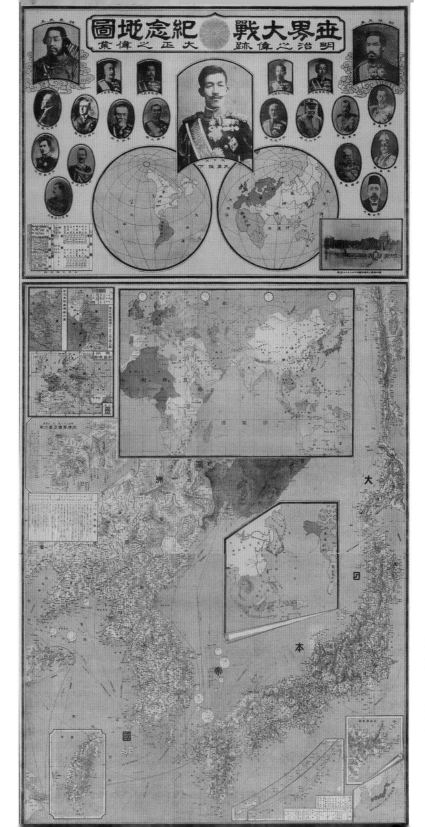

Map commemorating Japanese involvement in the First World War, 1918.

(*Opposite*) Pioneer Battalion performing a haka for Joseph George Ward at Bois-de-Warnimont, 30 June 1918.

# The war of islands

When Lieutenant Wilkes of the United States Exploring Expedition conducted his survey of what he called 'Pearl Harbor', known as Wai Momi and Puʻuloa by Hawaiʻians before Wilkes's work, he could not possibly have imagined the fate of the bay a century later. At the time of the survey Wilkes observed that the location had the potential to become one of the most significant strategic sites in the Pacific Ocean, providing access and protection for ships as well as the wider geopolitical advantages afforded by Hawaiʻi's location in the Pacific. Even before the annexation of Hawaiʻi, the United States government would act on this and other observations as part of a reciprocity agreement signed in 1875. This agreement, negotiated with the government of Kalākaua, provided Hawaiʻi with the ability to sell sugar to US markets and in turn gave the US Navy access to the site they would call Pearl Harbor.

In the wake of the First World War, Japan's geopolitical ambitions had continued to grow, increasingly butting up against American interests in the Pacific. Added to this was the continued racism expressed towards Japan

The attack on Pearl Harbor, 7 December 1941.

and its people: the draconian immigration policies directed towards Japanese migrants hoping to settle in the United States were an extra, and growing, point of discord. Tensions would boil over into war, with Japan attacking the United States in December 1941. The focus point of the initial attack would be the strategic heart of the Pacific identified by Wilkes in 1841, Wai Momi, now the US Naval base, Pearl Harbor. Japan's attack on Pearl Harbor was the beginning of a concerted campaign to further expand the geopolitical reach and strategic resource base of the empire across the western Pacific and mainland Asia. As a consequence, Japan would attack and occupy Pacific islands as far south as Australia.

The war brought a scale of conflict hitherto unknown to the Pacific islands, spreading destruction and grief across a large part of the Pacific. The forces of Japan, the US and the Allied nations would also bring new interactions, technologies and cultural exchanges to many Pacific islands. The scale of the logistics as well as the armies of personnel introduced to the islands wrote indelible changes onto a number of Pacific cultures, many of whom interpreted what they saw in ways unique to the culture of their island and the part it had played in the soon-to-recede Pacific of empires. Contacts such as those between Pacific islanders and African American marines encouraged ideas of later independence movements, as islanders saw that dark skin need not prohibit them from fulfilling the same roles as white people.

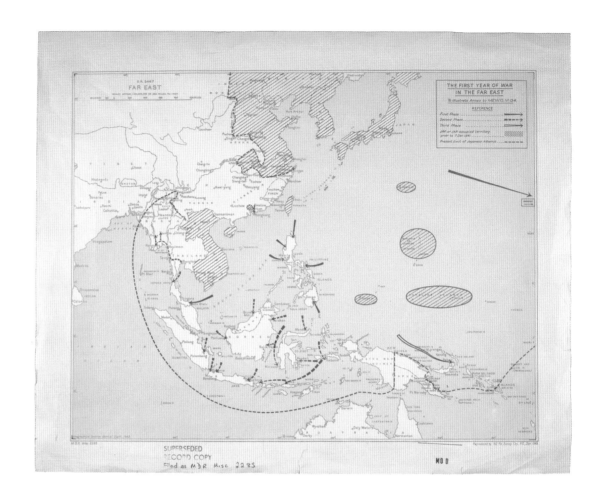

While the end of the war would confirm the United States as the dominant power in the Pacific, the victory came at great cost. Conflict in the Pacific would drag on longer than that in Europe and become a bloody war of attrition and island hopping. War would rage across the western Pacific, with Japan's temporary territorial gains extending as far south as the Solomon Islands; it would cost millions of lives, many of them civilian, to push back these Japanese advances. The

fighting would end only when the war was brought back to the heart of Japan's Pacific Empire, the islands of Japan itself. Here the war was ended through the use of an unparalleled destructive force. The shadow this cast over the Pacific would loom over the world throughout the twentieth century and beyond.

Map of 'The First Year of War in the Far East', Ministry of Defence, 1943.

# Hiroshima and Nagasaki

The end of the war in the Pacific was precipitated by the dropping of two bombs of unprecedented power. Since 1942 the United States had been working on the 'Manhattan Project' which aimed to develop the first nuclear weapons. These were used in the summer of 1945. Hiroshima was bombed first, on 6 August 6, and 80,000 people died from the immediate impact of the blast. Three days later a further bomb was dropped on Nagasaki, killing 40,000 people on impact. Thousands more were to die in the days, months and years after the bombs were detonated, victims of the radioactive after-effects of nuclear weapons.

The conflict ended quickly after the bombings, with Emperor Hirohito referring to the devastating and 'cruel' power of the bombs in his call for peace. The scale of the devastation of the bombs, their ability to render so much destruction and loss of life in such a short period of time, had been unimaginable to many prior to their first use. The map shown here, by Nihon Kotsu Kosha, was an attempt to convey the geographical destruction of the bomb dropped on Hiroshima. The sickly, black mark in the centre of the map marks the area

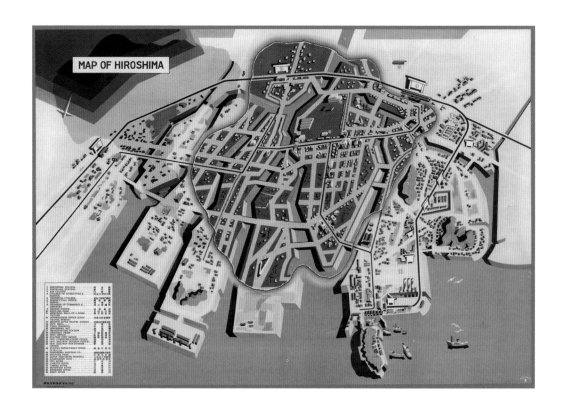

MAP OF HIROSHIMA

of destruction wrought by the bomb 'Little Boy', and it covers the most densely built and populated areas of the city.

With the dropping of these weapons, the Pacific and its islands became the place where a new world was born – one that deeply feared the use of nuclear weapons and, later, the possibility of escalating nuclear conflicts. While the majority of the world has since been spared the effects of nuclear weapons, these bombs were not yet done with the Pacific, which became the arena for their later testing and development. And Pacific islands would form the core of the twentieth-century push against the development and use of nuclear weapons (see pp. 188–9).

Detonation of the atomic bomb over Nagasaki, 1947.

(*Left*) Nihon Kotsu Kosha's map showing the impact of the atomic bomb on Hiroshima, 1947.

(*Left*) Hiroshima from the top of the Red Cross Hospital looking northwest. The frame buildings had been recently erected.

(*Below left*) Nagasaki before and after the bombing; (*below right*) Hiroshima before and after the bombing.

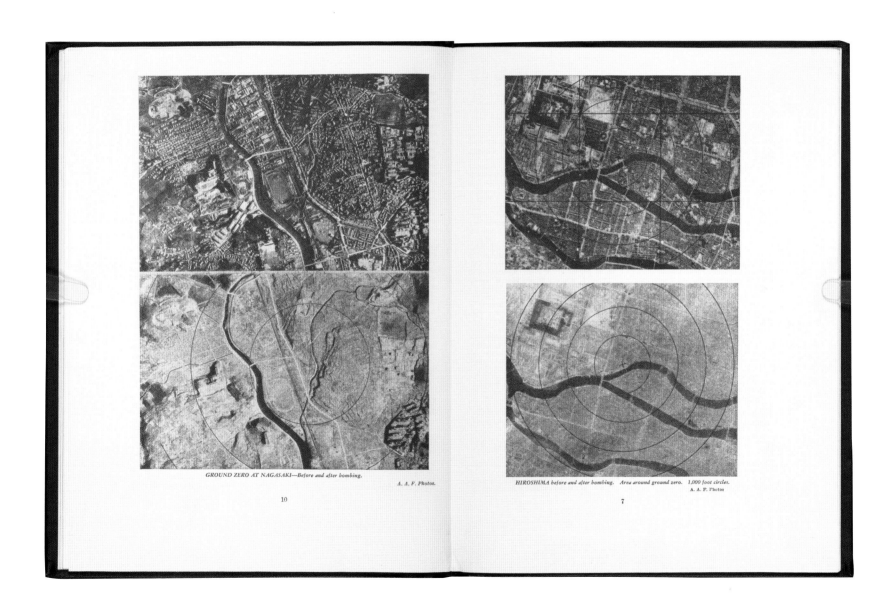

GROUND ZERO AT NAGASAKI—*Before and after bombing.*

A. A. F. Photos.

10

HIROSHIMA *before and after bombing. Area around ground zero. 1,000 foot circles.*

A. A. F. Photos.

7

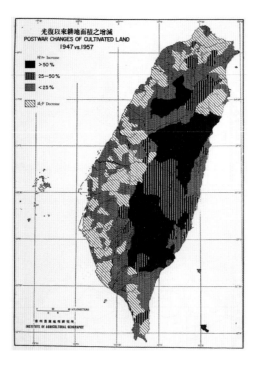

光復以來耕地面積之增減
POSTWAR CHANGES OF CULTIVATED LAND
1947 vs. 1957

增加 Increase
■ >50 %
▨ 25—50 %
▦ <25 %

▨ 減少 Decrease

INSTITUTE OF AGRICULTURAL GEOGRAPHY

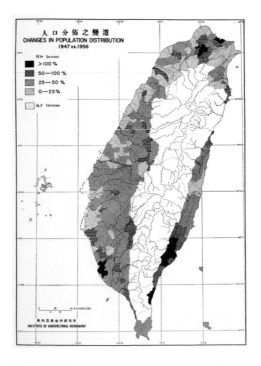

人口分佈之變遷
CHANGES IN POPULATION DISTRIBUTION
1947 vs. 1956

增加 Increase
■ >100 %
▨ 50—100 %
▦ 25—50 %
▨ 0—25 %

□ 減少 Decrease

INSTITUTE OF AGRICULTURAL GEOGRAPHY

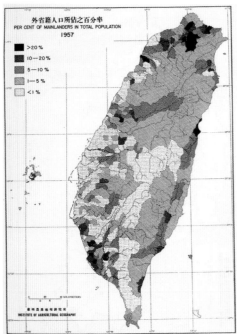

外省籍人口所佔之百分率
PER CENT OF MAINLANDERS IN TOTAL POPULATION
1957

■ >20 %
▨ 10—20 %
▦ 5—10 %
▨ 1—5 %
□ <1 %

INSTITUTE OF AGRICULTURAL GEOGRAPHY

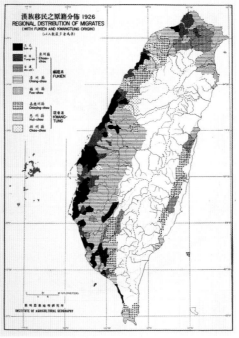

漢族移民之原籍分佈 1926
REGIONAL DISTRIBUTION OF MIGRATES
(WITH FUKIEN AND KWANGTUNG ORIGIN)

三邑 Sam-yi
同安 Tong-an
安溪 An-ch'i
泉州 Chuan-chou
漳州 Chang-chou
福州 Foo-chou
嘉應州 Chiaying-chou
惠州 Hui-chou
潮州 Chao-chou

福建系 FUKIEN
廣東系 KWANGTUNG

INSTITUTE OF AGRICULTURAL GEOGRAPHY

A series of plates showing Taiwan's changing population and land use. From *Geographical Atlas of Taiwan*, 1959.

# Taiwan and the Chinese Civil War

Taiwan had formed part of Qing Dynasty China since the late seventeenth century, but the decline of the Qing saw Taiwan become deeply embroiled in the political movements of eastern Asia and the wider Pacific Ocean. The rise of a Japanese Empire and its associated conflict with the Qing Dynasty, in the form of the Sino-Japanese War of 1894–5, led to Taiwan being ceded to Japan in the peace accords of 1895. As a result, the island became part of Japan's rapidly growing pelagic empire in the Pacific, and the coming years would see significant Japanese settlement on the island. This, however, was not to be the status quo for Taiwan during the twentieth century. Taiwan was of great strategic importance to the Japanese military and navy during the Second World War, providing ports for operations, and so it became a focus for US military activity during the campaign to roll back Japan's expansion across the islands of the Pacific. The tail end of this campaign saw troops from the Republic of China shipped to the island by the US Navy in order to accept the surrender of Japanese troops on the island. The Republic of China had been formed in 1912 in the wake of the collapse of the Qing Dynasty. The rise of the Republic of China was strongly challenged by the Communist Party of China, which fought a campaign for control over the country that lasted, albeit with pauses and periods of co-operation between the two republics, from 1927 to 1950.

The Second World War saw the two antagonists co-operate against Japanese aggression, but conflict broke out subsequently, and by 1949 Mao Zedong's Communist Party of China was in control of the capital on the mainland. The government of the Republic of China moved wholesale to the island of Taiwan and its capital, Taipei. It is important to note that the end of the Second World War and the peace accords signed with Japan had left Taiwan with an unclear international standing. American naval forces had landed Republic of China troops on the island of Taiwan, and at the peace accords the prevalent view was that the administration of Taiwan and its smaller neighbouring islands should pass to the government of mainland China. However, the Japanese renounced their claims to the island and made no specific mention as to who the claim would pass to. As a result, there was ambiguity about whether the Republic of China administration that was now established in Taipei was a legal government, capable of being internationally recognised, or whether the internationally recognised administration should be the People's Republic of China. The People's Republic regarded Taiwan as being under illegal occupation by the government and military of their opponent in a civil war.

What transpired in the wake of 1949 was an uneasy state of ongoing, but largely non-violent, conflict between the government of mainland China and the government on the island of Taiwan. The relocation of the Republic of China government included two million associated politicians, social elites and military personnel, who were added to the six million people who already lived on Taiwan. This group of people were added to a complex demographic, social and economic situation which had developed since foreign settlement started on the island in the seventeenth century. The atlas shown here is an attempt to grapple with the impacts of this. Since 1949, then, Taiwan has occupied a similar geopolitical space to that created by Zheng Chenggong (Koxinga): a thorn in the side of the government of mainland China.

# Marxism and the Pacific

In the wake of the Second World War, communist states had a significant presence around the Pacific, with both the USSR and the People's Republic of China having lands and territorial waters that bordered the ocean. During the latter part of the twentieth century many strands of Marxist theory would circulate around the Pacific, which would all be resisted by American geopolitical power in the region. American fears of communist and socialist governments developing around the Pacific went hand in hand with the end of colonial occupations around the ocean. While this presented opportunities for an expansion of influence by the United States and organisations such as the United Nations, the process of decolonisation was complex, contested and open to numerous influences. Running parallel to attempts to influence the Pacific islands through democratic or authoritarian political systems were strains of political thought which leant towards socialism, and the Pacific War had led to communist groups in the Philippines, Java and other locations resisting both Japanese and American colonialism. American foreign policy, and that of many other democratic nations, was deeply concerned about the development of a domino effect in eastern Asia. The thinking behind this was that the collapse of any state to communism in eastern Asia could lead to a cascade effect through other nations on the mainland and into the islands of Indonesia, Micronesia and on into the wider Pacific. This, in turn, led the United States and other nations to become embroiled in the ongoing conflicts in Korea and Vietnam in the 1950s and 1960s, and it also meant that political changes on Pacific islands were viewed warily.

The perspective of communist nations on the islands of the Pacific was, arguably, more complex. The People's Republic of China was at a standoff with the island of Taiwan and the resident government throughout the second half of the twentieth century. Meanwhile, the USSR viewed many Polynesian and Melanesian islands, and their ancestral socio-political structures, as victims of colonial, capitalist aggression perpetrated by European and American powers. The book seen here is a curious work that embodies some of these ideologies. Published in 1923 by the Petrograd State Publishing House, *Tihookeanskie Skazki* ('Pacific Tales') is a translated and abridged version of the 1916 German publication, *Südseemärchen: Aus Australien, Neu-Guinea, Fidji, Karolinen, Samoa, Tonga, Hawai'i, Neu-Seeland*. Whether it was published with the consent and support of the original editor is unknown, but it is clear that the Soviet edition was re-presented to fit within the intellectual and aesthetic climate of Russia at the time, hence the striking Constructivist title page.

*Tihookeanskie Skazki*'s exact purpose is difficult to determine, but it is worth noting the heritage of the Petrograd State Publishing House. Formed in the wake of the Revolution in Russia in 1917, it was an important early printer associated with the Constructivist movement and attempts to promote a deeper understanding of communist and Marxist principles across Russia. Within this canon *Tihookeanskie Skazki* seems to be an outlier, but it perhaps speaks to the pre-colonial and capitalist history of the Pacific islands that many in the USSR believed to closer to a state of 'natural' government that fit with communist beliefs. In this case the publication can be seen as part of the wider work of attempting to develop an understanding of the world that rolled back the structures and histories of capitalism in order to create intellectual space for ideas that supported communist expansion. In short, while the domino effect would fail to materialise as American policy-makers feared, democratic capitalists were not the only ones attempting to articulate a future for the Pacific islands in the twentieth century.

Title page from *Tihookeanskie Skazki* ('Pacific Tales'), 1923.

# A shadow over the Pacific

The bombs dropped on Hiroshima and Nagasaki were not the only ones to detonate on Pacific islands in the twentieth century, even though they were the only ones used in armed conflict. Numerous world powers, but in particular the United States, used the waters and lands of the Pacific as a space to test subsequent generations of atomic weapons with greater explosive yields, while also investigating the after-effects of nuclear weapons, the effect of mushroom clouds on surrounding aircraft and many other factors. The result was a huge volume of tests that occurred in and around Pacific islands.

Enewetak Atoll, part of the Marshall Islands group, was the site of extensive tests starting in 1952, the same year as the map shown here was published. Charting great circle distances, maps such as this were used to plot the shortest distance between points for aviators and would have been used by those involved in conducting or observing the nuclear tests at Enewetak Atoll. In the coming decades Enewetak Atoll would be subjected to dozens of nuclear tests, with a total yield of over 30 megatons. This resulted in ecological devastation, the re-landscaping of the atoll (a giant concrete dome was created to house highly radioactive material) and the dislocation of islanders who had called Enewetak Atoll home. The assumed legal right to forcefully remove the islanders had been received by the United States as part of the Trust Territory of the Pacific Islands, established in the wake of the war in 1947. This was exploited to depopulate the atoll so it could be used for nuclear testing. Such dispossessions would occur on a number of Pacific islands, as well as in the deserts of Australia, during this period, all in the name of testing new generations of nuclear weapons and their impacts. The resulting ecological devastation from the tests was exacerbated by poor understanding of the long-term consequences of radioactive fallout from the weapons. As a result, any people who were allowed to return to testing grounds developed degenerative illnesses that would cascade down through generations. These problems were made worse by haphazard attempts (often forced by domestic and international politics, as well as external organisations) to clean up the waste and toxicity resulting from the tests. Legal cases attempting to enforce clean-up operations of nuclear testing nations are still ongoing in the twenty-first century.

*Godzilla* poster, 1954.

(*Right*) 'Great Circle Distances and Azimuths from Eniwetok (Enewetak) Atoll', 1952.

Such devastation has left a lingering health, economic, political and cultural impact on the Pacific. Out of the devastation arose movements that helped define the twentieth century's political and environmental campaigns, such as the Campaign for Nuclear Disarmament and Greenpeace, which was formed in response to planned US government nuclear tests on Amchitka island in the northern Pacific. These were not the only cultural phenomena which arose as part of a broad effort to articulate the terror and understand the destruction of these tests and the atom bomb in general. During US testing on Bikini Atoll, the Japanese tuna fishing boat *Daigo Fukuryū Maru* ('Lucky Dragon 5') was caught up in the nuclear fallout from the testing zone. The horror of the effects on the crew, as well as the continuing effects of the bombs dropped on Hiroshima and Nagasaki, required articulation – the character of Godzilla (*Gojira*) was born as a metaphor for the destructive power of the weapons. For the producer Tomoyuki Tanaka, a movie monster that embodied the destructive effects of the weapons dropped on Japan and the horrors faced by the *Daigo Fukuryū Maru* was a sure-fire hit in Japan. What was perhaps unexpected was the draw that (a recut) *Godzilla* would have for American producers and audiences.

Nuclear weapons changed little of how empires and foreign powers had engaged with the Pacific over the previous centuries. They still brought death, disease and environmental destruction. What the bombs changed was the speed of action and scale of devastation.

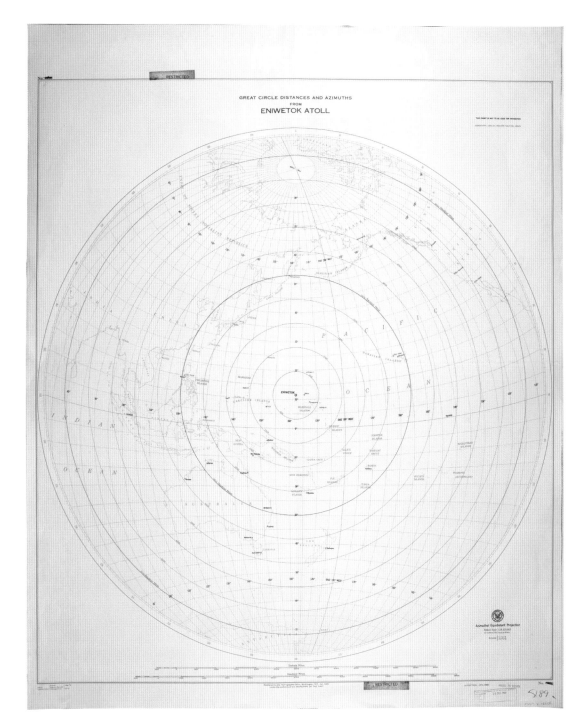

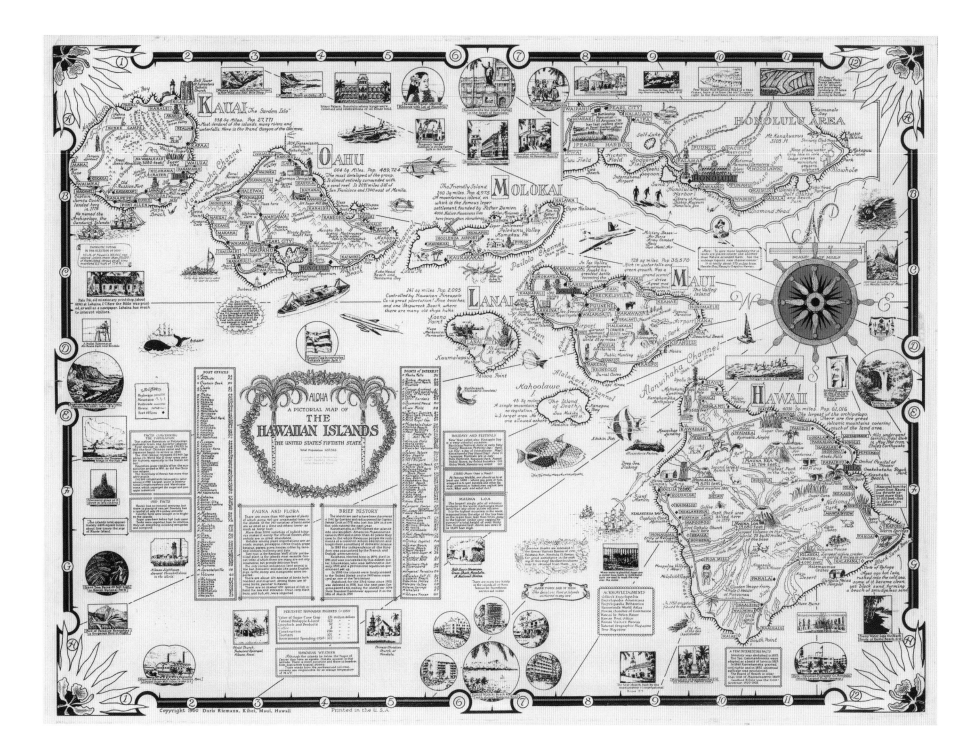

ALOHA

A PICTORIAL MAP OF
THE
HAWAIIAN ISLANDS
THE UNITED STATES FIFTIETH STATE

# The fiftieth state

Hawai'i played a crucial role in the Second World War as a focus of Japanese attempts to undermine American military power. In spite of this, it continued to be a hub for the United States throughout the war years and beyond. The expanded sphere of US influence on the ocean, not to mention a determination to control any potential communist expansion in East Asia or the islands of the Pacific, meant that Hawai'i would continue to be the heart of the American presence in the ocean. However, Hawai'i remained an annexed territory and, as such, peripheral to the politics and administration of the federal United States.

Many on the islands desired statehood, and the associated influence on US politics which by now had a significant impact on the islands. Statehood would also restructure many of the laws of the Hawai'ian islands and, crucially, this could be used to undermine some of the vested interests that had sprung up after the events of the late nineteenth century. These interests were inevitably

'Aloha: A Pictorial Map of the Hawaiian Islands, the United States' Fiftieth State', 1960.

colonial, and involved groups such as the white American plantation owners who controlled sugar production and the wider economy of the islands. These plantation owners were one major impediment on the route to statehood – as were people diametrically opposed to them, those who argued for the illegality of Hawai'ian annexation and sought independence. Politics in the mainland United States played a role too, with many Democrats reluctant to admit what they believed would be a Republican-leaning state to the Union.

Nonetheless, by the late 1950s Hawai'i's political momentum was headed towards statehood. Given the location of the islands in the Pacific, their central role in American power in the region and their economic value for plantation agriculture and tourism, this was always likely. Moreover, broader events of the twentieth century, such as America's push for the disbandment of European empires and the structures supporting the independence of small nations being developed by the United Nations, also suggested that Hawai'i, realistically, had only two potential trajectories: independence or statehood. The resolution of mainland

political issues (Alaska, a Democrat-voting state, was added to the Union just ahead of Hawai'i) and a well-organised campaign to vote for statehood on the Hawai'ian islands meant that from March 1959 there was an American state in the heart of the Pacific.

Given the difficult road to statehood, it is unsurprising that there have been subsequent efforts to promote the statehood of the Hawai'ian islands as being inevitable. After the vote, maps such as that seen here began to spring up, ostensibly promoting the islands for economic development and greater tourism but also creating a distinct (and enduring) narrative about the relationship between the islands and the rest of the United States. Here, the deposition of the monarchy is recorded as inevitable, part of the American belief in the redundancy of monarchies, while Dole's installation as governor is similarly unproblematic. A final touch is found in 'Patriotic Voting of the Election of 1959', which suggests that the 93% turnout for the election was a unanimous vote in favour of the creation of a Hawai'ian state. This was far from the case, and the body that did not vote was dominated by indigenous Hawai'ians.

# Indigenous voices and memory

In spite of the efforts of missionaries, colonial administrators and other outsiders to record and remove islander heritage, by the twentieth century many Pacific islands still had vibrant traditions and histories that were held and articulated by indigenous scholars. Significantly, this period saw a shift in which a growing number of islander scholars published their own histories and theories under their own names, in contrast to the experience of Te Rangikaheke with George Grey. Such a pivot is hugely significant, as an expression of control over the histories, legends and memories of a culture goes hand in hand with twentieth-century attempts to reassert control over the lands of the Pacific islands themselves. As missionaries, Grey and others had illustrated, the dispossession of memory is an integral part of the dispossession of people from their lands.

The intellectual work and monarchic reign of Queen Sālote Tupou III is a case in point. Sālote Tupou III was a member of a constitutional monarchy that evolved from the Tu'i Tonga system and has ruled in Tonga for centuries. The narrative that the islands of Tonga have never been colonised, only ever becoming a British protectorate, has formed an important part of defining their place in the world, especially during the twentieth century. Within this narrative the role of rulers like Sālote Tupou III in maintaining the memory of traditions of the islands is significant. During her rule the court patronised the arts, history and archaeology, and Sālote Tupou III herself was a poet and songwriter, her works focusing on life, history and the role of the monarchy in Tonga. As a result, when the islands moved beyond their protectorate status in 1970, Tongan identity was coherent and independent, as well as being identified positively with the Tongan monarchy.

Many Pacific islands did not have the structures of tradition and history that Tonga had been able to maintain during the colonial period. Islands such as Aotearoa/New Zealand and Hawai'i had suffered the erosion of memory and the ownership of memory described earlier. However, there were still individuals across the islands who maintained traditions, oral histories and legends, and there were those who sought to preserve this knowledge for future generations. Mary Kawena Pukui was a Hawai'ian scholar who worked for the Bernice Pauahi Bishop Museum from 1938 to 1961. During this time she collected numerous histories and legends from Hawai'ian communities. She also co-authored publications on the place names of Hawai'i and a Hawai'ian–English dictionary. The recording of place names is particularly important, as the overwriting of Hawai'ian landscapes with colonial names is another part of the disenfranchisement of indigenous peoples from their lands. This is particularly true in cultures where naming and naming practices are important and freighted with meaning, as is the case in Hawai'i.

From the works of individuals such as Sālote Tupou III and Mary Kawena Pukui, strands of thought and intellectual criticism have grown. Their works have also underpinned decolonising movements and efforts to reassert islander agency in their own lands, helping the world to see the Pacific islands from an indigenous point of view.

Photographic portrait of Queen Sālote Tupou III.

# Land rights in the Pacific

While the twentieth century saw an erosion of colonial government and administration in numerous parts of the Pacific, there are still many islands where indigenous communities are dispossessed of their land and disenfranchised from the political processes that administer it. Hawai'i is discussed at length in this part of the book but it is not the only place where a colonial government has not just established itself but absorbed an island as part of a larger, settler–nation state. Vancouver Island, today part of the Province of British Columbia, Canada, is home to and supports twelve First Nations groups who have been dispossessed since the Hudson's Bay Company set up a factory on the island in the nineteenth century.

Dispossession from the land of their ancestors means that contemporary communities on islands such as Vancouver Island no longer have the political and cultural control over island spaces and the surrounding seas they once did. They are also often marginalised in national decision making that will affect the continued development of current and former tribal lands and waters, such as the routing of oil pipelines and the allotting of fishing quotas. Crucially, there is also a pervasive belief that indigenous groups have forsaken such claims to agency on the land, and that it is now the domain of colonial governments and the white majority of these nations.

To counteract this, the histories and knowledge discussed above, which people like Mary Kawena Pukui have sought to preserve, are crucially important, as is communicating these narratives and using them to subvert colonial histories. Lawrence Paul Yuxweluptun is an artist of Coast Salish and Okanagan descent who uses his art to encourage change in how indigenous history and contemporary indigenous agency are perceived. His works intermingle indigenous and colonial artistic traditions and often focus on issues of land and sovereignty, with titles like 'Ceremonies of Possession' operating in a

colonial vernacular to assert that indigenous performance of sovereignty has as much weight as that of explorers, traders and colonial governments.

Artists like Yuxweluptun also work to refocus colonial views of indigenous culture. 'Untitled Drawing – Longhouse Interior' is based on a geometric perspective of a longhouse interior, similar to those constructed by colonial

artists, such as Webber, but it remakes the scene. Instead of a flat, reductive view of a space and culture, Yuxweluptun's work is populated by living First Nations culture, providing depth of perspective. In so doing, he breaks the colonial lens and provides an indigenous perspective on the site, one which is freighted with spirituality and meaning. Through this, Yuxweluptun underscores the central point of his work, that islanders

and other indigenous peoples predate colonial cultures and will continue to exert an influence on how these islands are seen and understood, and how they will operate into the future. They are another important part of decolonising Pacific islands and our imaginations of them.

(*Above*) Lawrence Paul Yuxweluptun's 'Untitled Drawing – Longhouse Interior'. (*Left*) *The inside of a house, in Nootka Sound*, by John Webber, 1778.

195

# The voyagers

A recurrent theme in this book has been the fact that relationships with the ocean are crucial for Pacific island societies, none more so than those that make up the Polynesian cultural group. While Polynesian seafarers sailed the world in the wake of contact with ships from outside the Pacific, on whaling ships, trading vessels and so on, the long-range voyaging that led to the settlement of islands such as Aotearoa/ New Zealand and Rapa Nui had waned by the nineteenth century. Significantly, the influence of colonial attitudes towards navigation also undermined the significance of Polynesian methods of boat building and wayfinding on the ocean.

During the twentieth century a number of attempts were made to reassert the historic significance of Polynesian navigation, its technical achievements and its potential for ranging across the Pacific Ocean. Of those that set out, arguably the most significant are the wide-ranging and evolving voyages of *Hōkūleʻa*, a reproduction of a historic *waʻa kaulua* (double-hulled voyaging craft). Originally the inspiration of artist the Herb Kāne, *Hōkūleʻa*'s original aim was to reinvigorate the voyaging tradition in Hawaiʻi.

In 1976 the vessel departed Hawaiʻi to sail for Tahiti, using traditional methods of navigation, under the leadership of a Micronesian navigator called Mau Piailug. With its successful arrival in Tahiti the vessel highlighted the potential of Polynesian navigation and also underlined the exchange of skills between islands and communities that has historically allowed Pacific islanders to thrive.

Since the original voyage, *Hōkūleʻa* has sailed to Aotearoa/New Zealand and Rapa Nui, recreating the seminal voyages of settlement that led to the creation of the Polynesian Triangle. The ship has also undertaken

voyages to Japan and North America, in turn embodying the connectedness of the Pacific which existed long before Europeans encroached onto the ocean. And it has all been done using traditional Polynesian techniques of wayfinding across the ocean. *Hōkūleʻa*, then, embodies much of what this book has been about, illustrating the interconnectedness of the Pacific and the different ways of understanding its cultural interactions and histories.

In 2014 *Hōkūleʻa* and a sister-ship, *Hikianalia*, set out on a voyage that expanded the horizons of wayfinding once more, a three-year circumnavigation of the world. Named 'Mālama Honua' ('To Care for Our Earth'), the voyage emphasised that Polynesian voyaging was capable of the same endeavours as colonial ships and crews had been – and laid down a challenge. This task was to move away from a worldview of consumption and destruction, underpinned by Western colonialism and facilitated by the history of Western navigation, and shift to one which cares for and respects the Earth, its oceans and a globe of peoples who rely on them.

(*Left* and *right*) *Hōkūleʻa*'s sister ship, *Hikianalia*, under sail.

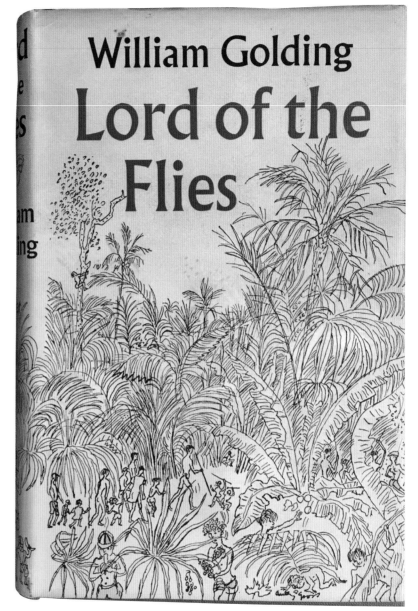

Covers of Damon's *Cocos, the Island of Blood and Treasure* (*left*)
and Golding's *Lord of the Flies* (*right*).

# Islands of mystery

By the twentieth century the islands of the Pacific had become firmly embedded in the literature and broader culture of Europe and North America. We have seen how many seminal works of eighteenth- and nineteenth-century fiction in English use the beach, desert island and castaway motifs of the Pacific islands to drive their narratives and stimulate the imagination of those who had not seen the ocean. This trend continued into the twentieth century and was influenced by other events in Pacific history from the period. William Golding's *Lord of the Flies* (1954) takes place on a remote Pacific island that provides the lush and feverish setting for the boys' descent into anarchy and murder. Golding's Pacific island setting builds on the literary imaginations constructed in previous centuries and, in earlier drafts, was connected with broader Pacific and global concerns. While the final version of Golding's novel alludes merely to an ongoing war, earlier drafts made mention of a nuclear aspect to the conflict.

During the later twentieth century, Pacific islands, real and imaginary, had a significant impact on the world of film, as did the particular imaginative geography of the Pacific. The imagined isolation of Pacific desert islands sets the scene for Tom Hanks' isolation on a Pacific island following a plane crash in the film *Cast Away* (2000). The grand scale of volcanic Pacific islands, such as Hawai'i and those off the coast of South America, also provided spaces in which twentieth-century imaginations could run riot. In Michael Crichton's novel *Jurassic Park* (1990), an imaginary Pacific island by the name of Isla Nublar is turned into a fantastical world filled with resurrected dinosaurs, meant to be caged for the enjoyment and fascination of future visitors. In Crichton's novel and its sequel, Isla Nublar is located just off the coast of Costa Rica, sharing a similar location to its real-life inspiration, Cocos Island or Isla del Coco. Isla del Coco rises precipitously out of the Pacific. Covered with dense vegetation and often shrouded in mist, it was the perfect setting for Crichton's out-of-control menagerie. As a result, he joined the ranks of authors for whom accounts, stories, maps and photographs of Pacific islands had provided inspiration in previous centuries.

What is particularly interesting about *Jurassic Park* is how complex and multilayered the relationship between the Pacific islands, the book and the film is. Crichton may have been inspired by Isla del Coco but this was not a suitable location to film the movie that would follow the best-selling book. Instead, another Pacific island with precipitous volcanic cliffs and evocative weather patterns was used as a more accessible stand-in: the Hawai'ian island of Kaua'i. It is also interesting to note how depopulated twentieth-century imaginations of Pacific islands were. *Lord of the Flies* occurred on a desert island (albeit one with pigs, suggesting some form of voyager settlement in the island's past), as did *Jurassic Park*, while the movie derived from the book served up a depopulated Hawai'i as the location for Spielberg's dinosaur rampage. Anglophone literary and cinematic imaginations continued to view Pacific islands as spaces where the imagination could run riot, ignoring the presence and agency of indigenous peoples. Books and bombs, then, both depopulated the islands of the twentieth-century Pacific.

# Surfing the Pacific

In May 1769 Sir Joseph Banks, travelling with James Cook on the *Endeavour* expedition to track the transit of Venus, witnessed something he thought remarkable. As he recorded in his journal, 'In the midst of [the] breakers 10 or 12 Indians were swimming who whenever surf broke near them divd [*sic*] under it with infinite ease, rising up on the other side; but their chief amusement was carried on by the stern of an old canoe, with this before them they swam out as far as the outermost breach, then one of two would get into it and opposing the blunt end to the breaking wave were hurried in with incredible swiftness. Sometimes they were carried almost ashore but generaly [*sic*] the wave broke over them before they were half way, in which case they divd and quickly rose on the other side with the canoe in their hands, which was towd [*sic*] out again and the same method repeated.'

Banks, like many Europeans of the time, swam poorly. For someone witnessing something so alien to him, Banks grasped the technique and enjoyment of surfing remarkably well in his description. The description of the practice of surfing recorded by Banks did not stimulate mass enthusiasm for this way of being on the water in the way that European articulations of Polynesian physical relationships or practices of *tatau* (tattoo) did, for example, did.

This would change during the nineteenth century, especially as greater numbers of Europeans and Americans visited the islands of Hawai'i. From the 1860s onwards growing numbers of visitors and settlers on Hawai'i experienced surfing and became enamoured with it. Mark Twain, during his travels on the islands in the 1860s, was taken with the grace and elegance of islanders who 'surf bathed', as Twain called it, and he decided to try it for himself. The result was not elegant, as Twain recounts in *Roughing It*: 'I got the board placed right, and at the right moment, too; but missed the connection myself. The board struck the shore in three-quarters of a second, without any cargo, and I struck the bottom about the same time, with a couple of barrels of water in me.' Twain, by all accounts, never tried to surf again, but many did, and a number of colonial clubs on Hawai'i began to incorporate the practice of surfing into their oceanic leisure pursuits. This represented an about-turn from the attitudes of missionaries and other colonials in the eighteenth and early nineteenth centuries, many of whom discouraged surfing on account of its connections to pre-Christian Polynesian traditions.

The appropriation of surfing into European and American colonial cultures has had a tremendous impact on the twentieth century. Surfing has developed its own subculture which has challenged generational norms in many countries and has spawned environmental movements that campaign for better treatment of oceans across the globe. Nonetheless, and in spite of the sport reconnecting with its Polynesian heritage and now having a greater Pacific island presence in its professional organisation, twentieth-century surf culture was deeply connected to colonial actions in the Pacific. As a result, while surfing reflects one of the most significant impacts Pacific islands have on the day-to-day life of many around the world, its expansion was not necessarily driven by the islanders themselves.

(*Top*) Illustrations from Twain's *Roughing It*: the women surfing (*left*) contrast with the depiction of Twain's wipe-out (*right*).

(*Bottom*) Webber's 'A View of Karakakooa, in Owyhee', which depicts a surfer in the foreground, 1784.

# The science of colonialism

Advancement of scientific knowledge in the Pacific had an established relationship with exploration and colonialism. The most famous exploring expedition of the eighteenth century, that of James Cook, Sir Joseph Banks and the crew of the *Endeavour*, having been sent to the island of Tahiti to chart the transit of Venus, was rooted in expanding scientific knowledge. Since then, the majority of exploring expeditions had a scientific element, if not an entire scientific corps, as evidenced by the expeditions that took Charles Darwin, James Dwight Dana and others around the Pacific Ocean and its islands. The United States Exploring Expedition, which brought James Dana to the Pacific, took the conducting of scientific enquiry very seriously, and it went together with the expansion of American influence in the nineteenth-century Pacific. As seen earlier, Wilkes's expedition, with its bloodshed in Fiji and charting of places like Wai Momi (Pearl Harbor), had long-term impacts on the islands of the Pacific which cascaded into the twentieth century and beyond. Hawai'i, in many ways, bore

the brunt of this impact, with Wilkes's observations of sites such as Pearl Harbor framing the potential of American activities on the island in the century to come. Another place where Wilkes's activities have an ongoing impact is the summit of Haleakalā, which Wilkes climbed and surveyed as part of the expedition's activities on the island of Maui.

Haleakalā means 'House of the Sun'. According to Hawai'ian tradition, it is the home of the grandmother of the demigod Maui, both of whom worked to capture the sun and slow its journey across the sky. For Hawai'ians, Haleakalā is a sacred site and Wilkes's climbing and charting of the mountain and its crater was the beginning of a continuing process of disrespecting and, many argue, desecrating the sacred site. Today, the Haleakalā Crater forms part of a US national park which is open to visitors and home to a growing number of scientific observatories. The observatories have been located at Haleakalā because of the prevailing atmospheric conditions at the crater and the lack of invasive light pollution that can obscure observations of the night sky. For astronomers and other scientists the

observatories are an invaluable piece of a global landscape of scientific research which works to develop a deeper understanding of the universe around us. For Hawai'ians the observatories and proposed construction of new, larger telescopes deface a sacred landscape and represent a violation of the rituals by which Hawai'ians welcome non-indigenous people onto their lands.

Debates around Haleakalā's status as a sacred and scientific site will continue, but it is important to remember that the debate around the use of sacred and other indigenous sites for scientific observation has a long and contested history. Cook's 'Camp Venus' was a site of contest and complex interaction between the *Endeavour*'s crew and the people of Tahiti who welcomed them onto the island. While the observations and scientific work produced by Cook's expeditions and today's Haleakalā observatories have been invaluable in developing the world's understanding of the earth and universe around us, these observations have come at the expense of island peoples from around the Pacific. For them, scientific progress has brought the desecration of sacred sites and much more since the *Endeavour* expedition.

The Haleakalā Observatory.

# Polluting an ocean

Human impacts on the Pacific Ocean and its islands have been developing for thousands of years, with all groups bringing significant environmental change to the spaces they settle and use. Early navigators who settled islands for the first time changed their ecosystems directly and indirectly, through land management and cultivation as well as the introduction of invasive species into island ecosystems. Similarly, islanders who have lived off the ocean engage in activities that can change the delicate balance of oceanic systems, especially when those activities involve the hunting of animals such as whales. These impacts are necessary for island societies to thrive and have mostly, with the exception of notable cases such as Rapa Nui, been managed sustainably.

At the very least, these actions have largely avoided catastrophic consequences and environmental decline.

The environmental damage initiated by the encroachment of Europeans on the Pacific, however, has operated on a different scale. Traders attempting to monopolise spice resources destroyed island biomes and created ecologically moribund monocultures on affected islands. Fur traders decimated populations of animals around the Pacific and whalers pushed populations of cetaceans to the brink of collapse. The impacts were driven by the political, economic and social structures which outsiders introduced to much of the Pacific. These disrupted local economies of exchange and opened up regional commodities to rapacious global

markets whose demand exceeded sustainable supply, if sustainable use was ever possible in cases like the hunting of sea otters. Added to this is the human and environmental catastrophe of nuclear weapons testing.

A defining part of the twentieth century was the mobilisation of groups who seek to highlight the dangerous exploitation of the natural world and to lobby for change. The pressure for change is also linked to other areas of campaigning on issues that deeply affect the Pacific. For example, Greenpeace, intimately linked with the campaign to ban the testing of nuclear weapons, was a key lobbyist in the campaign to end the commercial hunting of whales in the Pacific and globally. As a result, significant progress has been made in highlighting the dangerous

exploitation of the natural world in the Pacific, reining in impulses that have largely operated unchecked since the sixteenth century. However, while progress has been made in some areas, the habits of capitalism continue to deeply affect the Pacific Ocean, particularly industrialised fishing practices and our culture of disposability and waste.

The 'Great Pacific Garbage Patch' was first authoritatively described in the 1980s but had been observed in previous decades. Usually located at the midpoint between California and Hawai'i, the patch is an accumulation of human waste brought together by the same gyre currents that drove early European expansion into the Pacific. The patch is largely composed of plastic waste and discarded fishing gear from trawlers and other vessels, which has been drawn together by oceanic currents to cover an area of roughly 1.6 million square kilometres – about the same size as Texas. It is also slightly larger than the Hawai'i Oceanic Reserve created by the United States under the Obama administration. The Great Pacific Garbage Patch is not just an accumulation of rubbish but a reminder of the effects colonialism and Western capitalism have had on the Pacific. Removing the waste there is not enough; we must drastically change how we act.

A knot of consumer waste floating in the ocean in Puerto Princesa, Palawan Island.

(*Left*) A can of Budweiser, a plastic bag and a can of Spam photographed at the bottom of the Mariana Trench.

# Disappearing islands

A significant theme of this book has been the great diversity of biological life and human culture that Pacific islands support. It is also clear that these are fragile spaces, where the delicate balance of an island's ecosystem can be disastrously altered by invasive species, human communities or natural phenomena, such as earthquakes and volcanic eruptions. There should be no surprise, then, that Pacific islands stand to be dramatically affected by the results of global warming and climate change. As James Dana and others illustrated, the existence of many Pacific islands is somewhat miraculous, as they developed through volcanic processes, the actions of coral reef formation and sedimentation and a number of other processes that can function independently or combine to form the bedrock of a Pacific island. These resulting spots on a vast ocean are fragile; shifts in wind patterns can change the amounts of rainfall on islands with little natural groundwater storage: storms and storm surges can deeply alter island ecosystems; and changes in oceanic food webs can markedly affect the migration patterns of maritime animals that island communities rely on for food. Today, the greatest risk to Pacific islands is climate change. Not only

does the changing climate make extreme weather patterns and violent storms more likely to occur, but the meta-scale of changes to the Pacific is also life-threatening to islands, their ecosystems and their societies.

These changes threaten not just to make islands uninhabitable but also to make them disappear altogether. In recent decades a number of small islands in the western Pacific have been destroyed as a result of the changes in sea level that are associated with climate change. The islands of Rapita and Kakatina were specks offshore from Santa Isabel Island, part of the Solomons group, seen on this map produced by HM Surveying Ship *Dart* in 1902. Today they are no more, destroyed by the rise in global sea levels that has occurred between the 1990s and the 2010s. The size of this rise is around 2½ inches. For islands like Rapita and Kakatina that was enough to reduce coastal profiles and enhance erosion, through events like gales and king tides, to such a point that both of these specks on a map are now no more. Kakatina, Rapita and other disappeared islands in the Solomons were small and, while they were used by fishermen, uninhabited; but their disappearance is a warning to islands

across the Pacific. At the time of writing recent severe weather faced by Hawai'i and Japan has also resulted in the destruction of two small islands, losses that will impact the biodiversity and oceanic territory claims of both island groups.

Back in the Solomons, communities have been forced to relocate as changing sea levels and tides have inundated fresh water supplies. This is a small taste of the changes awaiting other islands in and around the Pacific. Nations with small populations will not be the only ones facing heightened risks. The cities of Hawai'i and Japan are already being impacted by greater tropical storms and at a higher frequency than before, while around the Pacific the populations of other island nations live predominantly in cities near the coast. For those of us outside the Pacific region, it is important to remember that, even in an age where empires have largely receded from this ocean, our politics, economies and daily habits still have a dramatic effect on those who live on islands around the Pacific. Collective responsibility for what we consume and how we live is the only thing that will limit how many of the Pacific Ocean's islands disappear below the waves.

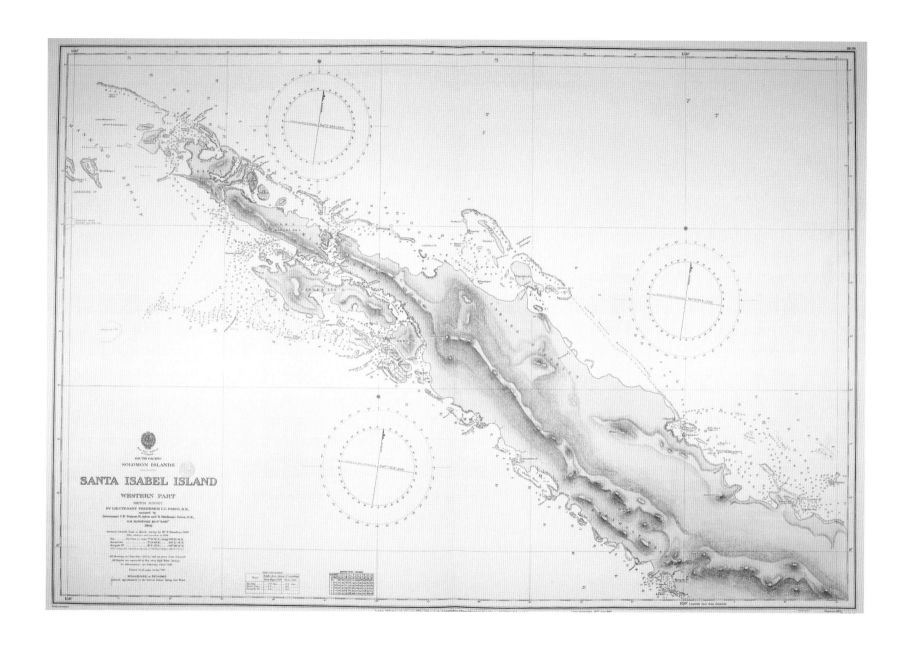

'Santa Isabel Island, Western Part', Admiralty chart from
1902 survey by HM Surveying Ship *Dart*. Two populated
islands that have recently disappeared, Rapita and
Kakatina, are noted on the map.

# Conclusion: Contested islands

The islands of the Pacific have drawn people to them for thousands of years, creating a complex web of human interactions with the environment and across their own societies. The cultural heritage artefacts that make up this book have a shorter history but they speak, nonetheless, to the interconnected histories of the Pacific, its islands, ecosystems and peoples. *Pacific* draws heavily from the collections of the British Library; this is a deliberate choice. The 'British' in British Library could make an incautious observer assume that the collections held there are a repository of anglophone knowledge, where Cook, Banks, Raleigh, and so on loom large. While these names are significant – Sir Joseph Banks, for example, being a founder collector of the material now held by the British Library – they do not impose a monolithic way of seeing on the collections.

Even in the libraries of individuals such as Banks, emphasis was always placed on collecting a global view of knowledge, covering a wide geography, many languages and perspectives. Since the founder collectors have passed on, their vision of developing the polyglot and cross-cultural nature of these collections has progressed and continues to expand to this day. Such collections will always have significant blind spots, reflecting a colonial perspective more than that of indigenous peoples, favouring the printed word over spoken heritage, and so on, but they can still challenge us to see the world differently.

While researching my previous book, *Lines in the Ice* (which told the history of the search for the Northwest Passage), the question I came back to repeatedly was, 'Why go to the Pacific?' This was the genesis of *Pacific*, but in digging through the British Library collection to locate answers, what I actually found was a view of the Pacific that shifted many historic perceptions of the ocean. What emerged was not a singular story about the likes of Cook and the developing British Empire in the Pacific, but something much more complex and multifaceted. The many strands of collecting the Library has engaged in for over two centuries have covered Asia, Europe, Russia, the Americas, Australia, the islands of the Pacific and beyond, encircling the Pacific and providing myriad perspectives on this ocean of islands. The emerging view this provides, highlighted over these pages, is not authoritative, but it unsettles many views of the Pacific that are common in the anglophone world. Clearly, this is not an ocean defined by James Cook or Sir Joseph Banks. It is one that was criss-crossed by voyagers and traders long before the arrival of Europeans, and that housed trading and cultural networks which have ebbed and flowed over time. The Pacific islands at large are not defined by Polynesian culture either, although European imaginations often still consider this to be the case.

Polynesian culture is, of course, an important part of what makes the Pacific islands unique and interconnected, in the context of not just early voyaging but also later endeavours – for example the Polynesian Confederacy idea of Kalākaua which, if successful, would have created an ocean of islands fundamentally different from that which we know today. Beyond this, it is clear that the Pacific is defined by the inhabitants of all its islands, be they North American First Nations, Aleuts from the north, Japanese, indigenous islanders of Formosa (Taiwan), Polynesians, Melanesians and many more cultural groups. Before the arrival of Europeans these groups were interconnected in various ways over

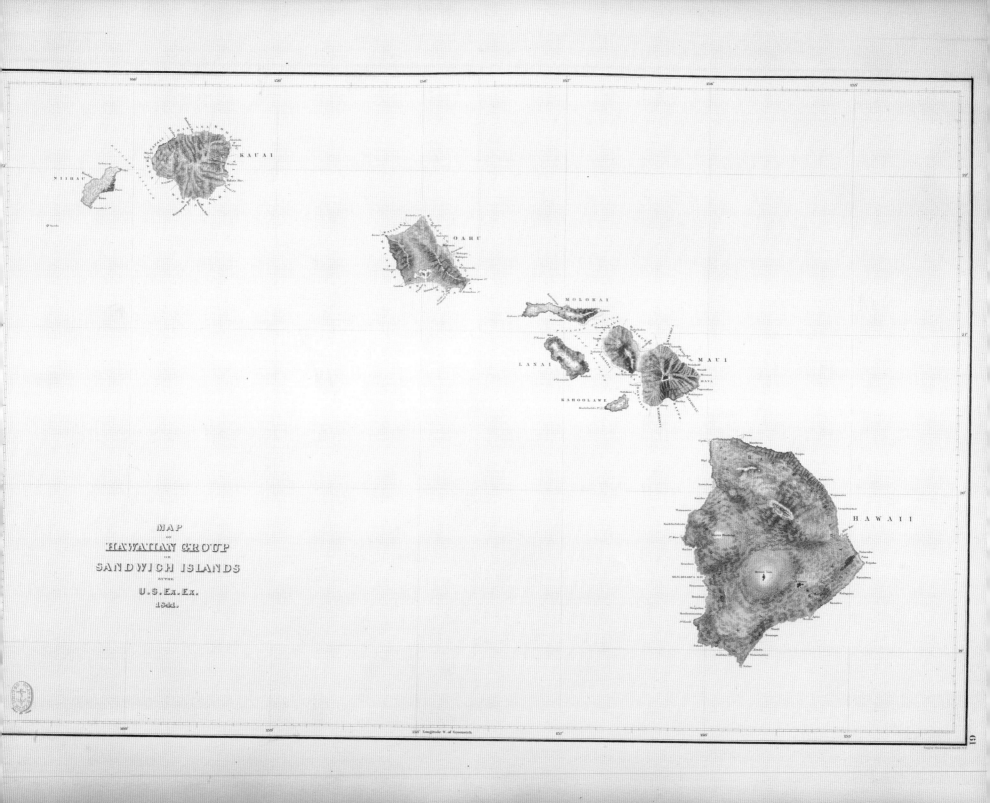

MAP
OF
HAWAIIAN GROUP
OR
SANDWICH ISLANDS
BY THE
U.S. Ex. Ex.
1841.

KAUAI

NIIHAU

OAHU

MOLOKAI

LANAI

MAUI

KAHOOLAWE

HAWAII

Longitude W. of Greenwich

time. After the arrival of Europeans those connections developed in new directions and, in some cases, existed over greater distances. This is a crucial point. The arrival of Europeans in the Pacific, along with all those who would come after, such as Americans, is not a moment of dramatic departure in terms of the complexity and interconnectedness of the Pacific Ocean. Europeans changed some of these networks, developed new ones and destroyed those that were antagonistic to them, but they did not invent the idea of an interconnected Pacific and its hinterland. The objects highlighted in this book, instead, connect to the theories of Epeli Hauʻofa and other Pacific scholars: that the ocean is one defined by islands and that it provides a complex matrix of interconnections and communication pathways between these dots of land.

While the interconnected Pacific is not the result of men such as Cook and Wilkes, these individuals did change the future direction of many islands of the ocean. They shifted balances of power and set in motion chains of events that would result in fundamental changes to island cultures, environmental degradation, disease and, often, death. Some

islands, such as Vancouver Island and Rapa Nui, were ravaged by disease and kidnapping, seismic events that affect their place in the world to this day. Even those islands that excelled at working with, around and against colonial powers, such as Japan and Hawaiʻi, eventually found themselves in situations where foreign powers exerted significant influence on their destiny and the power balance of the ocean around them. Pervasive memories of figures like Cook and Lapérouse encourage many to believe it was European powers who did and do hold the balance of influence in the Pacific. The reality is that the achievement of geopolitical primacy in today's Pacific was achieved by others: less well-known voyages such as that of the United States Exploring Expedition and the day-to-day activities of whalers, sealers, sandalwood traders and others who sailed from ports on the east coast of the United States.

The collections held in institutions like the British Library provide numerous insights into how the Pacific became an 'American Lake', in terms of who holds the balance of geopolitical power in the region. It is important to know about and understand these collections and the histories they

illustrate, not only because of how they help us understand the past but also because of how they help us interpret the future. In the twenty-first century, Pacific pollution and environmental degradation are critical issues for global governments to deal with, and we must understand how our historic engagement with the Pacific and other oceans has created a path that has led us to this point. The production of discarded waste and rising average global temperatures began with the trade in spices and ran through the selling of pelts and the burning of whale oil to where we are now. Similarly, a detailed understanding of the contested histories of islands in and around the Pacific helps us to understand contemporary geopolitical issues. We can see in these pages that Formosa (Taiwan) has been a strategically important island in the ocean across four centuries. Similarly, understanding the desire to control strategic waterways and islands in and around the ocean, such as the United States displayed when gradually taking control of the islands of Hawaiʻi, allows us to see that current tensions around island building in the South China Sea are, perhaps, further developments on the same trajectory.

*Pacific* also illustrates that the political intrigues and power struggles fought by those from outside or on the margins of the Pacific Ocean ebb and flow over time. American influence in the Pacific will not last forever, as was the case with Spain, China and many others. What does endure are the peoples and cultures of the Pacific islands. These develop through time, influenced by trade, migration, colonisation and other human forces, but so far the ocean of interconnected islands endured. This will be the case, however, only if those of us in the wider world change our habits to reduce the growing list of new environmental dangers that face this ocean and its peoples.

caido

qual questa terra
licota li spend ino
p: dina vj

quen zam

canpuso

cinhaguj

colinbaju

qua lihoua il
new aloj

GuenGuilo

abmGaia

poncoja

nan guj

GIAPAN
cauGoliuar
Galon

majacar

T    R    O         PICO DI CAN        CR      O

coin

anian
nanto

Ligo

anthnoja

pulomio

barbai      polino

# Select Bibliography

Andrade, T., *How Taiwan Became Chinese: Dutch, Spanish and Han Colonization in the Seventeenth century* (New York, 2007)

Armitage, D., and Bashford, A. (eds), *Pacific Histories: Ocean, Land, People* (London, 2014)

Beaglehole, J. C., *The Exploration of the Pacific* (London, 1966)

Bentley, J., *Seascapes: Maritime Histories, Littoral Cultures and Transoceanic Exchanges* (Honolulu, 2007)

Bockstoce, J. R., *The Opening of the Maritime Fur Trade at Bering Strait* (Philadelphia, 2005)

Borthwick, M., *Pacific Century: The Emergence of Modern Pacific Asia* (Boulder, 2007)

Camino, M. M., *Producing the Pacific: Maps and Narratives of Spanish Exploration, 1567–1606* (New York, 2005)

Campbell, I. C., *Worlds Apart: A History of the Pacific Islands* (Christchurch, 2003)

Chambers, N. (ed.), *Endeavouring Banks: Exploring Collections from the 'Endeavour' Voyage, 1768–1771* (London, 2016)

David, A., *The Charts and Coastal Views of Captain Cook's Voyages* (London, 1988)

Driver, F., *Geography Militant: Cultures of Exploration and Empire* (London, 2001)

Druett, J., *Tupaia: Captain Cook's Polynesian Navigator* (Santa Barbra, 2011)

Fischer, S. R., *Island at the End of the World: The Turbulent History of Easter Island* (London, 2005)

Fischer, S. R., *A History of the Pacific Islands* (London, 2013)

Flynn, D. O., and Giraldez, A. (eds), *The Pacific World: Lands, Peoples and History of the Pacific, 1500–1900* (London, 2009)

Frame, W., and Walker, L., *James Cook: The Voyages* (London, 2018)

Frankopan, P., *The Silk Road: A New History of the World* (London, 2015)

Gordon, A., *A Modern History of Japan: From Tokugawa Times to the Present* (Oxford, 2015)

Harris, P. R., *A History of the British Museum Library, 1753–1973* (London, 1998)

Hatfield, P. J., *Lines in the Ice: Exploring the Roof of the World* (London, 2016)

Hatfield, P. J., *Canada in the Frame: Copyright, Collections and the Image of Canada, 1895–1924* (London, 2018)

Hau'ofa, E., *We Are the Ocean: Selected Works* (Honolulu, 2008)

Haycox, S., Barnett, J., and Liburd, C. (eds), *Enlightenment and Exploration in the North Pacific, 1741–1805* (London, 1997)

Igler, D., *The Great Ocean: Pacific Worlds from Captain Cook to the Gold Rush* (Oxford, 2013)

Keighren, I. M., Withers, C. W. J., and Bell, B., *Travels Into Print: Exploration, Writing and Publishing with John Murray, 1773–1859* (Chicago, 2015)

Kirch, P. V., *The Lapita Peoples: Ancestors of the Oceanic World* (Oxford, 1997)

Kirch, P. V., *On the Road of the Winds: An Archaeological History of the Pacific Islands before European Contact* (Berkeley, 2000)

Lal, B. V., and Fortune, K. (eds), *The Pacific Islands: An Encyclopaedia* (Honolulu, 2000)

Lange, R., *Island Ministers: Indigenous Leadership in Nineteenth-Century Pacific Islands* (Canberra, 2005)

Lewis, D., *We the Navigators: The Ancient Art of Landfaring in the Pacific* (Honolulu, 1994)

Lidin, O., *Tanegashima: The Arrival of Europe in Japan* (Honolulu, 2002)

Mandelbrote, G., and Taylor, B. (eds), *Libraries within the Library: The Origins of the British Library's Printed Collections* (London, 2009)

Matsuda, M. K., *Pacific Worlds: A History of Seas, Peoples and Cultures* (Cambridge, 2015)

Murray, D., *Pirates of the South China Coast, 1790–1810* (Stanford, 1987)

Petersen, G., *Traditional Micronesian Societies: Adaptation, Integration and Political Organisation* (Honolulu, 2009)

Philbrick, N., *Away Off Shore: Nantucket Island and its People, 1602–1890* (New York, 2011)

Philbrick, N., *Sea of Glory: America's Voyage of Discovery, The US Exploring Expedition, 1838–1842* (New York, 2003)

Quammen, D., *The Song of the Dodo: Island Biogeography in an Age of Extinctions* (New York, 1996)

Salmond, A., *Two Worlds: First Meetings between Maoris and Europeans, 1642–1772* (Auckland, 1997)

Scarr, D., *A History of the Pacific Islands: Passages through Tropical Time* (Richmond, 2001)

Silva, N. K., *Aloha Betrayed: Native Hawaiian Resistance to American Colonialism* (Durham, 2004)

Slezkine, Y, *Arctic Mirrors: Russia and the Small Peoples of the North* (Ithaca, 1994)

Spriggs, M., *The Island Melanesians* (Oxford, 1997)

Taylor, J. G., *Indonesia: Peoples and Histories* (New Haven, 2004)

Thomas, N., *Islanders: The Pacific in the Age of Empire* (London, 2010)

Tonnessen, J. N., and Johnsen, A. O., *A History of Modern Whaling* (Berkeley, 1982)

Turner, J., *Spice: The History of a Temptation* (New York, 2008)

Van Dyke, P. A., *The Canton Trade: Life and Enterprise on the China Coast, 1700–1845* (Hong Kong, 2005)

Walker, B. L., *A Concise History of Japan* (Cambridge, 2015)

Worster, D., *Nature's Economy: A History of Ecological Ideas* (Cambridge, 1994)

# Acknowledgements

This book would not have come about without the questions arising from *Lines in the Ice: Exploring the Roof of the World*. As a result, I am particularly grateful to British Library Publishing for the opportunity to publish that book and to keep pursuing fascinating research through this one. In particular, Rob Davies and Abbie Day have been a great help and endlessly patient while a growing family and new jobs affected my focus on the book.

Colleagues around the British Library deserve thanks for their help or just listening to me muse over a lunch break. Tom Harper and Nick Dykes were helpful with a number of map-related queries, even going so far as to highlight notable works that I had missed, while Hamish Todd and colleagues have also been a great help while I researched the Japanese materials found in this book. Thanks are also due to colleagues from the reading rooms and basements at the Library: they are the ones who fetch the great volume of works any researcher requires to produce a book like this. Without their efforts this and many other books would never have come to fruition.

Similarly, there is a huge amount of effort that goes into the production of a book like this that often remains unseen. Abbie and Rob have overseen the editing of the book while Sally Nicholls has diligently organised further image research, photography and rights clearance. Having recently written a book for which I had to clear permissions in my own images, the amount of effort Sally and other picture researchers put into making sure the beautiful books of British Library Publishing happen is not lost on me. Similarly, we would not be able to produce books such as this without the hard work of the imaging team at the British Library as well as the support of those who have made their collections available to this book.

I am particularly indebted to Bob Paterson and David Rumsey for their support of the book. Bob kindly loaned his copy of *Tihookeanskie Skazki* ('*Pacific Tales*') and allowed the reproduction of its cover; he has also been a wonderful source of information and advice. I have enjoyed working with David Rumsey for a number of years, mostly while I was curator for digital mapping at the Library, and he has developed an astounding private map collection. His commitment to making the collection publicly accessible and usable is an inspiration and I am grateful to him for allowing the reproduction of a number of items in this book. You can find the rest of his collection online at www.davidrumsey.com. Thanks are due to my team at the Eccles Centre, too. While this has been a project for my personal time, the fact that my colleagues, Cara Rodway, Jean Petrovic and Philip Abraham, do such stellar work and make every day so enjoyable means I had a lot more energy for this book than I expected. I am lucky to work with them all.

I would also like to thank the readers of the early drafts of this book, particularly Madeleine Hatfield and Klaus Dodds. Their insights have made this a much better book. As usual, I am further indebted to Madeleine for her wide range of input on the book. Her thoughts, critical insights, keen eye and patience for evenings where I disappeared into the book were an integral part of completing this work. Joshua and Brendan, our two sons, loomed large in the writing of this, too. The history outlined here illustrates that much has been – and is now – lacking in our stewardship of the world around us; it also makes us question how long we can continue in this vein. For Joshua and Brendan, as well as the rest of their generation, this book is a promise that I will try to leave the world a better place than I found it.

# Illustrations

Front Cover. 'Vue des Iles Radak sous l'aspect du Vaquois'. Louis Choris, *Voyage Pittoresque du Monde*, Paris, 1822. British Library 803.m.19.

2–3. Gavriil Andreevich Sarychev, *Puteshestvie flota kapitana Sarycheva po sieverovostochnoi chasti Sibiri, Ledovitomu moriu i Vostochnomu okeanu [The Voyage of the Fleet of Captain Sarychev to Northeastern Siberia, the Frozen Sea, and the Eastern Ocean.]*, St. Petersburg, 1802. British Library 792.l.12.

4–5. Map of the South Sea. Claas Jansz Vooght, *De groote nieuwe vermeerderde zee-atlas ofte water-werelt*, Amsterdam, 1682. British Library Maps 7.Tab.126.

6. Aerial photo of Kiritimati, photo as seen by the crew of Expedition 4 aboard the International Space Station, 16 January 2002. NASA.

8–9. Tupaia, A Scene in Tahiti, *c*. 1769. British Library Add. 15508, f.14.

10–11. Sowek: A Pile-Village on the North Coast of New Guinea. Freidrich Ratzell , *The History of Mankind*, London, 1898. British Library 572*3343*.

12. Hokusai, *Fishing Boats at Choshi in Shimosa*, *c*. 1833–4, from the series 'One Thousand Pictures of the Ocean'. Art Institute, Chicago.

15 top left. Javanese canoe, drawing by John Webber, *c*. 1779. British Library Add. 15514 (54).

15 centre. Double canoe, drawing by John Webber, *c*. 1777. British Library Add. 15513 (26).

15 top right & bottom right: 'Bateau des Iles Carolines'; centre left: 'Bateau du port de San Francisco'; centre right: 'Vue d'une ile dans le groupe Krusenstern'. Louis Choris, *Voyage Pittoresque du Monde*, Paris, 1822. British Library 803.m.18.

15 bottom left & centre. 'Parao, Bateau de Passage

de Manille, and Sarambeau, Radeau de Pêche de Manille'. *Voyage de La Pérouse autour du Monde ... rédigé par M. L. A. Milet-Mureau*, Paris, 1797. British Library, 1899.r.27.

16. Newly reconstructed Lapita pot at the Vanuatu National Musem. Photo Stephen Alvarez/National Geographic.

19. Carving from the Waipapa Marae showing Kupe holding a paddle. Waipapa Marae, University of Auckland. Photograph by Melanie Lovell-Smith, sourced from Te Ara – the Encyclopedia of New Zealand.

20. Hokusai, *Whaling of the Coast of the Goto Islands*, *c*. 1831–3, from the series 'One Thousand Pictures of the Ocean'. Art Institute, Chicago.

21 top. Aleutians whaling. Henry Wood Elliot, *Our Arctic Province. Alaska and the Seal Islands*, New York, 1886. British Library 10412.ff.28.

21 bottom & 22–23. Ezu Saiyudan, Whaling, 1803. British Library 16054.d.5.

24. Indigenous Californian fishing from a raft. John Harris, *Navigantium atque Itinerantium Bibliotheca*, London, 1764. British Library G.7040–41.

25. Salmon Weirs of the Kenaitze. Henry Wood Elliot, *Our Arctic Province. Alaska and the Seal Islands*, New York, 1886. British Library 10412, ff.28.

26. John Webber, 'Poulaho, King of the Friendly Islands, drinking Kava', *c*. 1779–80. British Library Add. 23920, f.101r.

28. Zheng He on a boat. *Records of the Western Ocean*, *c*. 1600. British Library 15331.f.2.

29. Zheng He's ship. *Wu Bei Zhi*, *c*. 1644. Library of Congress, Washington, D.C.

30. Miniature of the Great Khan. Marco Polo, *Le devisement du monde (Travels)*, *c*. 1333–40. British Library Royal 19 d.1., f.61r.

31. Paolo Forlani, Map of the World, 1571. British Library Maps K. Top.IV.5.

32. Joan Martines, Chart of Indonesia, 1578. British Library Harley 3450, f.5.

35. Map of Banda Islands. François Valentijn, *Oud en Nieuw Oost-Indien Vervattende…*, Amsterdam, 1724. British Library G.7027–31.

36–37. Petrus Plancius, Map of the Spice Islands, 1617. State Library of New South Wales, Sydney.

38. Ache, Sumatra. P. Barretto de Resende, *Maps and Plans of Portuguese and other fortresses in S. Africa and E. India*, 1646. British Library Sloane 197.

39. Mosque at Ternate. Jules Sébastien César Dumont D'Urville, *Voyage au Pole Sud et dans l'Océanie sur les corvettes l'Astrolabe et la Zélée, exécuté ... pendant les années 1837 ... 1840*, Paris, 1846. British Library 1262.k.13.

41. Battista Agnese, Map of the world showing the track of Magellan's fleet, 1540. British Library Egerton MS 2854, ff.13v–14.

42. Sketch of the Retinue of the Dutch Envoy. British Library Sloane 3060, f.501.

43. Taishokkan's Chinese envoys approaching Japan. British Library Or.12440 Vol. 1, f.12v.

44. World Map. British Library Harley 3450, f.3.

45. Drake's Passage. Nicola van Sype, *La heroike enterprinse faict par le signeur Draeck d'avoir cirquit toute la terre*, Antwerp, 1581. British Library Maps C.2.a.7.(1.).

46. Father Michael Rogerius and Matteo Ricci

arriving in China. Cornlius Hazart, *Kerckelycke Historie van de Gheheele Werldt*, Antwerp, 1682. British Library 4520.e.3.

47. Johannes Vingboons, Bird's-eye view of Manila, *c.* 1665. Dutch National Archives.

48. 'A View of Cape Espíritu Santo, on Samal, … his Majesty's Ship the Centurion engag'd and took the Spanish Galleon call'd Notra Seigniora de Cabadonga, from Acapulco to Manila'. George Anson, *A Voyage Round the World*, London, 1748. British Library 212.e.1.

49. Map of the route of a captured galleon. George Anson, *A Voyage Round the World*, London, 1748. British Library 212.e.1.

50 left. Drake's capture of galleon Nuesta Señora de la Concepción (the Cacafuego) in March 1579. L. Hulsius, *Collection of Voyages and Travels*, Frankfurt, 1626. British Library C.114.c.21.

50 right. Map of the Galápagos. John Harris, *Navigantium atque Itinerantium Bibliotheca*, London, 1764. British Library G.7040–41.

51. Spanish Galleon in Manila Bay, the Philippines. Theodor de Bry, *America*, Frankfurt, 1601. British Library G.6626.

52. *Nova Guinea et Insulae Salmonis*, 1602. British Library Maps C.39.a.4.

55. Map of Quirós's 'Espíritu Santu' copied by William Hack in 1698 (orig. 1606). British Library Harley 4034, f.245.

56. New Guinea Islanders. François Valentijn, *Oud en Nieuw Oost-Indien Vervattende…*, Amsterdam. 1724. British Library G.7027–31.

57. Dampier's map of 'Nova Guinea and Nova Brtiannia'. John Harris, *Navigantium atque Itinerantium Bibliotheca*, London, 1764. British Library G.7040–41.

58. Map of Manila. Hipolito Ximeniz, *Topographie de la ciurdad de Manila: capital de las yslas Philipinas*, Manila, *c.* 1739. Maps K.Top.116.40.

59. Map of the Philippines. Pedro Murillo Velarde, *Carta hydrographica y chorographica delas yslas Filipinas*, Manila, 1734.

60. Macau. John Harris, *Navigantium atque*

*Itinerantium Bibliotheca*, London, 1764. British Library G.7040–41.

61. Jakarta. P. Barretto de Resende, *Maps and Plans of Portuguese and other fortresses in S. Africa and E. India*, 1646. British Library Sloane 197.

62. Dutch Portolan chart of Island of Formosa (Taiwan), 17th century. British Library Add. 34184, f.96.

63. Chinese boat with defences against pirates. British Library Add. Or. 1976.

64. Map of Nagasaki, *c.* 1680. British Library Or.75.g.25.

65. *Bankoku Sozu*, Nagasaki, 1645. British Library Maps *920 (485.).

66. Attrib. Albert Eckhout, *East Indian Market Stall in Batavia*, 1640–66. Rijksmuseum, Amsterdam.

67 top: Painted map of Ambon, *c.* 1606; bottom: Arms of the Dutch East India Company. Rijksmuseum, Amsterdam.

68. 'Ile de Cocos'. Willem Shouten, *Journal ou Description du Merveileux Voyage…*, Amsterdam, 1619. British Library G.6736.

69 left: Map; right top: Shooting at indigenous boat; right bottom: Trade between Dutch and indigenous islanders. Willem Shouten, *Journal ou Description du Merveileux Voyage…*, Amsterdam, 1619. British Library G.6736.

70–71. Map. Willem Shouten, *Journal ou Description du Merveileux Voyage…*, Amsterdam, 1619. British Library G.6736.

72. Sir Joseph Banks' copy of Abel Tasman's diary. British Library Add. 8946, f.72.

73. 'Fyland Moar' & 'Fyland Insous' [sic]. Sir Joseph Banks' copy of Abel Tasman's diary. British Library Add. 8946, f.129.

74. William Hack, Map of the Galápagos, 1687. British Library Sloane 45, f.39.

75. Isle of Chiloé. William Hack, *Description of the Coast & Islands in the South Sea of America … From the original Spanish manuscripts & our late English Discoverers A Description of all the Ports Bays Rivers Harbours Islands Sands Rocks & Dangers from the Mouth of Calafornia to the Straghts of Lemaire as allso

*Peyps' [sic] Island in the North Sea near the Straghts of Magellan*, 1698. British Library Maps 7.tab.122.

76. Portrait of Hasekura. Scipione Amati, *Relation und grundtlicher Bericht von dess Königreichs Voxu gottseliger Bekehrung*, Ingolstatt, 1617. British Library 1369.g.9.

78–79. 'Débarquement à travers les Recifs de l'Isle de Roamnzoff'. Louis Choris, *Voyage Pittoresque du Monde*, Paris, 1822. British Library 803.m.19.

80. Japanese depiction of the ship 'The Brothers'. British Library Or 14755.

82. New Guinea flora and fauna. William Dampier, *A Collection of Voyages*, London, 1729. British Library 673.c.12.

83. Map of the 1699 voyage. William Dampier, *A Collection of Voyages*, London, 1729. British Library 673.c.12.

84 left: Herman Moll, *A New and Exact Map of the Coast Countries and Islands within the Limits of the South Sea Company*, London, 1726. British Library Maps K.Top.124.7.84; right: *Lucipher's New Row Barge*, *c.* 1721. Satire on Robert Knight. Wellcome Collection.

87. The Moai of Easter Island. *Voyage de La Pérouse autour du Monde … rédigé par M. L. A. Milet-Mureau*, Paris, 1796. State Library of New South Wales, Sydney.

89. Alexander Johnston, *Physical Chart of the Pacific Ocean*, London, 1856. British Library Maps 48.f.17.

90. *A Map of the Discoveries made by the Russians on the North West Coast of America. Published by the Royal Academy of Sciences at St. Petersburg … Republished by Thomas Jefferys*, London, 1761. British Library 981.e.17.

93. Tupaia, Marae in Tahiti, *c.* 1769. British Library Add. 15508, ff.16 and 17.

95. Herman Spöring, *Fort Venus*, 1769. British Library Add. 7085, f.8 (a–d).

96. Mezzotint of Benjamin West's portrait of Sir Joseph Banks, 1773. Museum of New Zealand Te Papa Tongarewa.

97. Sydney Parkinson, Maori portraits, *c.* 1769. British Library Add 23920, f.54a.

98. Tupaia, Chart of the Islands surrounding Tahiti, *c.* 1769. British Library Add. 21593C.

101. Charles Meryon, *Death of Marion Du Fresne*, *c.* 1842. Alexander Turnbull Library/National Library of New Zealand.

102. Gerald Fitzgerald, *The Injured Islanders*, London, 1779. British Library 643.k.24.

105 top left: Missionary House and Environs in the Island of Otaheite; top right: Great Morai of Temarre in Pappare in Otaheite; bottom left: Morai and Altar in Attahooro with the Eatooa and Teees; bottom right: The Afiatookas of FuttaFaihe at Mooa in Tongataboo. William Wilson, *A Missionary Voyage to the Southern Pacific Ocean*, London, 1799. British Library G.2861.

107. Portrait of Mai. British Library Add. 23921, f.45r.

108. 'Idoles des Iles Sandwich'. Louis Choris, *Voyage Pittoresque du Monde*, Paris, 1822. British Library 803.m.18.

109. John Webber, *A view of Morai on O'Whyhee*, *c.* 1779. British Library Add. 15513, f.27.

110. John Webber, *View of Nootka Sound*, *c.* 1779. British Library Add. 15514, f.7.

112. Breadfruit. Louis Choris, *Voyage Pittoresque du Monde*, Paris, 1822. British Library 803.m.18.

113 top: The cargo area of HMS *Bounty*. William Bligh, *A Voyage to the South Sea*, London, 1792. British Library L.R.293.b.5; bottom: *Description of a Slave Ship*, a broadside, London, 1789. British Library 1881.d.8.

114. Friday Fletcher October Christian, drawn and etched by John Shillibeer. John Shillibeer, *A Narrative of the Briton's Voyage to Pitcairn Island*, London 1818. British Library 566.d.21.

115. Pitcairn Island, drawn and etched by John Shillibeer. John Shillibeer, *A Narrative of the Briton's Voyage to Pitcairn Island*, London 1818. British Library 566.d.21.

116 left: 'Fritz levelled his rifle, and fired with so much success and address that he hit the creature on the head'. Adrien Paul, *Willis the Pilot A sequel to the Swiss Family Robinson*, London, 1857. British Library

12842.ee.11; right: 'Queequeg and his Harpoon', illustration by I. W. Taber. Herman Melville, *Moby Dick*, London, 1900. British Library 012622.ee.10. (4.).

117. 'Terrible Encounter with a Shark', illustration by R. M. Ballantyne. R. M. Ballantyne, *The Coral Island*, London, 1858. British Library C.194.a.540.

118. 'Sketch of Friendly Cove in Nootka Sound taken by Mr Wedgborough'. John Meares, *Voyages made in the years 1788 and 1789, from China to the north west coast of America*, London, 1790. British Library G.2281.(1).

119. 'The Launch of the North West America at Nootka Sound. Being the first Vessel that ever built in that part of the Globe'. John Meares, *Voyages made in the years 1788 and 1789, from China to the north west coast of America*, London, 1790. British Library G.2281.(1).

120. Aleutians. Gavriil Andreevich Sarychev, *Puteshestvīe flota kapitana Sarycheva po sieverovostochnoi chasti Sibiri, Ledovitomu moriu i Vostochnomu okeanu [The Voyage of the Fleet of Captain Sarychev to Northeastern Siberia, the Frozen Sea, and the Eastern Ocean.]*, St. Petersburg, 1802. British Library 792.l.12.

121. Map of the Bering Strait. Gavriil Andreevich Sarychev, *Puteshestvīe flota kapitana Sarycheva po sieverovostochnoi chasti Sibiri, Ledovitomu moriu i Vostochnomu okeanu [The Voyage of the Fleet of Captain Sarychev to Northeastern Siberia, the Frozen Sea, and the Eastern Ocean.]*, St. Petersburg, 1802. British Library 792.l.12.

122. Frigates off Maui. *Voyage de La Pérouse autour du Monde … rédigé par M. L. A. Milet-Mureau*, Paris, 1796. State Library of New South Wales, Sydney.

123. 'A Chart of the World exhibiting the Track of M. de La Pérouse and the route of M. Lesseps across the continent'. *Voyage de La Pérouse autour du Monde … rédigé par M. L. A. Milet-Mureau*, Paris, 1797. British Library 1045.f.14.

124. King Kamehameha I of Hawaii. Louis Choris, *Voyage Pittoresque du Monde*, Paris, 1822. British Library 803.m.18.

125. Wife of King Kamehameha I. Louis Choris,

*Voyage Pittoresque du Monde*, Paris, 1822. British Library 803.m.18.

126. Captain David Porter. David Porter, *A Voyage in the South Seas, in the years 1812, 1813, and 1814, with particular details of the Gallipagos and Washington Islands …*, London, 1823. British Library 10493, ff.51.

127. Madisonville. David Porter, *A Voyage in the South Seas, in the years 1812, 1813, and 1814, with particular details of the Gallipagos and Washington Islands …*, London, 1823. British Library 10493, ff.51.

128. New Archangel [Sitka], trading post of the Russian-American Company. State Archive of the Russian Navy, St. Petersburg.

129. Honolulu. Louis Choris, *Voyage Pittoresque du Monde*, Paris, 1822. New York Public Library.

130. Nagasaki. A. J. von Krusenstern, *Voyage round the world in the years 1803, 1804, 1805 & 1806*, London 1813. British Library V.10129.

132–33. Japanese depiction of the ship 'The Brothers', its crew and objects. British Library Or 14755.

134. Chart of Van Diemen's Land and Hobart, 1838. British Library Maps 92488.(3.).

135. *Hobart Town, on the river Derwent, Van Diemens Land*, painted by W. J. Huggins & engraved by E. Duncan, London, 1830. British Library Maps 188.r.1.(2.).

136. A prison interior, New Caledonia. *Picturesque Atlas of Australasia*, Sydney & Melbourne, 1861. British Library Maps 151.a.1.

137. Convicts making roads, New Caledonia. *Picturesque Atlas of Australasia*, Sydney & Melbourne, 1861. British Library Maps 151.a.1.

138 left: Felice Beato, photograph of Prince Kung, 1860. British Library Photo 353/26; right: Felice Beato, photograph of Sir James Hope Grant, 1860. British Library Photo 353/(25).

139. *The East India Company's iron steamship Nemesis, Lieutenant W H Hall RN, Commander, with boats of Sulphur, Calliope, Larne and Starling destroying Chinese war junks in Anson's Bay, January 7th 1841*, coloured aquatint by and after E. Duncan, 1843. Courtesy of the Council of the National Army Museum.

140. *A Chart of Nantucket Island and Part of Martha's*

*Vineyard*, London, 1775. British Library Maps 184.m.3.

141. Entry to the Bay of Islands, with American consul, James Reddy Clendon's American flag flying. National Library of Australia.

142. Sperm Whale being harpooned. Robert Hamilton, *The Natural History of the ordinary cetacea or whales*, London, 1843. British Library 1150. a. 4.

143. M. F. Maury, Whale Chart, 1852. Barry Lawrence Ruderman Antique Maps.

144 left: Comparison of the beaks of finches. Charles Darwin, *Journal of researches into the natural history and geology of the countries visited during the voyage of H.M.S. Beagle round the world, under the command of Capt. Fitz Roy, R.N.*, London, 1860. British Library RB.23.a.4931; bottom: Galápagos Marine Iguana. Charles Darwin, *The Zoology of the Voyage of H.M.S. Beagle, under the command of Captain Fitzroy, R.N., during the years 1832 to 1836 ...*, London, 1832. British Library 791.l.18.

145. Galápagos Finch. Charles Darwin, *The Zoology of the Voyage of H.M.S. Beagle, under the command of Captain Fitzroy, R.N., during the years 1832 to 1836 ...*, London, 1832. British Library 791.l.18.

146. Map of the Oregon Territory. Charles Wilkes, *Narrative of the U.S. Exploring Expedition*, Philadelphia, 1850. British Library Map 145.e.7.

147 top: Chart of the World shewing the Tracks of the U.S. Exploring Expedition in 1833, 39, 40, 41 & 42. Charles Wilkes, *Narrative of the U.S. Exploring Expedition*, Philadelphia, 1850. British Library Map 145.e.7; bottom: Charles Wilkes. New York Public Library.

148. Fijian club dance. Charles Wilkes, *Narrative of the U.S. Exploring Expedition*, Philadelphia, 1850. British Library Map 145.e.7.

149. Map of the Fijian Islands. Charles Wilkes, *Narrative of the U.S. Exploring Expedition*, Philadelphia, 1850. British Library Map 145.e.6.

151 centre top, bottom left and right: Zoophytes drawn by J. C. Dana. Charles Wilkes, *Narrative of the U.S. Exploring Expedition*, Philadelphia, 1850. British Library 14000.i; top left: 'Aprosmictus splendens' and 'Aprosmictus personatus' drawn by T. R. Peale;

top right: 'Corvus hawaiiensis Peale' drawn by T. R. Peale; bottom centre: 'Todirampphus vitiensis' drawn by T. R. Peale. Charles Wilkes, *Narrative of the U.S. Exploring Expedition*, Philadelphia, 1850. British Library 14000.i.

152. South Sea Islander labourers planting sugar cane at a plantation in Mackay in the 1870s. State Library of Queensland.

153. Sketch showing the recruitment of South Sea Islander labourers in New Hebrides, 1892. State Library of Queensland.

154 left: Drawing showing the forced recruitment of South Sea Islanders to work on the plantations in Queensland, 1893. State Library of Queensland; right: Seizure of the Schooner Daphne by HMS Rosario. State Library of Victoria.

155. South Sea Islanders on the deck of a ship arriving at Bundaberg, 1895. State Library of Queensland.

157. George Grey, *Polynesian mythology, and ancient traditional history of the New Zealand race as furnished by their priests and chiefs*, London, 1855. British Library 4505.c.11.

158. Japanese scroll depicting the arrival of Commodore Perry's ships. British Library Or.16453.

159. A Japanese man and boy standing on the shore of a harbor in which is docked an American steamship, possibly Commodore Perry's ship, print by Hiroshige, 1861. Library of Congress, Washington, D.C.

160. Chart of Vancouver Island. George Vancouver, *Atlas*, London, 1798. British Library 1899.r.42.

161. British Camp, San Juan Islands. Beinecke Library, Yale University.

163. *U.S. Air Force. Political and time chart ... Northern hemisphere. Polar stereographic projection*, 1947. British Library Maps 920.(430).

164. Photo of King David Kalakaua, *c.* 1882. Hawaii State Archives.

165. King Kalakaua and Suite Paying a Formal Visit to the President in the Blue Room of the White House. King Kalākaua of Hawaii meets President Ulysses S. Grant at the White House in the first state

visit for a ruling monarch to the USA in December 1874. Frank Leslie's Illustrated Newspaper, 2 January 1875.

166. 'Another Shotgun Wedding with Neither Party Willing'. Puck Magazine, 1 December 1897. Library of Congress, Washington, D.C.

167 top: Map of the Pacific Ocean showing the Relation of Naval Stations and Principal Ports to the Hawaiian Islands. Lorrin A. Thurston, *A Hand-book on the Annexation of Hawaii*, St. Joseph, Michigan, 1897. British Library 8176.bb.37; bottom: Map showing the parties of the Pacific within which Hawaii is the only supply station. Lorrin A. Thurston, *A Hand-book on the Annexation of Hawaii*, St. Joseph, Michigan, 1897. British Library 8176.bb.37.

168. Kisaburō Ohara, Europe and Asia Octopus Map, 1904. Cornell University Library.

169 top: The Battle of Chempulo, 1905. British Library N.Tab.2005.(12); bottom: Uchida Kuichi, *The Meiji Emperor*, 1871. British Library Photo 1224//5 (1).

170–171. Hiroshima: Extent of Fire and Limits of Bomb Damage. *The Effects of Atomic Bombs on Hiroshima and Nagasaki*, United States Strategic Bombing Survey, Washington, 1946. British Library A.S.760/4 (1.).

172. Riding the surf, favourite pastime in Honolulu's reefing encircled harbour. Stereographic photo, 1915. Library of Congress, Washington, D.C.

175. Map of the Japanese Empire, 1919. Private Collection.

176. Pioneer Battalion performing a haka for Joseph George Ward at Bois-de-Warnimont, 30 June, 1918. Royal New Zealand Returned and Services' Association: New Zealand official negatives, World War 1914–1918. Alexander Turnbull Library, Wellington, New Zealand.

177. Wall map of the world commemorating Japanese involvement in World War I, 1918. The David Rumsey Map Collection, www.davidrumsey.com.

178. Pearl Harbour naval base and U.S.S. Shaw ablaze after the Japanese attach, December 1941. Library of Congress. Washington, D.C.

179. 'The First Year of the War in the Far East' 1943. British Library Maps MOD MDR Misc 2285.

180. Nihon Kotsu Kosha, Map of Hiroshima, 1947. The David Rumsey Map Collection, www. davidrumsey.com.

181. "… the power of the atomic bomb is beyond belief…" Nagasaki Prefecture Report. *The Effects of Atomic Bombs on Hiroshima and Nagasaki*, United States Strategic Bombing Survey, Washington, 1946. British Library A.S.760/4 (1.).

182. Hiroshima from the top of the Red Cross Hospital, looking northwest. Frame buildings recently erected. *The Effects of Atomic Bombs on Hiroshima and Nagasaki*, United States Strategic Bombing Survey, Washington, 1946. British Library A.S.760/4 (1.).

183. Ground Zero at Nagasaki, before and after bombing. Hiroshima before and after bombing. Area around ground zero. *The Effects of Atomic Bombs on Hiroshima and Nagasaki*, United States Strategic Bombing Survey, Washington, 1946. British Library A.S.760/4 (1.).

184. Chen Zhengxiang, *Taiwan dili tuji* [*Geographical Atlas of Taiwan*], Taipei, 1959. British Library (KB) CA 085 (T).

187. 'Pacific Island Fairytales', Petrogad, 1932. Private Collection.

188. Tomoyuki Tanaka, *Gojira* [*Godzilla*], poster, 1954. Toho co. Ltd.

189 Great Circle Distances and Adzimuths from Eniwetok Atoll, 1951. British Librayr Maps X.12606.

190. Ernest Dudley Chase, *Aloha. A Pictorial Map of the Hawaiian Islands, The United States' Fiftieth State*, Maui, 1960. The David Rumsey Map Collection, www.davidrumsey.com.

193. Queen Sālote Tupou III, 1968. Photo Luis Marden/National Geographic/Getty Images.

194. *Longhouse interior*, engraving after John Webber, *c.* 1780. British Library Add. 23921, f.83.

195. Lawrence Paul Yuxweluptun, *Untitled (Longhouse Interior)*, Reservation, 1987. Courtesy of Lawrence Paul Yuxweluptun. Photo Scott Massey/Site Photography.

196 & 197. Hikianalia. © Polynesian Voyaging Society.

198 left: Peter Damon, *Cocos. Island of blood and treasure*, Dublin, 1946. British Library 012635.b.32; right: William Golding, *Lord of the Flies*, London, 1954. British Library Cup.409.c.59.

201 top left: 'Surf-Bathing – Success'; top right: 'Surf-Bathing – Failure'. Mark Twain, *Roughing It*, Hartford, 1872. British Library 1560/629; bottom: 'A View of Karakakooa In Owyhee', engraving after John Webber. James Cook, *A Voyage to the Pacific Ocean*, London, 1784. British Library Maps 36.f.8.

202. Haleakala observatory, Maui, Hawaii, 2018. Photo dronepic.

204 left. A beer can seen at 3,780 meters depth at Enigma Seamount. Courtesy of 222. 204 centre: A plastic ice bag, likely blown overboard from a fishing vessel, was also found at Enigma Seamount; right: A food container, seen resting at 4,947 meters on the slopes of a canyon leading to the Sirena Deep. Courtesy of NOAA Office of Ocean Exploration and Research, 2016 Deepwater Exploration of the Marianas.

205. Plastic, rubber, polystyrene and other garbage floating in the ocean in Puerto Princesa, Palawan Island. Photo southeast asia/Alamy Stock Photo.

207. 'Santa Isabel Island, Western Part', Admiralty Chart from 1902 survey by HMS Dart. British Library Maps B. A. C.12(3402).

209. Map of the Sandwich Isles [Hawaii]. Charles Wilkes, *Narrative of the U.S. Exploring Expedition*, Philadelphia, 1850. British Library Map 145.e.6.212.

212. Joan Martines, Chart of Japan and the coast of China, 1578. British Library Harley 3450, f.16.

221. 'Vue de l'Isle de St. Paul dans la mer de Kamtchatka (avec des lions marins)'. Louis Choris, *Voyage Pittoresque du Monde*, Paris, 1822. British Library 803.m.19.

224. 'Pirogue douhle sous son Hangard (Ile Vavao)'. Jules Sébastien César Dumont D'Urville, *Voyage au Pole Sud et dans l'Océanie sur les corvettes l'Astrolabe et la Zélée, exécuté … pendant les années 1837 … 1840*, Paris, 1846. British Library 1262.k.13.

# Index

EQVINOC
beleiton
amandura
calapara
bambam
tiban
c: Guinapao
iaua majori
beru
nucopara
pallo
tabana
Gulino
sibaira
zolon
sibua
timor
ISOLI MALV
cimara
Isola di iauaminori
lap